WATER DEVELOPMENT, SUPPLY AND MANAGEMENT

Series Editor: ASIT K. BISWAS

Volume 2

UNITED NATIONS WATER CONFERENCE

SUMMARY AND MAIN DOCUMENTS

Other titles in the series:

Vol. 1	UNITED NATIONS	Water Development and Management: Proceedings of the United Nations Water Conference, 4 part set
Vol. 3	WORTHINGTON, E. B.	Arid Land Irrigation in Developing Countries: Environmental Problems and Effects
Vol. 4	PACEY, A.	Water for the Thousand Millions
Vol. 5	UNITED NATIONS	Register of International Rivers
Vol. 6	GOLUBEV, G. and BISWAS, A. K.	Interregional Water Transfers

UNITED NATIONS WATER CONFERENCE

SUMMARY AND MAIN DOCUMENTS

Edited by
ASIT K. BISWAS
Director, Biswas & Associates, 3 Valley View Road, Ottawa, Canada

Published for the
UNITED NATIONS
by
PERGAMON PRESS
OXFORD · NEW YORK · TORONTO · SYDNEY · PARIS · FRANKFURT

U.K.	Pergamon Press Ltd., Headington Hill Hall, Oxford OX3 0BW, England
U.S.A.	Pergamon Press Inc., Maxwell House, Fairview Park, Elmsford, New York 10523, U.S.A.
CANADA	Pergamon of Canada Ltd., 75 The East Mall, Toronto, Ontario, Canada
AUSTRALIA	Pergamon Press (Aust.) Pty. Ltd., 19a Boundary Street, Rushcutters Bay, N.S.W. 2011, Australia
FRANCE	Pergamon Press SARL, 24 rue des Ecoles, 75240 Paris, Cedex 05, France
FEDERAL REPUBLIC OF GERMANY	Pergamon Press GmbH, 6242 Kronberg-Taunus, Pferdstrasse 1, Federal Republic of Germany

Copyright © 1978 United Nations

All Rights Reserved. No part of this publication may be reproduced, stored in a retrieval system or transmitted in any form or by any means: electronic, electrostatic, magnetic tape, mechanical, photocopying, recording or otherwise, without permission in writing from the copyright holders.

First edition 1978

British Library Cataloguing in Publication Data

United Nations Water Conference: summary
and main documents. — (Water development,
supply and management ; vol.2).
1. Water — Congresses
I. Biswas, Asit K II. United Nations III. Series
333.9'1   HD1691   77-30461
ISBN 0-08-022392-3

In order to make this volume available as economically and as rapidly as possible the authors' typescripts have been reproduced in their original forms. This method unfortunately has its typographical limitations but it is hoped that they in no way distract the reader.

*Printed in Great Britain by William Clowes & Sons, Limited
London, Beccles and Colchester*

This book is dedicated to
YAHIA ABDEL MAGEED
Secretary General, UN Water Conference
A token of esteem for a great statesman and engineer,
and
A mark of true regard for a friend.

Contents

Preface	ix
Introduction *Asit K. Biswas*	xi
Opening Statement *Yahia Abdel Mageed*	1
United Nations Water Conference: A Perspective *Margaret R. Biswas*	7
Resources and Needs: Assessment of the World Water Situation	25
Policy Options	71
Overview of Thematic Papers	111
Mar del Plata Action Plan:	147
Recommendations	147
Annex	186
Resolutions	192
Index	207

Preface

The beginning of the preparation for a world water conference dates back to June 1972, when the Economic and Social Council of the United Nations, commonly known as ECOSOC, adopted a resolution requesting studies be undertaken on the "desirability of, and possible topics for, an international water conference.". In December 1975, the General Assembly of the United Nations adopted a resolution endorsing the recommendation of the ECOSOC that a United Nations Water Conference should be held. This world Conference was held at Mar del Plata, Argentina, during 14th to 25th March, 1977.

The Water Conference is the fifth world conference held under the aegis of the United Nations, where political leaders from member countries assembled to discuss major global problems. The earlier world conferences were on the Human Environment (Stockholm, 1972), Population (Bucharest, 1974), Food (Rome, 1974) and Human Settlements (Vancouver, 1976). It would be followed by conferences on Desertification (Nairobi, 1977) and Science and Technology (venue yet to be decided, 1979).

It would be a serious error if the Water Conference is considered in isolation, without any reference to the world conferences that have been held earlier or will follow later. For example, the Stockholm Conference recommended farsighted actions to ensure preservation of water quality and protection of the environment from large scale water development projects. The World Population Conference discussed the interrelationships between population, resources — including water — and environment. Increase in population and the satisfaction of basic human needs of each individual will need more food, energy and raw materials, and water is a basic requisite for production of all these components. The World Food Conference recognized the importance of water for agricultural development, and the need for further expansion of irrigated agriculture. It specifically recommended a comprehensive action programme by Governments and international organizations to expand irrigation, to promote efficient water conservation and use, and to control more effectively damages caused by floods, droughts, waterlogging and salinity. Similarly, the Vancouver Conference on the Human Settlements discussed the lack of clean water for the vast majority of the rural population of the world, and recommended a target of 1990 to provide clean water to all communities.

Just as the prior UN world conferences had an impact on the Water Conference, so will it on the conferences following. For the Desertification Conference that concluded in Nairobi, in September, 1977, water management in arid lands was an important consideration, and a resolution was passed at Mar del Plata, specifically for this conference.

The Water Conference produced many valuable documentations. Among these were four conference background papers, reports of five regional meetings, consolidated action recommendations, papers from different UN organizations, special papers commissioned by the Secretariat, and some 250 thematic papers prepared by individual countries. I was directly involved with the preparation of one of the major background papers — analysis of the present and future activities of the UN system in the area of water, and also for the consolidated action recommendations, which eventually became known as the Mar del Plata Action Plan. All these papers are available in the full Conference proceedings, in four volumes, also edited by myself and published by Pergamon Press. The Proceedings would provide authoritative information to the world community, much of which is not easily available. The present summary volume contains selected essential papers prepared for the Conference, which should be of interest to everyone engaged in water resources activities. In other words, the summary volume is an attempt to provide to individuals essential documents of the Conference at a reasonable price.

Finally, no discussion of the Water Conference can be complete without a word about its Secretary General, Yahia Abdel Mageed, currently Minister of Irrigation of Sudan. Appointed less than a year before the Conference, he did the impossible task of holding one of the most successful world gatherings held so far. Compared to other world conferences, there was very little political bickerings at Mar del Plata, which was undoubtedly due to the behind the scene activities of an extremely competent and efficient Secretary General. What is even more remarkable is that Mr. Mageed made it all possible with a very small Secretariat and a shoe-string budget, which was even less than one-third of the total budget for the audio-visual projects alone for the Vancouver Conference on Human Settlements! Everything considered, it was an outstanding achievement.

Asit K. Biswas
Editor

Editor's Introduction

> *All the rivers run into the sea,*
> *Yet the sea is not full;*
> *Unto the place from whence the rivers come,*
> *Thither they return again.*
>
> *Ecclesiastes 1:7*

Water, said the Greek philosopher Pindar, as early as the fifth century B.C., is the best of all things. It may perhaps be an overstatement, but it is certainly not surprising, especially when it is considered that it has been one of the most precious commodities throughout man's recorded history. Water makes life – human, animal or plant – in the biosphere possible, and without it life and civilization can not develop or survive. Wars have been fought in the past over the availability of water, and even now relations between several countries are strained due to disputes over management of shared water resources.

Because of the important role water plays in human survival, it has always been a subject of great interest, and the entire history of mankind can be written in terms of its need for water. From the very beginning, man realized that water is essential for the satisfaction of basic human needs, and hence early civilisations flourished on lands made fertile by major rivers: Tigris and Euphrates in Mesopotamia, Nile in Egypt, Indus in India, and Huang-Ho in China. As early as 3000 B.C., the Egyptians had already developed intricate water resources networks, especially irrigation systems. The historian, Herodotus, provides a vivid description of these early Egyptian water development works, and he was so impressed by the role of the River Nile in the country's survival that he called Egypt "the gift of the Nile".

The importance of water can be further amplified by the fact that the Greek philosopher, Empedocles of Agricentrum (490-430 B.C.), considered water to be one of the four primary elements or roots (*rhizomata*) from which all the materials of the world were constituted. The other three basic elements were air, fire and earth; the last two in the present day can be interpreted as energy and land. One can thus argue that such a concept was the forerunner of the molecular theory of materials, and water was considered to be so important that it was accepted as one of the fundamental building blocks of nature. Even great philosophers like Plato and Aristotle accepted this concept of water as a fundamental element, with only minor modifications.

The magnitude and complexity of water resources development and management problems in the early days were not complex. Population was small, *per capita* demand was low and water was plentiful. When there were water-related problems like droughts or floods, man simply migrated to a better location. Pollution loads were low, mainly of an organic nature, and water courses assimilated whatever load that entered without serious deterioration of water quality. Thus, right from the beginning man tended to treat water as gift from God — a "free" resource — and his birthright to use and squander as he saw fit. This freewheeling concept, until recent times, did not pose serious management problems. Hence, until the early twentieth century, the demand for water, its efficiency of use and its quality were generally secondary issues.

This scenario started to change in the developed countries with the advent of the Industrial Revolution. Workers from agricultural sectors in rural areas started to migrate to urban centres, attracted by burgeoning industrial employment. One of its undesirable side-effects was the development of centres of dense population. As the industries in the cities developed, more workers migrated from the rural areas, which in turn attracted more industries, and this created a somewhat vicious circle.

Industries were often unfortunately located in close proximity to water bodies because of the ease with which waste products could be discharged to the receiving waters at no direct economic cost. Furthermore, cities discharged their sewage into the water bodies without much treatment, thus compounding the problem. Even today, some major cities like Montreal, Canada, discharges sewage to nearby watercourses without even primary treatment. Such developments contributed to growing water pollution near centres of dense population. In medieval Paris, the streets were often like open sewers, but the River Seine was clean, and one could see fish swimming in the clear water. Times have now changed. Today the streets of Paris are clean, but the Seine is murky and gray, and one would indeed be fortunate to see any fish.

The situation in developing countries was somewhat different. From a global perspective, the water situation can be visualized within two extremes. At one extreme are the highly urbanized cities of advanced industrialized countries, where the vast majority of population have inhouse connections and sewerage services, backed by adequate infrastructure and institutional arrangements, having access to adequate financing, high level technology and necessary service personnel. At the other extreme is the rural sector of developing countries, having no service of any kind for either potable water or excreta disposal. Herein lies a major development dilemma, the rich get richer, the poor, poorer. In many urban centres, if one can afford the capital costs, clean piped water could be cheap enough for the rich to fill their swimming pools, while the poor may have to pay two or three times as much, per unit quantity of water, to buy by the bucket from a tanker. Even then, these urban poors may be luckier than their rural counterparts, who get their water, often contaminated, from whatever sources they can.

There is no doubt that the total amount of water available globally, if used efficiently, can meet vastly higher human needs. Current estimates indicate that the total volume of water on earth is 1.4×10^9 km^3, 97.3 per cent of which is ocean water, and, therefore cannot be used by man except for fisheries and navigation. Only 2.7 per cent is fresh water, 77.2 per cent of which is stored in polar ice-caps and glaciers, 22.4 per cent as ground water and soil moisture (about two-third lies deeper than 750 metres below the surface), 0.35 per cent in lakes and swamps, 0.04 per cent in the atmosphere and less than 0.01 per cent is in streams. In other words, nearly 90 per cent of fresh water is stored in ice-caps, glaciers and as deep ground water, and as such is not easily accessible. For all practical purposes, it is surface water in rivers, streams and lakes, amounting to less than half of 1 per cent of available fresh water, that constitutes the basic available supply for man, even though ground water has been heavily developed in certain parts of the world.

While reasonably accurate estimates of the total volume of water in the earth is available, information on its quality leaves much to be desired. Thus, with very few exceptions, even approximate continental or global assessments of the different water quality parameters are not known. Nor is much known about the magnitude and type of organic wastes from municipalities and industry that are entering water courses, and rapidly constituting growing hazard to human health and environment. Even in a major advanced industrialized country, like the United States, according to the 1976 report of its National Commission on Water Quality, 92 per cent of suspended solids, 37 per cent of biochemical oxygen demand and 98 per cent of the coliform bacteria will still remain uncontrolled in natural surface water, *even* when all discharges from point sources have been eliminated. This is largely due to agricultural activities. Currently there are no general measurements of volumes of synthetic organic compounds and heavy metals reaching water courses, and eventually the oceans.

Toxic chemicals and heavy metals are serious hazards to environmental health. They are gradually dispersed to ecosystems, other than the one intended, by evaporation and subsequent precipitation, or by drainage waters. For example, it has been estimated that England receives nearly 36 metric tons of chlorinated hydrocarbon as fallout per year. Such dispersal mechanisms mean that the toxic substances can be detected in areas far away from the points of application. Thus, significant quantities of pesticides, including DDT and its derivatives, have been found in animals in Antarctica, like penguins and their eggs, skua and fish, even though there is no agriculture, no insect life and no use of pesticides.

Water plays an important part as a medium through which toxic chemicals are dispersed to the ecosystems by selective concentration, as they pass relatively unchanged through successive levels of food chains and food webs. For example, in Lake Michigan, the concentration of DDT in lake sediments was 0.0085 ppm. Invertebrate primary consumers concentrated this to 0.41 ppm, their fish predators to 3 to 8 ppm, and the herring gulls predatory on the fish had levels no less than 3.177 ppm. This means the level of concentration increased by nearly 374,000 times between the lake sediments and the gulls.

The effect of such selective concentration means that the toxic effects of chemicals are more readily noticeable in top carnivores. Thus, discharge of mercury in the Minimata Bay, Japan, increased the mercury content of fish to dangerous levels, so much so that the fishermen who depended on fish as a major source of food, suffered heavily from mercury poisoning. Currently, this form of disease is often known as Minimata, and in addition to Japan, severe mercury poisoning, under similar circumstances, have been noted in Canada, especially among Indians having fish as their staple diet.

In addition to above environmental health implications, the quality of water available has direct relations to human health. Use of potable water will undoubtedly reduce health hazards like cholera, typhoid, infectious hepatitis and bacillary dysentery. It would further reduce human contacts with vectors of water-borne diseases like schistosomiasis, trypanosomiasis, and guinea worm. Some have estimated that the Gambian sleeping sickness can be reduced by 80 per cent by good water development schemes. While this figure may be somewhat optimistic, there is no doubt that the provision of potable water will significantly reduce the incidence of the dreaded sleeping sickness disease by reducing the exposure of human beings to Tsetse flies during the water collection journey. Similarly, guinea worm infection, which currently affects some 48 million people, chiefly in the Indian sub-continent and West Africa, can also be reduced. Currently, water and health situation, on a global basis, has been estimated as follows:

Gastro-enteritis, 400 million cases every year;

Schistosomiasis, 200 million cases every year;

Filariasis, 200 million cases every year;

Malaria, 160 million cases every year;

Onchocerciasis, 20-40 million cases every year.

These statistics clearly indicate that the health and economic costs of water-related diseases are considerable, and much of such costs can be reduced by rational water resources development and management. Availability of potable water in rural communities would eliminate the water collection journey, mainly of women and children of developing countries, who currently spend up to five hours every day collecting the family water requirements. Such chores take up to 12 per cent of daytime calorie needs of most carriers in non-dry areas, and up to 25 per cent or more in mountainous regions. Since women are not traditionally the most well-nourished members of the family, elimination of water collection journey, by the availability of potable water closer to home, has not only implications in terms of reduced disease propagation, but also in terms of nutrition, a fact often overlooked by planners and politicians. Furthermore, the time freed can be used for learning and productive work.

There is no doubt that the total amount of water available globally, if distributed equally, can meet much higher demands. The problem, however, is that water is not equitably distributed either in space or in time. In some parts of the world, there may be too much water and floods could be a perennial problem, whereas in other parts, especially in arid regions, there may not be enough water to sustain all water-related activities throughout the year. Thus, in areas of both water abundance and shortage, it is important to institute appropriate water resources development and management policies so as to alleviate the problems of floods and droughts, and to ensure in the process that adequate water of right quantity and quality is available on a long-term sustaining basis. Such policies would include implementation of rational conservation plans and pollution control strategies, so that deterioration of water quality can be prevented, thus ensuring the total stock of available water is usable for different purposes.

If the earlier general assessment of the world-wide conditions is considered in conjunction with the following factors, the urgency of immediate rational water development and management becomes apparent:

(a) It took nearly a million years for the first billion people to appear on earth, but the next billion is due in only another 15 years. The world population is expected to reach 6.5 billion by the year 2000. The basic human needs of the additional 2.5 billion people have to be satisfied in slightly over 3 decades. Basic human needs may be considered to be food, clothing and shelter, and public services provided by and for the community at large, such as safe drinking water, sanitation, public transport, and minimum health services. Satisfaction of basic human needs for the additional 2.5 billion people means more water to supply these goods and services.

(b) According to the World Health Organization, 1200 million people, or 30 per cent of the present world population, lack safe drinking water, and 1400 million people have no sanitary waste disposal facilities. Lack of proper excreta disposal has an immediate impact on water quality, especially in areas where safe water is in short supply. It contaminates the water sources, and thus contributes to spread of diseases. Currently some 5 million people die every year from such water-borne diseases as cholera, typhoid, diarrhea, dysentery, malaria and intestinal worm infections.

(c) Unplanned industrial expansion and population pressures in large urban areas are straining available water supply. As urban areas grow, more water becomes necessary and simultaneously more waste is being generated, some of which is disposed off in to watercourses, thus degrading water quality. In other words, more and more water becomes necessary, but at the same time the quality of available supply is being degraded.

(d) The daily water demand for a human being varies between 1.5 and 20 litres, depending on climate and physical activity. The daily *per capita* in-house water use varies from 3 to 700 litres. A ten-year study in Singapore indicates that as domestic water use goes up, disease rates go down. It concluded that 90 litres of high quality water seemed to be the "social minimum" for prevention of water-borne diseases.

(e) Agriculture is the greatest user of water, accounting for some 80 per cent of all consumption: comparable figure for the United States is slightly above 40 per cent. It takes approximately 1000 tons of water to grow one ton of grain and 2000 tons to grow one ton of rice. In addition, animal husbandry and fisheries require abundant water.

(f) In 1975, according to the Food and Agricultural Organization, the total area irrigated in the world amounted to 223 million hectares, of which 93 million hectares was in developing countries. Some 15 per cent of the world's cropland is irrigated, yielding from 30 to 40 per cent of all agricultural production. The amount of water used by irrigated crops is nearly 1,300,000 million cubic metres, but because of losses in storage, conveyance and use, the total amount used increases to almost 3,000,000 million cubic metres.

(g) By 1990, it is estimated that the total area irrigated in the world would increase to 223 million hectares, of which 119 million hectares would be in developing countries. Expanding and maintaining irrigated areas to 1990 is going to be a challenging task, and its magnitude can be judged by the following requirements for the developing market economy countries only:

22.5 million hectares of new irrigation;

45 million hectares of irrigation improvement;

78.2 million hectares of drainage improvement, including 52.4 million hectares on irrigated land;

438,000 million m^3 of additional water;

$97,800 million of investment at 1975 prices.

(h) Increased agricultural activities in marginal areas have often over exploited water availability. In many areas, more groundwater is being withdrawn than can be replenished naturally, thus contributing to major management problems.

(i) Industry is a heavy user of water. In the United States, industrial water demands account for nearly 40 per cent of the total water requirements, and five major industrial groups — food and kindred products, pulp and paper, chemicals, petroleum, coal products and primary metals — account for slightly more than 85 per cent of total industrial requirements. However, nearly 60 to 80 per cent of water required for industrial processing is for cooling and need not be of a high quality.

(j) Irrational use of water is contributing to the loss of productive soil due to waterlogging, salinization, alkalinization and erosion. On a global scale, at least 200 to 300 thousand hectares of irrigated land is lost every year due to salinization and waterlogging. In the Nubariya area of Egypt, water level is increasing at the rate of one mm every day. Current estimates indicate that 20 to 25 million hectares of land that is saline at present was fertile and productive at one time.

(k) Water conservation practices have not received adequate attention so far. The efficiency of use of irrigation water is still low in most countries, and losses of up to 70 to 80 per cent are not exactly uncommon. Overwatering is often endemic, and it is virtually certain that most current estimates of water needs for irrigation are grossly overstated to account for this loss. Similarly in the industrial sector, many products can be manufactured with significantly less water than currently being used. For example, water requirements to manufacture one ton of paperboard vary from 62,000 to 376,000 litres, the higher figure being over six times the lower one. In some urban centres of developing countries, as much as 50 per cent of all the water stored and conveyed is being lost due to leakages.

These and other aspects of water resources development affect different countries in different ways, and all go to prove that *rational management of water resources can no longer be considered as only desirable, it is now an absolute must*. But the overall tasks must be viewed in a wider context. Management of water is essential, but the fundamental question that must be asked is for what? Not for itself, but for those who inhabit this "only one earth", and to provide a better quality of life to those segments of society who have not had the opportunity for hundreds of years. In the case of water, as in that of energy or any other resource issues which confront the world today, the problems must be viewed in the wider context of rational use of natural resource for the achievement of a sustainable development process, as envisioned by the New International Economic Order proclaimed by the United Nations.

This may pose an important question: will enough water be available for future developments in the world? Some have already suggested that water, rather than land, will be the major constraint for increasing world food production during the final years of this century. Two comments can be made about such statements. First, the majority of such statements come from people who have no special expertise on water, and thus it becomes comparatively easy to make such rash forecasts. Secondly, such concepts are basically neo-Malthusian, and like other similar concepts, it has been discarded by serious scholars.

To conclude, the major problem in the area of water resources is not one of Malthusian spectre of impending scarcity, but one of instituting more rational and better management practices. Water resources of different regions for which adequate data are not available have to be assessed, and based on such assessments, long-term development and management plans have to be established. Water and land should not appear as constraints in the overall planning process of a country, rather realistic development and production targets should be matched to their availability. What is urgently needed is the formulation of long-term development policies, on a sustaining basis, that reflect changing water supply and demand patterns, consistent with efficient use, and better understanding of the social and environmental implications so that adverse impacts can be minimized. In fact, it can be successfully argued that the time has come when the emphasis should shift to comprehensive land and water planning, treating land and water as an integrated and interacting unit, rather than water planning *per se*.

Opening Statement

Yahia Abdel Mageed

The convening of the United Nations Water Conference is an event of historic importance. For the first time, the range and complexity of the problems of water development confronting mankind will be taken up in their totality by a world forum in a systematic and comprehensive manner. Consideration of the fundamental aspects of water policy, as distinct from the exclusively scientific and technological, also lends uniqueness to this Conference.

Although historically, water development has influenced the growth of the great river civilizations of antiquity, it was only in the nineteenth and twentieth centuries that application of new technologies ushered in the modern era of massive development of water resources in the Americas, Europe, Africa, Asia and the Pacific. The Second World War temporarily halted this trend as national and international resources were diverted to other sectors. But the post-war period and accompanying independence of many nations led to a revival of interest in the development of water resources in all countries, notably in a great majority of the developing nations.

This renewed interest was rooted in the hope that water development would assure the much longed-for economic and social development. Since water is essential to industry and agriculture, its development was perceived as the symbol of all development. Accordingly, water problems merited varying degrees of attention in many countries. But subsequent achievements in this area seldom matched those of earlier years. Further, the degree of water development rarely kept pace with growing aspirations for socio-economic development, particularly in the developing countries.

We only have to consider that a quarter of the world's population is now starving; another quarter is severely undernourished; by the year 2000, we shall have to provide food for some 6000 million people. At the same time, two thirds of the world's population — some 80 per cent in rural areas — have no access to adequate or safe water supply, and that figure will double by the year 2000 unless remedial action is taken. The resolution of these problems is far beyond the capability of any single or fragmented effort.

While water undoubtedly has the potential for aiding profound social and economic change, it was soon recognized in many countries that the prevailing forms of socio-economic organization tended to create critical constraints of capital and manpower. These have severely retarded efficient utilization and development of water resources. The resulting gap between potential and performance, between promise and progress, between ambition and achievement must be reckoned with in several countries today.

SOME PRINCIPAL CONCERNS

With this background in mind, it is pertinent to review some basic problems or issues which must engage our attention. I shall not attempt to deal with all these numerous and complicated problems exhaustively but shall confine myself to certain areas that merit priority.

First, the problem of community water supplies. When we recall the spectacular advances in science and technology that have occurred in our own lifetime when it has been possible to send man to outer space, it is surely paradoxical that here on earth, people should be denied a fundamental human right — a readily available supply of clean water for healthy survival and betterment.

Second, the problem of self-sufficiency in food production. Hopes of redressing the imbalance between the rich and poor in food production have come no closer to reality. Despite the efforts and achievements of the past decades, the general condition of the people in the developing countries has not improved. The 460 million deprived and hungry people of 1974 have now increased by a further 24 million and, in the absence of a dramatic breakthrough in the expansion of food and agricultural production, they will continue to increase by more than 12 million yearly.

At present about a tenth of the land area of the world is cultivated, and only about a sixth of this cultivated land is currently under irrigation. Yet this same irrigated land produces between 40 and 50 per cent of all agricultural output. It is clear that, if future famines are to be avoided, more land will have to be placed under irrigation.

Third, the problem of pollution. Many rivers and lakes are being increasingly polluted, as a result of the uncontrolled discharge of untreated effluents, both from industry and agriculture. This is contributing enormously to a rapid diminution of available supplies of good quality water for various domestic, industrial or agricultural purposes. Satisfactory remedies have yet to be formulated. Otherwise the results of our misuse will be passed on to future generations.

Fourth, the problem of shared water resources. It is a fact of contemporary life that there are important points of difference among many countries with regard to the problems of shared water resources. It appears that no significant progress can be achieved in the management and development of these resources without a more effective system or framework within which the differing national positions, interests or approaches can be harmonized so as to facilitate co-operation.

There are many opinions on the specific form such co-operation might take. But certainly, it may be stated quite unequivocally that these shared resources should be viewed as links to promote the bonds of unity, solidarity and fraternity among the nations sharing a common destiny.

These, then, are only four principal concerns I have chosen to mention here. Others include the incidence of floods, droughts, the water needs of industry, hydroelectric power generation, inland navigation, environment and health concerns, all of which are no less important. The degree of their importance is dependent upon different national and regional situations, which I am sure will receive your detailed consideration during the Conference.

It is necessary at this stage to refer to one of the principal constraints to more effective action, namely, the scarcity of capital and foreign exchange, particularly in the less-developed countries. Ways and means will have to be found for more effective mobilization of financial resources, both internal as well as external.

PRESENT INTERNATIONAL CLIMATE

We are here today to consider these and other water-related problems in the context of a world situation where nations have pledged themselves to work towards a New International Economic Order — an order which we hope will usher in a new set of more rational and equitable international political and economic relations. Also, we are meeting in a new international climate created by the dialogues of conferences at Stockholm, Paris, Nairobi, Rome and Vancouver. Countries of the world are now working towards the New Economic International Economic Order through such means as economic and technical co-operation among the developing countries, with the object of attaining collective self-reliance in their developmental effort. These emerging concepts and trends mark the transition from an earlier era of dependence on former colonial or metropolitan powers, to a new era of collective self-reliance and a new pattern of interdependence in the comity of nations. This transitional phase is a historic necessity if we are to create a new world, free from poverty, hunger and malnutrition - in short, a world free from the present inequity of vast areas of under-development coexisting alongside others of affluence. In consequence, at this Conference, it behoves us to consider the problems of water development against this background of the world situation. It is incumbent on us to take into account the present climate of international relations in order that water might be considered as an instrument for the promotion of a greater measure of international cooperation.

I am suggesting that such a broad perspective will be helpful because water development, particularly at the policy and decision-making level, faces the same problems as all other sectors of economic development, and cannot therefore be treated in complete isolation as an independent domain unrelated to other areas of development. A consideration of problems of development in general is obviously beyond the scope of this Conference but, nevertheless, it will be useful to recall this broad interconnexion while considering problems specific to the development of water resources.

PREPARATORY PROCESS

This brings me directly to the point that while some aspects of the water problems have general dimensions, many aspects are, by and large, unique to specific river basins, lakes and aquifers in different countries and regions. Due recognition and consideration had to be and was, in fact, given to this aspect of water problems in the preparatory process for this Conference. The regional economic commissions spearheaded the preparations for the regional meetings according to the guidelines set by the Committee on Natural Resources acting as the preparatory committee for the Conference. It is a matter of gratification to all of us that these regional preparatory meetings invariably involved broadbased, high-level participation. Each meeting was successful in that its reports and recommendations embody the needs, hopes and aspirations of the respective regions. The vast fund of valuable expertise and experience accumulated by the various agencies of the United Nations system is presented in the special reports prepared by them on various subjects appropriate to their respective fields of competence. The preparatory work was, in fact, a combined effort of the whole United Nations system. The individual national experiences on specific aspects are outlined in the various thematic papers submitted by Governments. This preparatory process was devised to accomplish, and did in fact succeed in accomplishing, the extraction of the essence of the problems and their potential solution in the different geographic regions of the world and in the different sectoral uses of water, with due regard to the important infrastructural problems of education, manpower, training, research, etc., which underpin both the geographical as well as the functional areas of water problems.

The preparatory process had, in itself, many valuable lessons to offer:

First, it brought out the fact that water problems affect both the developed as well as developing countries. There are many similarities between the two sets of conditions but at the same time, there exist important dissimilarities in the nature of the problems. For instance, water pollution, a high-priority problem in developed industrial societies, has not yet reached the same dimensions in developing countries, given the relatively lower level of industrial development.

Second, the analytical review in the preparatory process showed that only 2 per cent of the water resources of Africa, and 3 per cent in Latin America, have so far been developed. It also showed that the present level of development of hydroelectric power in Africa and Latin America is only 6 — 8 per cent of the available potential — facts which point up the need for accelerated development.

Third, the very process of preparation for the Conference has generated a certain momentum on a global scale. A new consciousness was created. National committees were created or reactivated in some countries. New laws or decrees were promulgated in others. This momentum has not only to be maintained but further developed hereafter.

ROLE OF THE CONFERENCE

This Conference marks the culmination of a lengthy preparatory process involving your helpful participation. I am extremely happy to be able to extend to all of you the most cordial welcome and to express my sincere conviction that your participation in the Conference will impart a measure of unparalleled value to its subsequent recommendations and resolutions.

The Conference provides a unique opportunity for formulating an international consensus on a number of policy and operational measures. Should such a consensus emerge, you may consider the desirability and appropriateness of incorporating it in the form of a declaration which would provide a framework to guide the policies for future development of water resources — not with any rigidity but with sufficient flexibility to facilitate a consideration of differing situations and needs in different countries. Should it be possible to work towards such a declaration, that in itself would constitute an historic landmark in the field of water resource development.

In addition to this, I am sure that your deliberations will result in a number of practical recommendations for action in the various sectors and aspects of water development.

On the question of community water supplies and agriculture, here is an opportunity — may I say, even an obligation — to formulate a concrete plan of action with detailed, financial and manpower implications, and specific time-bound targets. You have already expressed your commitment at Vancouver to provide clean water for all by 1990, if possible. Let us now avoid generalities because there is no disagreement on objectives or strategies. Let us get down to specifics, assess what can be accomplished with our respective national resources and indicate specifically what we need by way of external assistance. Let there be no mistake that, in the ultimate analysis, real action lies at the national level — international assistance being essentially catalytic and effective only when there is dynamism and vigour in national action. There is a similar need to develop concrete action-oriented recommendations that will promote co-operation among developing countries specifically in the water sector, in order to combat pollution, floods and droughts specifically and to provide the capital and manpower needs essential for further development and management.

In relation to the problem of shared water resources, if there is general agreement on the need for a code of conduct, this will be a significant advance in facilitating greater co-operation in the future among co-basin countries. I am not suggesting that a code of conduct should actually be evolved in this forum, but only that there should be agreement on the *need* for such a code, so that appropriate steps can be taken in the future, to set in motion a process to facilitate the eventual adoption of such a code of conduct with common consent. This would be a limited, but significant, advance in a seemingly intractable subject.

I am sure I will be echoing a common sentiment if I were to say that the deliberations of the Conference should not result in a mere set of generalized recommendations full of platitudes and cliches. In contrast, the Conference should result in a blueprint for action at the national, regional and international levels, valid for the next few decades.

We hope that the Conference will mark the beginning of a new era in the history of water development in the world. We expect that it will engender a new spirit of dedication to the betterment of all peoples; a new sense of awareness of the urgency and importance of water problems; a new climate for a better appreciation of these problems; higher levels of flow of funds through the channels of international financial assistance to the cause of development; and, in general, a firmer commitment on the part of all concerned to establish a real breakthrough so that our planet will be a better place to live in.

IMPLEMENTATION

Another important question that merits our consideration is the problem of implementation of recommendations. While the formulation of correct and comprehensive recommendations is important in itself, much of the effectiveness of the recommendations is impaired in the absence of equally effective mechanisms for their implementation. The discussions during the preparatory process brought up the question of what was sometimes called the "implementation gap" and the need for closing this gap.

The question of implementation has to be considered at different levels — national, regional and international. At the national level, effective public participation is the key to success, for experience has shown that lack of participation by the affected population has frequently led to sterile inefficiency in execution, whereas the active involvement of the people produces a galvanizing effect all round. No amount of policy formulation, institutional reorganization or legislative action, important as these all are, will lead to success without the involvement of the population.

At the national, subregional, regional and international levels, the need for closer and more effective co-ordination of all bilateral and multilateral governmental as well as non-governmental organizations, both within and outside the United Nations system is also recognized to be an imperative necessity for successful implementation.

It is obvious that the United Nations system has an important role to play. In fact, the system has to its merit a record of commendable work over the last few decades which the world will acknowledge. At the same time, the opinion is unanimous that there is considerable room for more effective co-ordination. The system has itself worked out proposals to improve co-ordination and make it more effective. This is an unprecedented opportunity for the Governments to impart a new vigour to international action and to enable it to carry out its expanded role and function in a more dynamic manner in assisting the Governments in facing the challenges of the future.

May I, in conclusion, be permitted to remind us of the great ferment in the world today. Over the greater part of the globe, there is considerable turmoil largely impelled by the prevalence of what has come to be referred to as a state of "underdevelopment". It will be no exaggeration to suggest that the development of water resources is an important means to combat this "underdevelopment" and thus to contribute to the greater well-being of mankind. Let not history say that a golden opportunity for arranging an orderly developmental progress of mankind presented itself to this generation but was not grasped in time. For, in the ultimate analysis, the success of this Conference will be measured not here at Mar del Plata, not by us, but by posterity over the sweep of history and by the measure to which our deliberations during the next two weeks influence the course of events over the next two decades.

United Nations Water Conference: A Perspective

Margaret R. Biswas

The United Nations Water Conference convened at Mar del Plata, Argentina, from 14 to 25 March, 1977, and was attended by 116 governments, the various United Nations agencies and organizations, intergovernmental organizations, 58 non-governmental organizations, and several liberation movements. China was once again absent from the World Forum: they did not participate at Habitat either. Yahia Abdel Mageed, former Minister of Irrigation and Hydro-electric Power of the Sudan, was Secretary-General of the Conference. Luis Urbano Jauregui, Head of the delegation of Argentina, served as President.

The Water Conference was first proposed by the Committee on Natural Resources in New York in 1971. It was approved by the Economic and Social Council in 1973 and endorsed by the United Nations General Assembly in December 1975 in Resolution 3513 (XXX). Since the early 1970's, the United Nations has been holding a series of conferences to create global strategies to meet problems that are beyond the power of any single nation to resolve and are of concern to the international community in its attempt to improve the quality of life of its people. The work and recommendations of these preceding United Nations conferences, notably those on Environment, Population, (1) Food, (2) and Human Settlements (3) contributed to the preparations for the Water Conference.

According to the resolutions of the Economic and Social Council, the Conference was to be convened to:

- exchange experience on water resources development and water uses;
- review new technologies;
- stimulate greater co-operation in the field of water;
- discuss comprehensively the problems raised by growing water demands where the stock of the resource was constant;
- to consider specific economic and administrative, as well as technical aspects of water resources planning and development, primarily directed towards water policy-makers.

The main purpose of the Conference was to promote a level of preparedness nationally, regionally, and internationally which would help the world avoid a water crisis of global dimensions by the end of the century. It was to deal with the problem of ensuring that the world had an adequate supply of water, of good quality, to meet the needs of a world population which is not only growing, but is also seeking improved economic and social conditions for all people.

Although water is a renewable resource, the total amount of water available on a global basis is constant, and estimated at 1.4×10^9 km^3. Distribution of the world's water resources is shown in Table 1.

Table 1. Distribution of World's water resources

Location	Percentage
Ocean	97.3
Fresh	2.7
Distribution of fresh water:	
Ice cap and glaciers	77.2
Ground water and soil moisture	22.4
Lakes and swamps	0.35
Atmosphere	0.04
Stream channels	0.01

The water available for human use, though adequate in volume, is frequently available at the wrong place, at the wrong time and with the wrong quality. As population increases, the resulting demand for water for domestic, agricultural and industrial uses is causing serious strains on the planet's fixed water stock, while careless management, pollution and inadequate conservation threaten to reduce the availability of usable water. In addition, we have not yet learned to contain natural disasters, such as floods and droughts.

MAJOR CONFERENCE ISSUES

Kurt Waldheim, Secretary-General of the United Nations, in his opening address stated that the Conference was closely related to the aims of the United Nations concerning a more equitable and just world order. Every aspect of socio-economic development depends upon the availability of an adequate supply of water. More water will be necessary to provide food, manufactured goods and energy to sustain a world population which will have grown from 4 billion to 6 or 7 billion by the year 2000. Water development needs, he said, must be perceived in terms of comprehensive programmes; a project-by-project approach was no longer adequate. If world water resources are to meet human needs in the twenty-first century, radical new management approaches, like shifting water supplies from surplus to deficit regions, were necessary. New research such as utilization of polar ice-packs and improved technologies for such tasks as desalination of sea water must be fostered. This Conference demonstrated the ability to act before a disastrous crisis was upon us, but potential water crises may be faced in many parts of the world, unless the political will to co-operate in an unprecedented fashion is forthcoming.

The Secretary-General of the Water Conference, Y.A. Mageed, outlined four principal concerns:

(1). Community water supplies: Two-thirds of the world's population — some 80 per cent in rural areas — have no access to adequate or safe water supply, and that figure will double by the year 2000 unless remedial actions are taken.

(2). Self-sufficiency in food production: The number of deprived and hungry people has increased by 24 million from 460 million in 1974 to 484 million and, in the absence of a dramatic breakthrough in the expansion of food production, will continue to increase by more than 12 million yearly. At present, about a tenth of the land area of the world is cultivated and only one-sixth of this cultivated land is under irrigation, producing 40 - 50 per cent of all agricultural output. To avoid future famines, more land will have to be irrigated.

(3). Pollution: Satisfactory remedies for pollution from untreated effluents have yet to be formulated.

(4). Shared Water Resources: There must be a more effective system within which the differing national interests and approaches regarding shared resources can be harmonized. A general agreement on the need for a code of conduct, to be evolved later, would be a significant advance.

In many countries, he said, the prevailing forms of socio-economic organization created critical constraints of capital and manpower. Ways would have to be found for more effective mobilization of financial resources. Countries of the world were working towards a new economic order through such means as economic and technical co-operation among developed countries.

The preparatory process had highlighted regional problems. It showed that only 2 per cent of the water resources of Africa, and 3 per cent in Latin America had been developed. Only 6 — 8 per cent of available hydro-electric power in Africa and Latin America is developed. The process of preparation generated a momentum that must be maintained, if recommendations are to be implemented.

The question of implementation, according to Mageed, had to be considered at different levels — national, regional and international. Real action lay at the national level, international assistance being essentially catalytic and effective only when there was dynamic national action. At the national level, effective public participation is the key to success. At all levels, more effective co-ordination of all bilateral and multilateral governmental as well as non-governmental organizations is imperative. It was unanimously agreed that more effective co-ordination of the United Nations system was necessary.

Urging nations to take stock of their common destiny, Luis Urbano Jauregui, the Conference President, remarked that the United Nations Water Conference could mark the start of a new era: that of water rationally used, preserved and harmonized with the environment. The conservation and development of water are not isolated problems, nor can they be solved by any particular sector or region. They constitute a single theme: water as the heritage of mankind to serve the common good.

Gabriel Van Laethem, Under Secretary-General for Economic and Social Affairs of the United Nations, said that water was wasted too long since it was presumed to be abundant, renewable, and available at low cost of free of charge. Because its management has traditionally been within the public domain, it has not been the subject of a research effort comparable to that from which the great industrial technologies have benefited. Therefore, methods of water use have in many ways not developed since ancient times, and practices inherited from the Romans are still being used. While the solution of water problems depended in part upon scientists and engineers, it was primarily the responsibility of politicians who determined national measures and international co-operation.

The United States explained that recent water problems had led it to place more emphasis on water management. Instead of water development, and greater concern for environmental aspects. It recognized that water supply is affected by a host of factors that have nothing to do with hydraulic engineering. Foremost among such factors was population. Though global population will double in the next 25 years, demand for water would double in far less time due to the increased need for water, intensive argiculture, and industrial technologies. The location of people was another factor. Instead of settling in places where water was abundant, people have been encouraged to settle where they must rely on complex systems to bring water to them. Countries with less than abundant water supplies or with high population growth in areas of marginal water availability should emphasize policies to reduce rates of population growth, encourage resource-oriented internal migration, stimulate reclamation and conservation, and adopt development technologies appropriate to specific water needs. Recognizing the need for accurate data to avert a water crisis, the United States is prepared to provide assistance to other nations interested in designing information systems. Data are, however, of little use without trained people. Because water resources management requires familiarity with the specific region, training should be done in and by the countries concerned.

The USSR stated that its population was concentrated in the West, while 80 per cent of its water resources were concentrated in Siberia and the Far East, where only one-third of its population and agriculture is located. The USSR was waging a planned struggle against pollution, but will not have clean water if other countries continue to discharge improperly treated effluents into rivers. It suggested the Conference facilitate international agreements which would prevent countries from discharging effluents into rivers. All governments should control and end pollution. Countries should also recycle water and reduce demand. New technical means for agriculture and other installed technology that uses small amounts of water should be developed. A way must be found to reduce the demand for water for agricultural crops. Efforts should be made to concentrate on crops that use less water.

Having reached the limit of its natural water potential, Israel was doing its utmost to increase efficiency in water use. In agriculture, Israel started by moving from gravity irrigation to sprinkling. Now direct dripping at the roots of the plant and automatic irrigation systems which reliably supply the exact quantity needed by the crop were being employed. Unconventional methods such as cloud seeding were also being used.

H.M. Horning, of the Food and Agriculture Organization (FAO), expressed similar concern. Since water resources are finite, increased use must be equated with reduction in waste, especially in agriculture, which accounts for some 80 per cent of world water consumption. Efficiency of use in crop production will assume overriding importance, and must find response from institutions already unable to cope. He said that the World Food Conference had suggested countries undertake an inventory of water resources available for agriculture in order to determine potential irrigation. It had emphasized flood control, drainage, and reclamation, and advocated small-scale projects in which farmers could participate.

FAO, continued Horning, felt action to overcome food and crop deficits must include:

improvement of existing irrigation;

expansion of irrigation and drainage to new land;

improvement and extension of rainfed agriculture and livestock production through better soil moisture management and through the opening up of new land;

protection of agricultural land against flooding and waterlogging and where necessary its reclamation; and

introduction or expansion of fish rearing in conjunction with rural development.

In the case of irrigation and drainage, the magnitude of a 15 year global target is estimated at some 45 million hectares of improved and 22 million hectares of new irrigation development, at a total cost of nearly 100 thousand million dollars.

Milos Holy, President of the International Commission on Irrigation and Drainage, maintained securing sufficient supplies of water for large-scale irrigation projects will be one of the principal future tasks of water management. It is estimated that by the year 2000 the world area under irrigation will be about 500 million hectares, double that of 1975. At an average increment of 10 million hectares of irrigated land per year, an increased water supply of 45,000 million m^3 a year will be required globally. The increased demand on water resources by 2000 will be 1,125,000 m^3, which is roughly equal to the annual flow in the Congo River, only a little less than that which flows in the Rio de la Plata, almost 5 times more than flows in the River Indus and 14 times more than flows in the River Nile.

The importance of irrigation was further stressed by India:

"In the developing countries the preponderant use of water is for irrigation which accounts for more than ninety per cent of total consumption. This is because of the pivotal position that agriculture continues to occupy in their economies, both as the principal source of national income and the main source of employment. The pressure of population on land in these countries calls for both horizontal and vertical extension of areas that can be brought under cultivation and this means looking at water supply as the key input for maintaining the population/food balance. The great pressure of urbanization in these countries can be mitigated only by developing rural areas and there is no way to develop rural areas in many of these countries except by providing an assured irrigation facility."

Switzerland raised several salient questions. Is it wise to spend huge sums to provide water to the poor sections of major cities, or would the funds be better spent for rural development, which alone can halt the growth of these quarters? Should the provision of potable water be placed as most important, when 80 per cent of water utilization in the world is for agriculture? Is it sensible to spend millions on irrigation without trying to develop new types of grain requiring little water? Is the development of complex technology for fresh water more important than the development of new technology for conserving water? Switzerland concluded that more research was necessary, by both developed and developing countries, in order to answer these questions.

France, among others, maintained that, in agriculture, the main effort concerning proper use of water should be at the level of the farmer. Farming techniques must be well adapted to the climate and environmentally sound. All water management must be closely linked to land use planning, whether agricultural or urban, since harnessing water resources modified the land and the ecology.

Although selective aspects of environmental problems were mentioned by most delegations, Mostafa Tolba, Executive Director of the United Nations Environment Programme (UNEP) and Secretary-General of the United Nations Conference on Desertification, provided a comprehensive review of the environmental implications of water resources development. He stated that a prior assessment of probable environmental impacts should be mandatory in the planning of all water development projects. Alternative patterns of development should be studied. There may be complex impacts on human health and settlements, land and ecosystems, including fish and wildlife. Water-borne diseases, such as malaria and schistosomiasis are all the more prevalent when the characteristics of water bodies favour the abundance of their hosts, mosquitoes and snails. Careless waste-water disposal contaminates water, and the death rate from gastroenteritis is higher in areas with unsafe water supplies.

Water developments also have implications for human settlements since people must be resettled from impounded areas. Furthermore, inefficient use of water can cause waterlogging and salinity, which destroys arable land. Both proper land use and sound water management are also integral components of desertification control and reversal. Thus, the Water Conference and the Desertification Conference are closely interrelated.

Dr. Tolba concluded that water plays a major role in satisfying the basic and essential needs of food, shelter, clothing, health, education, and productive work. Satisfaction of the basic human needs of those billions who live below the level of subsistence is the most urgent challenge facing the international community.

Ibrahim Hussain, of the International Labour Organisation, told the Conference that productive employment is necessary to satisfy basic needs. Water resources development could provide work for millions, if appropriate technology were used. For small and large scale water projects, many activities in developing countries carried out by imported machines could be executed by relatively unskilled labour. Public participation in the planning process was also desirable.

The Netherlands suggested programmes in countries should not only be directed to the construction of the facilities, but also to preparatory and infrastructural elements. Among them are the education and involvement of the local population, promotional activities at various levels, the development and application of appropriate technologies and the establishment of institutional facilities, including those for training. Sharing of experiences between developing countries should be encouraged.

According to Martin Beyer, of UNICEF, the education of villagers was crucial for the proper use and maintenance of water supply installations. UNICEF encouraged the integration of health education into village water supply schemes and community participation. Its activities were based on the fact that up to 50 per cent of the population in developing countries are children and young people. The suffering and deaths caused by water-borne or water-related diseases are motivation enough for action. So is the drudgery of the women in many parts of the world, who with their children often have to spend large parts of their days only to lug water to their homes miles away from the sources, which are mostly contaminated.

Kenya described how its *Harambee* groups (*Harambee* means "let us pull together") had developed rural water supplies on a self-help basis. Women had played a major role in this development. Kenya saw money and manpower as the main obstacle to water development in developing countries. Donor countries should finance training of local manpower.

With its meagre resources, Tanzania realized that water and other services could best be provided if the rual population was concentrated in the villages. In 1973, about 2 million people lived in villages, today there are over 13 million people living in 7684 villages. The objective is to provide each village with clean water within 5 years and everyone in rural areas within 20 years.

Liberia regarded lack of adequate information about water resources as one of the chief obstacles to all types of development in that country. With regard to shared resources, no agreements with neighbouring countries can be made until the facts about the rivers in all countries are known.

Zambia felt the most effective means of contributing to water resources development in Africa would be the establishment of a Water Resources Development Institute for training of technicians and professionals. The most urgent need was for short courses to bring engineers up-to-date. Morocco regarded training as the real bottleneck in the Third World, but also suggested the Conference promote research benefiting developing countries. The Third World should also carry out research as, for example, solar energy for desalination of brackish waters. Nigeria said personnel training facilities must be established on a regional basis where none exist, and existing facilities strengthened where inadequate.

The Sudan endorsed the recommendations of the African regional meeting, later adopted by the Conference, that countries establish scientific institutes in common river basins to promote studies, formulate plans for basin development, and promote training, so as to reduce dependence on foreign consultancy. The Sudan also outlined the water situation in Africa: only 3 per cent of the irrigable land in Africa is under irrigation and 2.5 per cent of the continent's water resources are developed. Though Africa has a third of the world's hydropower potential, only 5.6 per cent of its potential is developed. The Sudan described its own long-term policy aimed at self-sufficiency in food production, and increased export of agricultural products.

Egypt stated it possessed the water and land resources and the man-power necessary to effectively solve its food problems. It was the responsibility of the rich and advanced nations to extend economic and technical aid such as soft loans and up-to-date technological methods, to Egypt and other developing nations.

Ethiopia said water losses by evaporation were higher in Africa than elsewhere in the world, and Africa was subject to highly variable seasonal water flows. Niger explained how the 1968-1975 drought marked the lives of 25 million Sahelians. A harvest of 4.5 million tons in an average year was reduced to only 2.9 million tons in 1973 and 1974. Loss of cattle, from 1969 to 1974, varied from 20 to 80 per cent, according to place, with an average of 30 per cent. The magnitude of the drought was due to the weakness of economic structures, especially the lack of water infrastructure that could have lessened its effects.

The difficulty facing the Sahel is not insufficiency of water: the irrigation potential is 1,500,000 hectares, while self-sufficiency in food by the year 2000 would require the irrigation of only 500,000 hectares. With regard to underground water, there are 10 billion m^3 per year for extraction, while the needs of men, livestock and industry to 2000 are estimated at 2.5 billion m^3 per year.

Chad pointed out that certain studies take too long to prepare. For a region such as the Sahel, studies must be rapid and produce concrete results, for the population cannot wait indefinitely.

Frequent references were also made to flood control. Faruk Berkol, Co-ordinator of United Nations Disaster Relief Office, said national development planning often overlooks the impact of natural water-related disasters. A primary aim of prevention is to restrict occupation of high-risk areas, in particular flood plains and low-lying coastal areas.

A few delegations complained of devastation by war. Vietnam stated that "war of aggression and sabotage" conducted by the United States against Vietnam largely interrupted large-scale water development which had now been resumed. Wells, pumping stations and dikes had been destroyed by bombings. Libya insisted only a small part of its water development plans had been realized because mine-fields from the Second World War still remain over large areas, making exploration for water resources difficult. The Colonial Powers "violated the innocence of our land and made it a playground for their armed conflict", Libya said. The mine-fields were still killing hundreds of people. Democratic Yemen said it is ironic that modern technology has been used to influence the environment for military purposes, when great areas of the world suffer from drought.

Great Britain said the solution to drought and other water problems in a developing country were not necessarily those which would be adopted in a developed country. Technology must be matched to the skills of those who are responsible for its operation. The drought of 1976 had reminded Great Britain that it still had much to learn.

France stressed that technology should not increase dependence. Technology of an advanced type should be promoted, provided that it is socially and economically adapted to the realities of each nation. Romania called for concrete actions to achieve a wide transfer of modern technology and technical assistance without political involvement. Libya and Mauritania advocated the transfer of research results at prices developing countries can afford. Pakistan recommended undertaking of research to improve the engineering economics of new techniques.

The Ukraine said broader use must be made of technologies that make little or no use of water and of non-polluting technologies. In Sweden, water requirements of industry had been greatly reduced by the use of water-saving technologies. At the same time, requirements of communities had stagnated with the over-all effect that water requirements in Sweden today are only half of that forecast just over 10 years ago.

The Philippines pointed out that to a large extent the technology to resolve many water problems already exists. What is required is the firm commitment at the national and international levels to provide financial and technical assistance, especially in the developing world. Indonesia and India, among others, suggested that water management was a field where technical co-operation between developing countries might be as important as the transfer of technology from developed nations. India has pioneered many labour-intensive technologies for water development, for example, stone masonry construction as opposed to concrete.

Bradford Morse, Administrator of the United Nations Development Programme and Secretary-General of United Nations Conference on Technical Co-operation among Developing Countries to be held in Buenos Aires in 1978, stated that the forthcoming Conference could help all to utilize technology in a way which would preserve and re-invigorate age-old values that protected and respected natural resources, like water. Small-scale irrigation projects are indispensable in most developing areas. Schemes requiring massive investment take a long time to build and may have less impact on farmers and villages than smaller schemes. One example of opportunity for new technology applicable to local situations is the development of special "low head turbines" enabling villages to obtain hydropower from local streams, as has already been done in China.

According to Morse, UNDP does not have the financial resources to facilitate the massive investment required to develop the water resources in developing nations, but the United Nations system does have a unique combination of human resources and skills to enable the planners in developing countries to focus on key issues and bring to them modern scientific knowledge. The UN system is a vehicle for aiding governments in mobilizing their own human and capital resources, although the major share of the development effort will have to come from within the countries themselves. Effective and stable water institutions must be created.

Saudi Arabia mentioned it is contributing more than 3 per cent of its gross national product for international assistance, of which 25 per cent is for water projects. It has made available $10,500 million in loans and grants to other countries for water-related projects between 1973 and 1976.

Canada cited the report by WHO and the World Bank (E/CONF.70/14) which indicated that 88 per cent of recent funding for community water programmes has been provided by individual countries. It pledged more than $361 million over the next 6 to 7 years for water projects in developing nations. Canada urged countries to give more priority to water development programmes when requesting assistance, and said it was taking a more active role in governing bodies in multilateral organizations to ensure that water projects are given sufficient priority.

The World Bank also maintained that water supply investment must compete more effectively in setting of national priorities. Every attempt must be made to mobilize funds through water charges in developing countries, but water supply rates should be designed to ensure that the poor can afford their needs. In 1976, the Bank lent $300 million for water supply and sanitation projects, mostly for urban areas.

According to Bernd Dietrich, of the World Health Organization, nearly 80 per cent of the rural population of the developing countries do not have access to safe water supply and more than 50 per cent of the urban population receive unsafe water. The situation concerning waste disposal is even worse. Globally, investments made since 1970 must be doubled; while for rural water supply alone four times more must be invested than in the last five years, if the Habitat target is to be reached. In this effort, governments will be faced with hard decisions, particularly in deciding whether to provide a high level of service to a few, or to aim at total population coverage rapidly through a lower level of service in quantity and possibly quality. Hard decisions are also needed with respect to financing and servicing of additional water supplies and the sharing of their costs between the rich and the poor, and between the urban and rural population.

Germany emphasized giving priority to a basic supply for the entire population rather than improving the supply to population groups already served. It has contributed 2 billion DM to replenish the International Development Association, which is appropriate for financing water projects, and $55 million to the International Fund for Agricultural Development which will support irrigation.

Arthur Davies, Secretary-General of the World Meteorological Organization, estimated that if an accurate assessment is to be made by the year 2000 of the world's water resources, about $1500 million will be needed for surface water investigations and five to ten times more for groundwater. These figures may seem high, but they were small in comparison with the benefits they will bring to national economies. To help accomplish this task, WMO is developing a new Hydrological Operational Multipurpose System (HOMS).

ISSUES INVOLVING RESOLUTIONS

While the delegates recognized that the massive finances required for development of water resources will have to come largely through domestic efforts, they also realized that even provision of safe drinking water required a level of investment far beyond the capability of many developing nations. Many developing countries therefore advocated the establishment of a fund for water development, and varying ideas were put forward as to its exact nature. Some suggested the creation of a voluntary fund under United Nations auspices, while others proposed a percentage of the United Nations annual budget. Tanzania, among others, suggested the creation of an "International Fund for Accelerating the Provision of Water to the Rural Areas in Developing Countries", and urged countries to reduce their armaments and credit to the fund part of the money thus saved. Most developed countries expressed reservations about the need for a separate fund, and indicated that their governments were prepared to increase financial assistance through their bilateral or existing multilateral agencies.

The final resolution on "financing arrangements" requested the Secretary-General to prepare a study of the most effective and flexible mechanism to increase the flow of financial resources for water development, for presentation to the General Assembly at its 32nd session through the ECOSOC at its 63rd session. It also recommended additional financial allocations be made to existing bilateral and international organizations.

With regard to institutional arrangements within the United Nations system, most of the African group proposed that one organization have sole responsibility for water. Most delegations, however, called for more effective co-ordination and a more productive use of existing institutions, rather than the establishment of a new organization at the intergovernmental and intersecretariat levels. While some representatives favoured the establishment of a new intergovernmental body under the Economic and Social Council to co-ordinate the activities of the United Nations agencies dealing with water, others felt that the existing Committee on Natural Resources could best serve the purpose.

At the intersecretariat level, some proposals advocated a new organization to co-ordinate activities, while most favoured the strengthening of existing structures, assigning a central role to the Advisory Committee on Co-ordination (ACC). Many countries endorsed the ACC recommendations for co-ordination presented to the conference, including the creation of an inter-agency Water Resources Board composed of all UN organizations dealing with water, including the Regional Economic Commissions.

At the regional level, there was unanimous agreement that the Regional Economic Commissions should be strengthened, as this was the level at which most of the work needed to be done, and the sharing of experience was most practical. Therefore, the establishment of regional training centres was recommended. At the country level, Germany and the Netherlands among others, proposed strengthening the role of UNDP representatives, as it was the main institution responsible for technical co-operation.

The resolution adopted called for strengthening of the Regional Commissions and co-ordination of projects and programmes under the leadership of UNDP representatives. At the intergovernmental level, the ECOSOC and the Committee on Natural Resources should play a central role in the promotion of co-operation as a follow-up to the Plan of Action adopted by the Conference. The Conference also recommended that the Committee on Natural Resources examine the proposals in the ACC report (E/CONF.70/CBP.4) at its May 1977 session and submit its recommendations to the ECOSOC at its 63rd session in July 1977.

Another international issue that received a great deal of attention at the Conference was the problem of shared water resources. Most representatives felt the questions of shared resources should be solved through negotiation between the states concerned on the basis of equal rights and mutual agreement. After lengthy debate, the Conference arrived at a consensus that in the absence of an agreement, relevant information should be exchanged rather than not starting any major works. Germany and several others pointed out that if an intermediary such as an international organization was necessary, the consent of all riparian states must be obtained. Bangladesh proposed setting up a United Nations Centre on International Rivers, with regional branches. Discussions concentrated on techniques for resolving conflicts rather than any specific disagreements, and generally underlined the inadequacy of international law for transnational water resources. Several representatives advocated defining codes of conduct based on experience gained in successful international litigation. Such codes should be flexible, allowing for evolution, free exchange of information and facilitate the evaluation of information among co-riparian states. They should also accommodate administration of water resources during various stages of socio-economic development.

Closely associated to the management of shared natural resources was the question of trans-frontier pollution. Norway and Sweden stated that transnational pollution should be dealt with on a regional basis, as national measures were insufficient. Sweden, like Norway, had been seriously affected by long-distance airborne pollutants, mainly sulphur from other European states. Russia requested the Conference to facilitate international agreements which would prevent other countries from discharging pollutants into rivers. Iran believed international standards for water quality should be developed for international rivers and rivers discharging into the sea.

Mostafa Tolba, of UNEP, reminded the Conference that the major issues of water resources had been identified in the Declaration on the Human Environment at Stockholm. The principles of law for regulating trans-frontier pollution have yet to be developed, but the whole question was under active consideration by organizations like the International Law Commission and the OECD, as well as by UNEP. It might be useful, he suggested, "to accelerate the study of international treaties, principles of international law, and international decisions widely accepted as binding, to help clarify the extent to which states may be prepared to accept principles that may put new obligations upon them". At present, when management of shared river basins is on a case-by-case basis, strengthened Regional Commissions, perhaps with the support of UNEP Regional Advisory Teams, could offer useful help.

A resolution on river commissions recommended to the Secretary-General to explore the possibility of organizing meetings between existing international river commissions. The Conference also called for a re-arrangement of priorities in the work of the International Law Commission, with a view to ensuring the codification of existing international examples of joint action to facilitate the progressive development of international law of shared waters. These activities should be co-ordinated with those of other international bodies with a view to the early conclusion of an international convention.

Pollution and other environmental aspects of water resources development were frequently mentioned. Excessive exploitation of resources in the absence of effective legislation and control could not continue. Waste-water treatment should also be backed with financial and legislative support. The Holy See pointed out the need to protect water against radio-active wastes. The spread of water-related diseases and loss of productive land to salinity and erosion must be prevented. Short-sighted forestry practices and over-grazing by livestock were destroying the capacity of land to absorb water, filter it, and recharge ground supplies. Water planning should be co-ordinated with land use, and be an integral part of overall development planning.

That most delegates from developing nations, however, regarded environmental considerations as a secondary issue to development was clearly demonstrated when a number of developing countries, led by Brazil, expressed strong opposition to a recommendation by the United States at the final plenary session, calling for an evaluation of the environmental costs of hydropower projects. Only industrialized nations, already developed, could afford such considerations, they contended. The Conference, however, adopted a comprehensive set of recommendations on environment, health and pollution control, and a resolution for development of industrial technologies, using little or no water, and facilitating recycling.

More efficient use of water was also emphasized and included development of technologies using less water and maintenance of existing water supply services. Sweden regarded transmission of information, whether to farmer or decision-maker, of utmost importance to improve utilization of water. Since agriculture consumed by far the greatest amount of water, accounting for up to 90 per cent, particularly in certain developing countries, the efficiency of its storage, distribution and application on the farm must be improved in project operations. France maintained that the main effort concerning efficient use of water should be at the level of the farmer. Other delegations, including the Netherlands, Sri Lanka and Indonesia, expressed the view that farmers should participate in the planning, operation and management of irrigation projects.

Public participation was regarded as essential in all forms of water development, especially the role of women, in community water supplies in developing countries.

There was unanimous agreement on implementation of the Habitat recommendation to provide clean and adequate water supplies for all, by 1990, if possible, and the parallel improvement of sanitation. The Conference endorsed this aim by approving an action plan to reach the goal, drafted by WHO and the World Bank. As a focal point for these efforts, the Conference approved the proposal by developing countries to designate the decade 1980-1990 as the *International Drinking Water Supply and Sanitation Decade*. A plan of action was also adopted for agricultural water use. Another resolution stressed the need for strengthening assessment of water resources if these plans of action are to be implemented.

Two other resolutions welcomed forthcoming United Nations Conferences. A resolution on the "Role of Water in Combating Desertification" urged governments to participate in the United Nations Conference on Desertification, and recommended action with regard to water in countries facing desertification. The other resolution urged governments to participate in the United Nations Conference on Technical Co-operation among Developing Countries in Argentina in 1978 and recommended the United Nations system promote such co-operation in water resources development. Two resolutions of a more political nature dealt with water policies in occupied territories and the Panama Canal Zone. The resolutions and other recommendations of the Conference comprise the Mar del Plata Action Plan contained in this volume.

CONFERENCE ANALYSIS

The recommendations approved by the Conference are based on a consolidated set of proposals which emerged mainly from five regional preparatory meetings held in 1976. They were modified only slightly by the delegations in Committee. The preparatory process had contributed significantly to raising the consciousness of governments and scientists regarding their national and the global water situation. As Secretary-General Mageed stated in his opening address: "The very process of preparation has generated a certain momentum on a global scale. A new consciousness was created. National committees were created or re-activated in some countries. New laws or decrees were promulgated in others. This momentum has not only to be maintained, but further developed."

It is this awareness they create which is the major contribution of World Conferences held under the auspices of the United Nations. Globally, we have the basic technology, human resources and finances to solve water problems, especially in developing countries. The problem is a lack of awareness and political will both nationally and internationally. A World Conference is one of the few options available for creating awareness and political will at a global level. Nothing has done more to raise global consciousness regarding the lack of basic needs of an impoverished billion than World Conferences held by the United Nations.

The Water Conference resulted in unprecedented stock-taking of the whole range of water problems at the national, regional, and international levels, especially in developing countries, and their consideration by a world forum. Some 215 thematic papers on various aspects of water development and management were prepared by individual countries for the Conference. Much of the data and other information contained in papers prepared by many developing countries is difficult to find and will be helpful to international organizations and bilateral donor agencies active in the water resources area.

The Conference itself provided a forum for exchange of experience, and doing business. One African delegate explained what the Conference meant to him: "I would have had to spend ten years travelling around the world in order to meet these people to discuss water problems with them". Present were representatives of all the United Nations agencies concerned with water, and members of most bilateral aid agencies, as well as the decision-makers and technical experts from respective nations. The representatives were the Ministers and other decision-makers responsible for policies and their implementation back home. Water resources planning, project authorization and the level of funding are all essentially political processes. Planners may decide the feasibility of the project, but politics decides the implementation of the plan.

It is frequently not realized that what distinguishes United Nations conferences from other international conferences is that they are action-oriented. There is considerable practical action before the conference, followed by implementation of the different recommendations to varying degrees afterwards. The Water Conference will have a profound impact on thinking and practice for the rest of this century.

Implementation of recommendations requires funding and the need for large-scale assistance to developing countries was repeatedly stressed. Documents prepared for the Conference indicate that for agricultural water use, the investment required for a 15 year programme is of the order of $97 billion, that for the assessment of resources $9 billion, and for community water supplies and sanitation $132,940 million to meet the 1990 Habitat target. Although most of this money is to be provided by national budgets, most developing countries indicated that this level of investment was far beyond their capability and stressed the need for financial assistance. While donor countries rejected a new fund and few pledges were made, governments did express their intentions to increase funding through existing multilateral institutions and bilateral programmes. In donor countries with a democratic system of government, pledges are not definite anyway, and have to be ratified by parliament. Some Western nations admitted privately their preference for increasing bilateral funding. Recipient nations, however, tend to prefer assistance from international organizations which comes with no strings attached. There are valid arguments on both sides.

Although the financial figures appear formidable, they can be obtained if there is the political will. Equal and more money is constantly being found for other areas of expenditure. The money could easily be obtained by diverting a fraction of the money from armaments expenditure. As Barbara Ward has frequently emphasized, the human race might have clean water and adequate food by the end of the century for $30 billion a year, one-tenth of the $300 billion spent annually on armaments.

As several delegations pointed out, the available resources could be used more efficiently both by governments and agencies. Costs could be reduced in many instances by resorting to local manpower and materials. Most developing countries manufacture little or no construction equipment and import it with scarce foreign exchange, while much of the work could be done by labour, also reducing unemployment. Measures to renovate irrigation schemes and eradicate water-borne disease can also be highly labour-intensive. Once countries train more of their own professionals, fewer expensive foreign consultants would be required.

Secondly, there is at present money available for water resources development which is not being used because developing countries have not requested assistance. Canada has repeatedly stated that it wishes to give more money to water development, but nations, having other priorities, do not request such assistance. Furthermore, many developing countries do not have adequate expertise to plan good projects and formulate properly the project documents requesting aid. This is often the real constraint, rather than a lack of funds.

The designation of the period 1980/1990 as the International Drinking Water Supply and Sanitation Decade should help to marshal international investment in support of national action. As Mageed stated, international investment from 1971-1975 has been too low; for example, for community water supply only 12 per cent of urban costs and 9 per cent of rural costs. If the Decade is properly planned and further interest generated, there is no reason why in many countries the Habitat objective should not be attained. Although ideally the provision of rural water supply and sanitation should be part of an integrated rural development programme, this approach, though cheaper, would add considerably to the time necessary for implementation. Estimated populations of Third World nations with services are shown in Table 2.

Table 2. Estimated populations* of developing countries in 1975 with reasonably adequate community water supply and sanitation services

	Total population (UN estimates)	Population served (from WHO survey)			
		Community water supply		Sanitation	
	in million	in million	%	in million	%
Urban	577	450	77	437	75
Rural	1419	313	22	209	15
Total	1996	763	38	646	33

* Not including the population of China
Source: Report on Community Water Supplies E/CONF. 70/14.

The situation varies considerably from country to country. In Africa, some countries like Tanzania and the Sudan are already implementing programmes for rural water supply, while in others not even plans have been formulated. The adoption of action programmes concerning drinking water supplies and agricultural water use were two of the major achievements of the Conference, affecting directly the basic needs of the most impoverished people.

The magnitude of the task of expanding and maintaining irrigated areas in the developing market economy countries is staggering, as can be seen from the programme to be executed by 1990 by the United Nations:

   22 million hectares of new irrigation.

   45 million hectares of improved irrigation.

   78 million hectares of drainage.

   440 thousand million cubic metres of additional irrigation water.

   97 thousand million dollars of investment, at 1975 prices.

These investment costs, it must be realized, do not include irrigation costs in the developed world of an estimated 23.1 million hectares of new irrigation and improvements of 41.3 million hectares of existing irrigation.

Will the world provide this funding? A more realistic question is whether the world can afford not to provide it, when the global consequences of the resulting starvation are considered. What action will be taken remains to be seen.

It is only now that we are beginning to see the concrete accomplishments of the World Food and Population Conferences. The International Fund for Agricultural Development which, at the Food Conference, appeared almost a lost cause, is about to commence operation. At its disposal over the first three years, is an initial operating fund of 31 billion, much of which will be available for irrigation. Although a fertilizer fund had been discussed for years, it was not until after the World Food Conference that the International Fertilizer Supply Scheme was created. Frequently World Conferences act as such a catalyst for action both internationally and nationally. The plan to make the Sudan not only self-sufficient in food production, but also the bread-basket of the Arab world is a case in point. Similarly, the Water Conference will undoubtedly contribute to the acceleration of water resources development.

It may be considered a concrete achievement of the Conference that no new organization was created. Currently, United Nations agencies cover a wide spectrum of water development and another body might well create more complications than facilitate water development. What is necessary is better co-ordination of the United Nations system. The report *Present and Future Activities of the United Nations System in the Water Sector* (E/CONF.70/CBP .4)* contained in the proceedings provides details of the constraints that must be overcome. Even though these constraints are rectified, problems will continue as long as governments give conflicting direction to the governing bodies of the different United Nations agencies and organizations, resulting in a competitive approach to development. For example, a Ministry of Health determines direction for WHO, while a Ministry of Agriculture gives direction to FAO, and so forth, but the approaches to water development of these Ministries are not co-ordinated by their national governments. Until governments co-ordinate their policies at the national level, co-ordination at the international level is unlikely to occur.

The Conference was too broad a forum to deal constructively with such a complex issue as shared water resources, and the problem remains a divisive political issue. Countries had difficulty in agreeing upon the term *shared water resources* and there was very little substantive discussion. Though many countries claimed to have co-operation policies, the reality of the situation is quite different.

In comparison to other UN World Conferences in recent years, the Water Conference was marked by little political confrontation and had by far the smallest budget among those which have been held. Much of the success of the Conference must be attributed to the Secretary-General, Mageed, who was appointed less than a year before the Conference. Considering the short time available and the rather modest budget, Mageed did an outstanding job. He was assisted in his efforts by a small, but highly competent secretariat, especially his technical secretary, Enzo Fano.

Since the Conference, the Committee on Natural Resources (CNR) decided at its May 1977 session to recommend to the ECOSOC that the CNR should meet in special

---
*See *Water Development and Management*, edited by Asit K. Biswas, Pergamon Press, Oxford, 1978.

session in 1978 in order to deal with the subject of water, as a follow-up to the Water Conference. As Mageed stated in his opening address to the Water Conference, the ultimate success of the deliberations of Mar del Plata will be determined by their influence on the course of events over the next two decades. The development of water resources, he concluded, was an important means of combating "under-development" and the turmoil it created in the greater part of the globe, thus contributing to the greater well-being of mankind.

REFERENCES

1. Margaret R. Biswas and A. K. Biswas, *World Population Conference: A Perspective*, Agriculture and Environment, Vol. 1, No. 4, December 1974, pp. 385-391.

2. Margaret R. Biswas and A. K. Biswas, *World Food Conference: A Perspective*, Agriculture and Environment, Vol. 2, No. 1, June 1975, pp. 15-39.

3. Margaret R. Biswas, *Habitat in Retrospect*, International Journal for Environmental Studies Vol.11, 1977.

Resources and Needs: Assessment of the World Water Situation *

INTRODUCTION

THE POTENTIAL WORLD WATER CRISIS: A CALL FOR ACTION

Leonardo da Vinci described water as "the driver of nature". An overstatement? Perhaps. Still the fact remains: water makes human life possible. And it is difficult to imagine any programme for human development or improvement that does not presuppose or require a readily available supply of water.

Readily available for much of the world's population, water has traditionally been regarded as an inexhaustible gift of nature by many societies. Such complacency about this life-giving resource threatens human welfare, livelihood, development, and indeed life itself in the years to come.

One only has to consider that right now population growth accompanied by agricultural development is straining water resources even in humid lands — not only in highly industrialized regions but also in less developed areas of the world.

The projected doubling and trebling of the world population, coupled with increasing world industrialization and agricultural development, accelerates this trend. At the same time, population growth together with industrial and agricultural development all contribute to a serious deterioration in the quality of water.

It is consequently a statement of fact rather than mere conjecture to say that there will be a critical shortage of water of suitable quality to sustain future growth unless water management is radically improved.

In any discussion about water, it is important to stress that we are speaking of a *fixed* total stock. Unlike other natural resources, the total global supply of water can be neither increased (as timber or fish) nor diminished (as petroleum or coal). Since water is continuously being renewed through nature's hydrological cycle, it is potentially inexhaustible. While this is so, locally available supplies can at the same time be quickly depleted or made unusable by inadequate conservation, pollution or over-all careless management.

In theory, the global stock of water could meet greatly expanded human needs. In reality, the traditional sources of water supply, surface run-off and groundwater stores, are inequitably distributed among peoples and countries. Some communities live where regular precipitation gives them an ample surplus at present. Others have far more water than they want or need, but not necessarily in the right place or at the right time. Still others have barely enough water for current needs, and drought is perennial through the wide belt of arid lands.

---

* This document has been prepared by the Conference secretariat in co-operation with the interested organizations and programmes of the United Nations system. The secretariat gratefully acknowledges the assistance of Professor Gilbert F. White, who acted as consultant in the preparation of the document.

In short, globally there may be potentially enough water to meet forthcoming needs. But, frustratingly, it tends to be available in the wrong place, at the wrong time, or with the wrong quality. And in one way or another, all societies are affected, however rich, however poor.

This general assessment of a world-wide condition becomes a specific reality when one considers:

(a) Reasonably safe supplies of drinking water are unavailable for at least one fifth of the world's city dwellers and three quarters of its rural people; in many countries, less than one half of the urban population and less than one tenth of the rural population are served with an adequate and safe water supply;

(b) Increasing and unplanned concentration of population and industry in large urban areas strains water supply: this leads to problems of waste disposal which, in turn, degrade the quality of life and environmental health;

(c) Proliferation of industrial processes, greater use of energy and increased agricultural activity are causing progressive and chronic degradation of the quality of available water by the increase of toxic compounds and other pollutants: the mutagenic and carcinogenic effect of these substances poses a potential threat to human life;

(d) Backwardness and relative isolation of rural areas where the great majority of the world population now lives aggravate the difficulty of providing adequate and safe supplies of drinking water, improved sanitation and waste disposal;

(e) Expansion of food production in water-short areas and in marginal lands has necessitated rapid development of irrigation and land reclamation, to the degree that water and land resources have been exploited to their limit in many areas;

(f) Ever-growing land degradation from such causes as water-logging, salinization and erosion is leading to losses in production potential, investment and employment;

(g) Ground-water supplies are being exhausted, while both surface- and ground-water sources are deteriorating in many areas;

(h) Water use is often needlessly inefficient and wasteful, considering the possible application of scientific knowledge and the setting of appropriate service levels;

(i) Expensive technology for water development to compensate for shortage is straining inadequate resources in many regions;

(j) Conflicts about rights and priorities among users intensifies as the demand for available water accelerates.

These problems affect different societies in different ways. The immediate concern may be unpotable water and human waste in the shanty town of a tropical city, multiplying wastes in an industrialized high-income country, shortage of water impeding agricultural development in an arid land, watershed destruction and ground-water depletion in an entire nation.

One may perceive these as local, regional and national problems. And indeed they are. But while it may be said that arid lands, for instance, have their exclusive set of problems — as have industrialized nations — still, many problems are common to many regions and communities. In many instances, the resolution of these problems would benefit greatly from the sharing of national experience and the rational management of whole river basins that know no national boundary. For this reason, it is useful and practical to view current local and regional problems about this global resource as a global concern requiring co-operation among nations. Without such collaboration, it will not only be difficult to alleviate current short-comings, but more important, to curb their proliferation and avert a world water crisis.

Obstacles to such salutary co-operation are deeply rooted. Water has traditionally been regarded as a local concern, and much past management has been exclusively limited to local programmes. The major constraint, however, to broader co-operation is complacency about a natural resource that may currently be perceived as inexhaustible in some areas. This constraint is compounded by varying policies, or even lack of policies, that stem from widely varying national priorities, opportunities and limitations. Today circumstances of population and industrial growth, as well as technological complexities, force us to take a more comprehensive international view.

Nations may attempt to solve water problems unilaterally. But this may result in unnecessary and wasteful duplication of effort. What is more, many nations are limited not only in their ability to estimate the long-term effects of any new local water system they may initiate but also in their capability to appraise the full implications of such a system on the future well-being of the entire nation and its neighbouring countries.

This preamble serves as a brief statement of a grave condition and as an introduction to matters that will be developed and expanded in subsequent papers prepared by the secretariats, interested organizations and programmes of the United Nations system.

The first of these papers, "Resources and needs: an assessment of the world water situation", is a preliminary step in the understanding of the problem and its possible solution. The second paper will treat technology and how it may best be used under different socio-economic conditions.* A third paper will explore policy options and consider how institutions and water policies may best be adapted to the physical, economic and cultural conditions of individual countries.**

Finally, it is expected that concern about this vulnerable resource will be translated into a series of concrete proposals for action at national and international levels. Water resources might then be efficiently and rationally developed and used for the betterment of all concerned nations and mankind. To quote from the conclusion of this first paper: "It should ... not be taken for granted that any sector of the world's population need drink contaminated water, that industry need continue its present pattern of largely unregulated water use and discharge, that agriculture cannot alter its current pattern of irrigation loss and misuse of water, or that productive soils need be destroyed and aquifers exhausted beyond our ability to replenish them in our own lifetime."

---

*See *Water Development and Management*, edited by Asit K. Biswas, Pergamon Press, Oxford, 1978.
**Included in this volume, see pp. 70-110.

I. AN OVERVIEW OF THE WORLD SITUATION

The total amount of world water is constant and can be neither increased nor diminished. Most is ocean water. Only a small proportion is fresh, and of this fresh supply, less than 1 per cent is available for human use in streams, lakes, swamps and in the ground; the rest is locked away in ice-caps and glaciers.

Estimates of the volume of fresh-water supply can be derived from observation and measurement of precipitation, evaporation and ground water. Short-comings in appraisal methods, however, and lack of basic hydrological data in some areas limit the accuracy of these estimates. Still, rough estimates can be made for continents and for the world as a whole. These reveal tremendous variations in local supply, ranging in scale from rocky deserts with virtually no water to tropical forests with a water surplus throughout the year. At any one place, the available supply may vary from day to day and from year to year. Water supply also varies in mineral, chemical and bacteriological quality.

Water is mostly used for domestic, industrial and irrigation purposes, and of these, irrigation often accounts for more withdrawal than all the other uses combined. Some water is used for on-site agriculture and mining. Livestock, fish and wildlife all require water. Lakes and streams are used for transportation, recreation, and the generation of hydroelectric power. Other water is stored, diverted or confined to reduce losses from floods. A rapidly growing use is for the conveyance and disposal of wastes from cities, factories and farms.

What will be the future demand for these uses? What effect will this demand have upon supply and its quality? How will this, in turn, affect human health and welfare?

These questions are crucial. Faced with fixed supply and growing demand, their solution in any area will depend upon prevailing economic and social conditions, administrative and judicial processes, the availability of funds to effect change, and the availability and suitability of technology in so far as it affects the environment and the health of the population.

Since these are dynamic considerations, any measure taken for the improvement of water supply and use in a country may become inappropriate in that country at a later time and may be entirely inapplicable to the aims and policies of other countries at any time.

In a world context, the long-term effects of man-inspired development are conjectural. Just as shifts in the relative properties of the land surface may influence climate, so may the construction of new water reservoirs and the diversion of streams and ocean currents. Further, alterations in the chemical content of streams flowing into the ocean may affect ocean life.

In the short run, the welfare of humanity is likely to be measurably affected by the success with which nations adapt their activities to the realities of available water supply and human needs in specific river basins or regions. With few exceptions, supply is highly variable in each region; information

about water resources is inadequate, potential uses are multiple and involve trade-offs in allocating supply; standards of quality tend to be determined by local or national preference; the application of scientific knowledge about water and its use lags far behind the findings of basic research.
These generalities only take on their full meaning when expressed in terms of concrete situations. However important global statistics may be, they have more significance when expressed in terms of a specific water basin or country. Only then do they reveal the problems affecting the capability of peoples and nations to develop and even survive.

II. ASSESSMENT OF FRESH-WATER SUPPLIES: PHYSICAL RESOURCES

A. *Water and Fresh Water in the Global Cycle*

Recent estimates show that the total volume of water on earth is about 1.4×10^9 cubic kilometres. More than 97 per cent is ocean water. At any given moment, an estimated 77.2 per cent of fresh water is stored in ice-caps and glaciers, 22.4 per cent is ground water and soil moisture, 0.35 per cent is in lakes and swamps, 0.04 per cent is in the atmosphere and less than 0.01 per cent is in streams (see table 1).

Table 1. *Total volume of water on earth*

	Percentage
Ocean water	97.3
Fresh water	2.7
Location of fresh water:	
Ice-caps and glaciers	77.2
Ground water* and soil moisture	22.4
Lakes and swamps	0.35
Atmosphere	0.04
Streams	0.01

Source: A. Baumgartner and E. Reichel, *The World Water Balance* (Munich, 1975).

* About two thirds lies deeper than 750 metres below the surface.

While ice-caps, glaciers and ground water account for most fresh water resources, for all practical purposes, it is surface water that constitutes the basic available supply for most people.

Through the hydrological cycle, water circulates from earth to atmosphere to earth: driven by the suns's energy, water moves endlessly from the oceans to the atmosphere to the continents, and back again to the oceans; much precipitated water that falls on land is evaporated into the atmosphere; some is absorbed by plant roots and re-enters the atmosphere via leaf-pore transpiration; some travels over or under the earth's surface and eventually reaches the sea. Because oceans cover seven tenths of the earth's surface, it is evident that a major part of precipitation falls directly into the sea; it has passed through the hydrological cycle without having been a natural resource at all.

With a few minor exceptions, the only water that can thus be considered as a potential resource for man is that portion of total precipitation that happens to fall on land. It is a usable resource only from the moment it strikes the land surface until the moment it re-enters the oceans or one of the land-locked seas or salt lakes, and only so long as it remains comparatively pure.

Although surface water provides most of man's available supply, ground-water use has been heavily developed in some parts of the world and this has resulted in the excessive exploitation of some water-bearing formations. With improved knowledge, reliance on ground water will undoubtedly increase. But there is much to learn about ground water and its rational use, and it will require particularly intelligent management. In contrast, surface water has been far more thoroughly and systematically studied.
Given favourable circumstances, water supplies can be increased by such techniques as watershed management and the direct harvesting of precipitation.

Less conventional sources of increased availability include cloud-seeding, desalination and waste water re-use. While these non-conventional sources may be important in a particular local context and may become more important in the future, surface and ground water will probably remain the most important supplies for some time to come.

The usefulness of water and its socio-economic value depend upon its quality. For this reason, any assessment of fresh water must take into account both quality and quantity.

B. Methods of Appraising Surface Water

All the water reaching the streams within a river basin is potentially available as surface-water supply. The degree of availability will vary at different places along the flow of a stream; the quantity of water available at any specific location can be determined by estimates of discharge flow, measurement of stage, velocity and channel section of the stream flow.

Since the design, planning and management of water resources require knowledge of the time characteristics of flow, it is important to have a continuous record of stream-flow data for many years at points of withdrawal or use. Of course, it is rarely possible to forecast the locations for which stream-flow data will be needed in the future. Moreover, lack of funds and trained manpower often preclude the possibility of maintaining extensive data-gathering networks. Great skill and care are required in the design and operation of basic data networks to maximize the benefits from limited expenditure. For these and other reasons, it is necessary to rely heavily on estimates. These may be derived either from measurements made at other locations or from analysis of the relationship between stream-flow and other hydrometeorological data and physiographic characteristics. Observations from similar locations may be judiciously pooled to provide better data than could be derived exclusively from any one location.

Whether estimated or directly measured, the mean annual flow of a stream over a period of many years will thus represent available surface-water supply. Full use of this supply would require that demand coincide with flow at any given time. The extent to which supply is in fact used will depend upon the interrelation of rate of flow at a particular time, areal distribution and the technology that can be applied by the people concerned.

Consequently, any appraisal of water supply must take economic and environmental as well as hydrological data into account if we are to develop plans that harmonize demand and supply within acceptable economic limits. The physical studies require frequency and sequential analyses of flow data, and should also pay heed to the availability of ground water supplies.

Annual analysis of discharge data will yield adequate information for the planning and management of very large reservoirs such as Lake Volta. In such large reservoirs, a series of *annual* discharge data may permit evaluation of the possibility of critically low inflow for periods of several years. In contrast, in the case of smaller water supply reservoirs, it is necessary to know the variability of discharge *within* the year. And for many projects it is even necessary to consider *daily* discharges and possible extreme flood conditions.

Although sufficiently reliable estimates of the volume and variability of stream flow can sometimes be made by direct comparison with flow at nearby locations, it is more often necessary to use relationships between flow itself and other factors.

Hydrologists and engineers have many scientific tools and methods for assessing water supply in the absence of direct measurements. The improvement of these methods and their dissemination was the main objective of the International Hydrological Decade (1965-1974) and of the International Hydrological and Operational Hydrology Programmes of UNESCO and WMO, respectively, particularly concerning the water balance.

Fundamental to the water balance concept is the equation of continuity. That is, for any hydrological unit and specified time period:

$$\text{Outflow} = \text{inflow} \pm \text{change in storage}.$$

This principle is applicable to a small catchment, a major river basin, a reservoir, a continent, or the world as a whole. Since changes in storage become negligible when projected over a long period of time, the mean annual water balance for a river basin can be stated:

$$\text{Run-off} = \text{precipitation} - \text{evapotranspiration}.$$

(Evapotranspiration may be defined as transpiration and evaporation from soil, water and other surfaces.)

Maps of average annual precipitation, evaporation and run-off, are best derived from systematic water balance analysis. The isolines can be constructed so that a balance of the three terms of the equation is achieved at all locations, thereby providing a quick, approximate estimate of the three terms on a geographical basis.

The water balance concept is basic to water resource analysis because it provides a means for estimating the value of hydrological and meteorological data in assessing the effects of proposed developments. The water balance is applicable for any period of time. For short periods of time, changes in storage become a predominant consideration and cannot be neglected. In such circumstances, it is helpful to apply conceptual modelling techniques in which factors and natural laws governing the movement of waters in a basin are represented by mathematical formulae. Modelling involves repetitive solution of complex functions requiring the aid of an electronic computer. Such techniques can provide estimated daily values of several components in the cycle and may serve many purposes. They are particularly helpful in evaluating the consequences of man's activities on water resources.

C. Methods of Appraising Precipitation and Evapotranspiration

Precipitation is the primary source of water supply for world food production: though irrigation places many demands upon stream flow and ground water, it only supplements precipitation in meeting the basic consumption requirement of crops. Precipitation data therefore play a vital role in water resource development and management. Records are generally more extensive and more numerous than those for stream flow, largely because the measurements can be made by lay observers and the equipment used is less costly. Consequently, measurement networks are often densely concentrated in some regions. Average annual precipitation values can be correlated with physiographic characteristics. The resulting relationships can then be used for interpolation of data in areas of sparse measurement networks. On the whole, however, precipitation is generally undermeasured and reliable averages are difficult to obtain.

The common methods of projecting water supply assume a continuation of prevailing climatic conditions. Since planning for the development and use of water supplies is, by necessity, based on the recently recorded past, the possibilities of significant changes in climate are of critical concern. For example, it is important to know whether widespread and prolonged drought — such as that experienced recently in the Sudano-Sahelian zone of West Africa — can be expected to occur within the natural year-to-year cycle or should rather be considered the result of climatic change.

There is abundant evidence that major changes in climate have occurred during the history of the earth (the ice-ages, for example), and there is no reason to presume that the present climatic régimes will not change within the next 1000-5000 years. More important, but less evident, is the magnitude and probability of natural changes which can occur within periods of, say, 50 to 100 years. Such information, if it were available, could be advantageously used for planning purposes. There is, therefore, an obvious need for improved understanding of the nature and causes of trends in climatic change.

Evapotranspiration is the most difficult term to evaluate in the water-balance equation. Observations are usually restricted to measurements of loss from tanks containing water, plants and soil, or soil alone. There are many techniques for computing free-water evaporation and *potential* evapotranspiration (the maximum water loss under prevailing meteorological conditions uninfluenced by soil-moisture deficiency). These techniques involved the observation of the influence of radiation, wind movement, temperature and humidity, for example. While it is hoped that ways will be found to improve methods of estimating evapotranspiration in the future, reasonably reliable analyses can be made, even at present, where an adequate data-gathering network exists. The techniques for estimating free-water evaporation are more reliable than for evapotranspiration. This is a matter of some importance in project planning and design. For example, the evaporation from Lake Nasser represents about one quarter of the normal flow of the Nile at Aswan.

D. Methods of Appraising Ground Water

Ground water and surface water commonly form a linked system. Flow can be in either direction, and the rate of flow varies geographically and chronologically.

The interchange is not significant for some aquifers (rock or soil containing and transmitting water). But it has been estimated that about 30 per cent of the total flow in surface streams is supplied from ground water, and seepage from streams is known to be a principal source of inflow to some aquifers. Water withdrawn from riparian wells along an alluvial stream can effect an appreciable reduction in surface flow, and the diversion of surface flow can reduce ground-water recharge. But in other instances, withdrawal from either source has no effect on supply from the other. Although the methods of appraisal are different for ground and surface water, supply from either source cannot be evaluated independently unless it is established that the interchange is minimal.

It is important to note that there are two distinct types of circumstances concerning the development and management of ground-water supplies. Normally, ground water is considered a renewable resource with optimal use restricted to the average rate of recharge. "Mining" of ground water, however, is sometimes carried out with fixed-term objectives: the aquifer which supports 1.5 million hectares of irrigated land in the Texas Panhandle will be exhausted within a few decades at current pumping rates.

Average annual recharge can in extreme cases be relatively insignificant, as in the large artesian basin of the intercalary of the northern Sahara. This basin contains immense quantities of fresh water, some of it with ages up to 40,000 years.

To reflect the possible mining of water in appraisals of total regional or global supply, it is necessary to assume withdrawal rates and take into account the total storage and planned development. The appraisal of aquifer storage in particular requires extensive on-site exploration.

The estimated rate of withdrawal of ground water on a continuing basis is a key factor in the appraisal of regional or global water supply. The maximum rate at which water can be withdrawn without adversely affecting the source may be termed "safe yield". Since supply recharge in many cases tends to increase with draw-down, the safe-yield concept must incorporate economic considerations if it is to serve any practical purpose. Safe yield may also depend upon the location, spacing and depth of the bore-holes in relation to the speed of movement of water underground.

Flow rates in aquifers are normally extremely slow, and time lags in underground phenomena can therefore be very long. It may take more than a century for an increase in water level in the recharge area of an extensive artesian aquifer to be transmitted to remote locations in the aquifer. It is important, therefore, that variations in pressure or water level be correctly related to causal factors, with due consideration given to lags in time.

The quantity of water available under specified conditions may be estimated from the water-balance equation. The equation can be written for surface and subsurface components of the basin as a whole, or for the ground-water reservoir only. The latter approach is essential for adequate understanding of the ground-water régime and for management purposes, while the former is more suitable for evaluation of total surface and ground-water supplies.

Either way, a sound estimate requires accurate hydrological data and extensive information about aquifer characteristics. Because of the interrelationships involved, the solution may become extremely complex and the results somewhat less accurate than for surface-water evaluation alone. Various types of models have been devised to cope with ground-water assessment — physical, analogue and mathematical — and these are acquiring widespread use.

E. Methods of Appraising Water Quality

The physical, chemical and biological properties of water determine the suitability of its quality for various uses.

Water is considered to be polluted when it is altered in composition, directly or indirectly, to the degree that it is less suitable or even unsuitable — for a particular use or function. Pollution increasingly results from man's activities, but water in its natural state is not always of sufficiently good quality to serve all uses. For example, saline waters are sometimes found in arid and semi-arid regions, some streams in their natural state carry heavy loads of silt in suspension or as bed load.

Pollutants reach water bodies from "point sources" such as power stations, factories, mines and city sewer outlets, and from "non-point sources" such as eroding banks and cultivated fields.

Measurement of the concentration of pollutants can be made at points of waste discharge and in downstream reaches or aquifers. The monitoring of quality is made difficult by two conditions. First the concentration of pollutants in aquatic ecosystems is affected by many external conditions, including stream flow, turbidity and temperature, and these episodic effects are rarely proportionate to the average volume of the pollutant. Secondly, it is uncertain how a given dose of a particular polluting substance will adversely affect humans, fish, benthic and other organisms in the environment.

It is impractical and incorrect to consider data from one measurement station as representative of the characterisitics of a long water stream. Accordingly, observations of water quality are made by collecting and analysing samples periodically at a network of stations along streams, lakes and at bore-holes. On a stream such as the Rhine or the Ohio, the analyses take into account: temperature, sediment load, dissolved solids, major nutrients such as phosphorous and nitrogen, organic material as measured by biochemical oxygen demand and dissolved oxygen, salts, acidity, bacteriological contamination as measured by coliform organisms, and heavy metals.

The difficulties of monitoring quality are intensified by the proliferation of man-made chemical compounds that find their way into water bodies. As a result, it is debatable whether existing networks and current monitoring methods are truly effective in identifying the existence and point of entry of potentially harmful substances. It should also be noted that some chemical pollutants are removed in conventional water-treatment processes, while others remain.

Table 2. Networks of hydrological stations

Region	Non-recording rain-gauges Number existing	Non-recording rain-gauges Existing density 1000 square kms/station	Self-recording rain-gauges Number existing	Self-recording rain-gauges Existing density 1000 square kms/station	Evaporation stations Number existing	Evaporation stations Existing density 1000 square kms/station	Discharge stations Number existing	Discharge stations Existing density 1000 square kms/station	Sediment stations Number existing	Sediment stations Existing density 1000 square kms/station	Water-quality stations Number existing	Water-quality stations Existing density 1000 square kms/station
Africa[a]	18 520	1.48	1 214	22.61	1 043	26.32	4 390	6.19	740	36.73	801	33.94
Asia[b]	17 815	1.69	2 489[c]	11.92	1 590	18.00	6 386	4.58	1 601	17.30	3 290	7.94
South America	12 200	1.05	2 106	5.92	1 091	11.72	3 709	3.45	701	18.24	374	34.20
North and Central America[d]	19 499	1.11	4 547	4.78	2 538	8.56	14 521	1.49	1 851	11.70	3 291	5.94
South West Pacific	16 419	0.69	1 795	6.13	569	19.32	4 801	2.19	749	14.06	2 399	4.39
Europe[e]	44 704	0.13	5 356	1.09	1 004	5.53	12 926	0.82	2 057	4.63	8 284	0.53

Source: Survey made by the World Meteorological Organization in 1975.

[a] Excluding Botswana, Congo, Ivory Coast, Sierra Leone, Somalia.
[b] Excluding Afghanistan, China, Democratic Yemen, Kuwait, Nepal, Yemen.
[c] Excluding Japan, which alone has 4,167 stations.
[d] Excluding British Caribbean Territories, Cuba, Haiti, Honduras, Panama, St. Pierre and Miquelon.
[e] Excluding USSR except for discharge and sediment stations.

F. Reliability of Water Supply and Quality Appraisals

The reliability of appraisal varies according to the method used and the amount and accuracy of the data available for study.

1. Surface water

At gauged stations, surface-water supply may be reliably estimated depending upon how long records have been kept and the accuracy of the measurements themselves.

At ungauged stations, reliability will be contingent upon the historical length of records and the accuracy of measurement for other components in the water-balance equation as well as the relative density of observation stations in the area.

2. Precipitation

As a rule, reasonably accurate measurements of rainfall can be made with less than 10 per cent error, but wide margins of error are to be expected in measuring snowfall under windy conditions. Here again, an adequate network density is crucial. Precipitation is extremely variable in a mountainous terrain where network density is usually low, while snowfall may be high.

3. Evapotranspiration

Although evapotranspiration is less variable, measurements from pans and tanks serve only as an indication of potential evapotranspiration. Actual evapotranspiration is also a function of the evaporation of soil moisture and is difficult to estimate. When estimated from one of many equations, then reliability also depends upon the adequacy of whatever other types of data are used: radiation, temperature, rainfall, humidity and wind, for example.

4. Ground water

While appraisals of ground-water supply reply in part on the same observation networks as surface water, they are largely dependent upon measurements of aquifer characteristics, artificial withdrawals and water levels, as well as geological studies of the formation. The accuracy of these measurements varies widely according to the nature of the aquifer and the thoroughness with which the study is conducted. Even well executed surveys sometimes result in estimates of recharge which later prove to be from 50 to 100 per cent wide of the mark.

5. Water quality

The accuracy of quality measurement varies considerably among the many parameters observed and with the methods of sample analysis. The long-term goal in the United States of America and the United Kingdom is for a system accuracy within 1 per cent. Automatic water quality monitors will certainly gain widespread use in the future, at least for the more common parameters. The achievable accuracy of such instruments at a reasonable cost is within 1 to 5 per cent variant. But most observation networks currently have a much wider range of error. The reliability of appraisals once again depends to a great extent on the network density, the parameters observed and the degree of standardization achieved.

In short the reliability of all water appraisals depends heavily on the adequacy of national observation networks. The present status of stream-flow, water-quality and sediment networks is presented in table 2. Ground-water networks (water levels) exist in a few countries but for the most part the only data on ground-water resources are those collected in connexion with water development projects or with oil prospecting.

Table 2 compares the existing density of stations with the densities recommended in the World Meteorological Organization (WMO) *Guide to Hydro-meteorological Practices*. Because these "required" densities are for average conditions, and because more than 20 countries, including China and the USSR are omitted, the resulting measurements are, at best, very rough. They suggest that networks are conspicuously in excess of the minimum in Europe, less so in Central and North America and the south-west Pacific, least dense in Africa, and generally less than minimum both in Africa and Asia. The more obvious deficiencies are in rain gauges and discharge stations for the latter two regions. But it should be stressed that network density in excess of the recommended minimum does not imply that this is unwarranted. The optimum density is always greater than the minimum, and the statistics in table 2 include many stations required for operating purposes.

The inadequacy of networks is not restricted to deficiencies in the number of stations and their period of record. In both developing and industrialized countries, it is often the areal distribution of stations and the over-all network design that limit the accuracy of assessment.

It is also important that the various types of network (water-quality, water-quantity, precipitation etc.) and related services be closely co-ordinated to take advantage of the physical relationships involved. Although much has been written about network design, practical application has lagged behind knowledge gained through research and experience.

The organization of comprehensive national networks and data-processing services remains one of the most urgent tasks in water development and management. At the international level, this is the core of the WMO Operational Hydrology Programme. Such services may sometimes be advantageously organized on a regional basis. The operation of unified networks is critical wherever basins or aquifers are shared by two or more countries that require commonly accepted data for management. Several UNDP/WMO projects have taken this approach.

G. *Global Supplies of Fresh Water*

The study of the global water balance was the principal topic of the International Hydrological Decade (IHD) and three important monographs on the subject were published towards the end of the Decade (Baumgartner, 1975; Lvovich, 1974; the USSR National Committee for IHD, 1974). Although the methodology used in the three studies differs to some extent, the results are relatively consistent (see table 3).

Table 3. **Average annual water balances of the world according to authors published since 1970.**

P = Precipitation
E = Evaporation
R = Run-off

Volume of water
(thousands of cubic kilometres)

Region	Baumgartner 1975 P	E	R	USSR Monograph 1974 P	E	R	Lvovich, 1974 P	E	R
Europe	6.6	3.8	2.8	8.3	5.3	3.0	7.2	4.1	3.1
Asia	30.7	18.5	12.2	32.2	18.1	14.1	32.7	19.5	13.2
Africa	20.7	17.3	3.4	22.3	17.7	4.6	20.8	16.6	4.2
Australia	7.1	4.7	2.4	7.1	4.6	2.5	6.4	4.4	2.0
North America	15.6	9.7	5.9	18.3	10.1	8.2	13.9	7.9	6.0
South America	28.0	16.9	11.1	28.4	16.2	12.2	29.4	19.0	10.4
Antarctica	2.4	0.4	2.0	2.3	0	2.3	...	...	...
Land areas*	111	71	40	119	72	47	113	72	41
Oceans	385	425	−40	458	505	−47	412	453	−41
World	496	496	0	577	577	0	525	525	0

Depth of water
(Millimetres)

Europe	657	375	282	790	507	283	734	415	319
Asia	696	420	276	740	416	324	726	433	293
Africa	696	582	114	740	587	153	686	547	139
Australia	803	534	269	791	511	280	736	510	226
North America	645	403	242	756	418	338	670	383	287
South America	1564	946	618	1595	910	685	1648	1065	583
Antarctica	169	28	141	165	0	165	...	...	...
World	973	973	0	1130	1130	0	1030	1030	0

Sources: USSR, National Committee for IHD, *World Water Balance and Water Resources of the Earth* (Leningrad, 1974); Lvovich, *Global Water Resources and the Future* (Moscow, 1974); A. Baumgartner and E. Reichel, *The World Water Balance* (Munich, 1975).

*Values are adjusted upwards to include Antarctica for comparison with corresponding volumes derived by the other two authors.

The major differences among the estimates stem from the difficulty of calculating precipitation and evaporation in the ocean basins. In contrast, estimates for land areas, where more stations record both precipitation and evaporation, are very close.

1. *Surface run-off and run-off to the sea*

The run-off of roughly 40,000 to 47,000 cubic kilometres, annually occurs chiefly in Asia and South America. The heaviest concentration in terms of average depth by region is found in South America. The volume in Africa, Australia, Europe and North America combined is less than 40 per cent of the total (see table 3).

Frequently "run-off to the sea" is treated as a limiting measure of water available for the support of human needs. Run-off to the sea may, however, be the best available measure of the real water resources of human society, provided one considers and understands the underlying possible deficiencies. For instance, it must be assumed that:

(a) Land areas which do not contribute run-off to the sea are without water supply;

(b) Losses from streams and ground-water storage, such as non-beneficial evapotranspiration by vegetation in the valley bottom, are either inconsequential or would not be reduced by upstream withdrawals;

(c) Possible mining of ground water is inconsequential;

(d) Average consumptive use during the period analysed is inconsequential unless observed discharges are not used in the analysis or adjustment is made for measured withdrawal.

It must also be considered that there are many closed basins, some as large as the Caspian drainages, which contribute no run-off to the sea but do, however, experience surface run-off and ground-water recharge. Non-beneficial evapotranspiration from ground storage is a serious problem in some areas, and lowering the water table tends to reduce such losses. Much water is lost in transit to the sea, particularly in swampy areas such as the Sudd of the Sudan, and constitutes available supply at upstream locations. Moreover, while the quantities of water involved may not be significant on a regional or global scale when considered individually, yet they all constitute incremental increases to the supply as measured by run-off to the sea. They cannot be presumed to be inconsequential when one considers available supply for an individual basin or any other relatively small area. In these cases, as with other sources of supply, the definition of available water is shaped by demand in relation to technology and cost. The estimated volume of water that can be abstracted from a stream or aquifer is influenced by judgement concerning feasible storage facilities, pumping lifts and the like. The demand component, as will be shown in the following section, should not be obscured by physical calculations.

2. *Lakes and reservoirs*

The total volume of fresh water stored in lakes (about 2×10^5 cubic kilometres) represents about four times the average yearly run-off from all land areas. The volume of water accumulated in man-made reservoirs (about 5×10^3 cubic kilometres) represents about 11 per cent of the yearly run-off.

Lakes and reservoirs play an important role in regulating stream flow and thus facilitate its use, although they do not themselves constitute a major source of supply. The "mining" of water in lakes would lower their levels and adversely affect the water balance. Lowering of lake levels can result from changes in upstream areas. The Caspian Sea is a classic example of this.

3. *Ground water*

Except for Europe, part of Africa, part of North America and small parts of Asia, the availability of ground-water resources is not well established.

Recent estimates of the global store of fresh ground water above 4000 metres in depth range from 8.1×10^6 to 10.5×10^6 cubic kilometres. Ground-water reserves, however, only have significance where conditions are favourable for their exploitation.

A relatively small quantity of ground water (about 13×10^3 cubic kilometres or roughly 0.1 per cent of total reserves) participates in the hydrological cycle in the average year. Most of this takes place through contribution to stream flow and is therefore included in the appraisal of surface supply.

There are no available estimates for global or continental recharge, or the difference between recharge and contribution to stream flow. Detailed studies have been made, however, for selected areas such as the Lake Chad basin.

H. *Climate and Human Activity*

Just as there is no substantial agreement among the world scientific community whether or not climate is changing at a rapid rate, there is similarly no general agreement that human activities *per se* have a significant effect upon climatic change.

Some scientists believe, however, that some activities are likely to effect significant climatic changes: burning of fossil fuels, burning of grasslands and forests, cultivation of semi-arid lands, cutting of forests, ploughing of grasslands, and transfer of pollutants destructive to the ozone into the stratosphere, for example.

These potential material changes seem to warrant a major and continuing endeavour to improve our ability to assess the present and predict the possible future consequences of human activities upon changes in climate. Unfortunately, the extensive lag in time between cause and effect, the difficulties in limiting or even isolating possible causes, and the complex relationships involved virtually preclude our arriving at positive conclusions through correlation analysis of climatic and other relevant data.

Models have been developed which depict the principal features of global climate with limited application. Once it is possible to develop models which simulate climate accurately, it may be possible to determine how specific activities of man influence the input parameters and thus stimulate how these activities correspondingly effect changes in climate. This approach could also be used to test hypotheses for modifying climate, such as the damming of the Bering Strait.

Water-resource development might conceivably induce changes in climate. Irrigation of large tracts of land, for example, affects the climate down-wind of the area, but appreciable effects appear to be relatively local. Proposals to divert immense quantities of water from rivers feeding into the Arctic Ocean have caused some concern, since these rivers constitute a heat source for the ocean. There are divergent views on whether the resulting increase in ice-cover would materially affect the climate of inhabited regions.

World-wide concern about climatic change led the WMO Seventh Congress to undertake, with the co-operation of other concerned bodies, an integrated international effort to study the question.

I. *Global Assessment of Water Quality*

Of the numerous water quality parameters relevant to water use, our knowledge and available data are both so limited that, with few exceptions, even approximate continental or global assessment is not possible. Figure 1 presents estimates of the erosion products from continents. The total of dissolved solids carried to the oceans is estimated at more than 2480 million metric tons annually; a total of 3905 million metric tons of soluble material has been calculated (D.A. Livingstone, 1964).

The total products of erosion carried by streams have been estimated between 12 and 51 thousand million metric tons annually (Lvovich 1974, pp. 246-257). The sediment comes largely from Asia, where removal may average as much as .16 millimetres per year from the land surface.

Organic waste from cities and factories constitutes a rapidly growing hazard to health for urban populations, especially for those in squatter settlements on the peripheries of tropical cities which are not supplied with purified water. Even in an industrialized nation such as the United States, 92 per cent of the total suspended solids, 37 per cent of the biochemical oxygen demand, and 98 per cent of the coliform bacteria will remain uncontrolled in natural surface water once all discharge has been eliminated from point sources; this is largely the consequence of agricultural activity (United States National Commission on Water Quality 1976). There are no general measurements of volumes of synthetic organic compounds and heavy metals reaching the oceans.

Ground water usually contains far more dissolved salts than surface water. The chemical composition of precipitation is gradually modified as it infiltrates and moves through soil and rock, the water taking up soluble compounds of the medium. The main compounds are calcium, magnesium, fluorides, sodium, potassium, iron, bicarbonate, sulphate, chloride and nitrate ions. Their combined concentration in water is measured as salinity. And in arid regions, salinity is increased as a result of high evaporation.

Irrigation tends to increase the load of salts in streams by leaching salts from the soil and returning them to the stream by drainage. At the same time, irrigation concentrates salts by removing part of the water that would otherwise dilute the load.

Salt-water intrusion from the sea to coastal aquifers can cause a drastic increase in the salinity of ground-water supply. Intrusion can result from the lowering of the water table through the exploitation of fresh water. Since

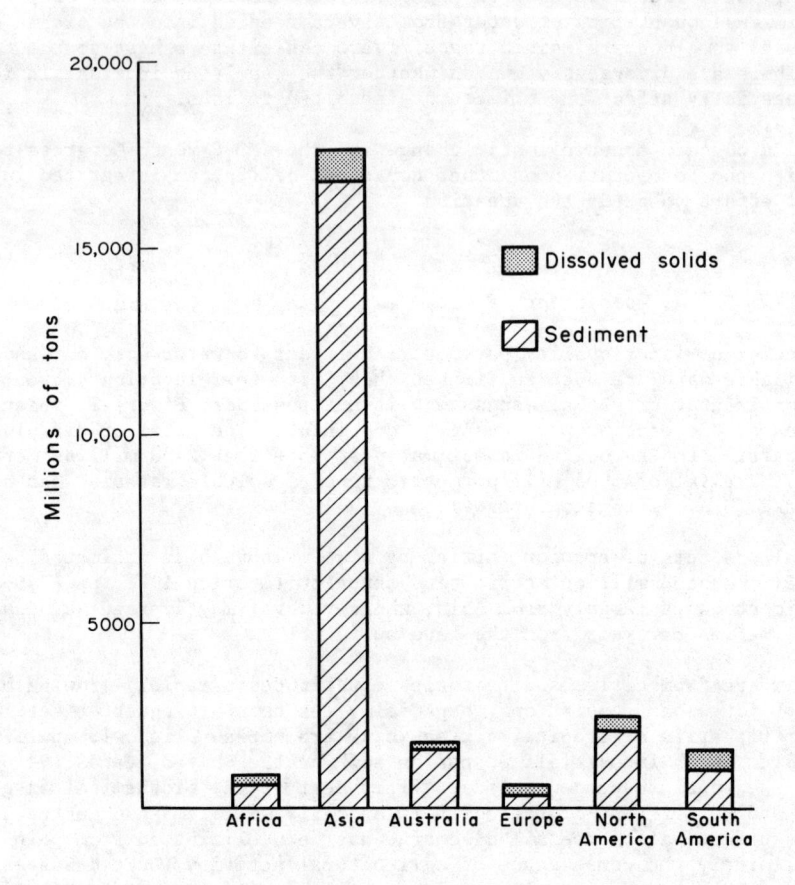

Fig. 1. Estimated erosion products and dissolved solids carried by streams.
Source: Lvovich, *Global Water Resources and Their Future* (Moscow, 1974).

coastal zones are generally heavily populated, with growing demands for water supply, salt-water intrusion can become a serious problem. While the encroachment process may be slow, it tends to become irreversible.

Ground-water pollution induced by man is also an increasing concern. Fecal pathogenic organisms die off relatively quickly and seldom constitute a hazard, except in limestone areas where underground water may travel long distances relatively rapidly. On the other hand, drainage waters from urban or agricultural lands may contain objectionable chemicals which percolate into the soil and irreversibly contaminate the adjacent aquifer. Since surface water is a source of ground-water recharge, this, too, is a source of contamination. Here again, the process may evolve slowly, but the effects are persistent.

J. Non-conventional Sources of Water Supply

Many technological devices are used either to change salt water into fresh water or to change the place of water in the hydrological cycle so as to increase its availability. These technologies include: desalination, weather modification, phreatophyte modification, evaporation suppression, waste water re-use, geothermal water exploitation, and the transport of icebergs.

Of these, only desalination has had a significant, yet moderate result. A few islands and countries, such as Kuwait, derive virtually all their fresh water from desalination plants. Between 1961 and 1971, the output of large desalting plants for brackish or ocean water expanded at an annual rate of 18 per cent. By 1972, the output from 812 land-based plants was 1.39×10^6 cubic metres daily. By 1975, the number of plants of 100 cubic-metre capacity or greater had increased to 1036 and world capacity had risen to 2.1×10^6 cubic metres.

Weather modification has been practised on such a limited scale so far that it is difficult to make a sound assessment of its potential effect on the water balance of large areas.

Waste water re-use is a growing source of supply. Already well established in Chinese agriculture, it is now more widely applied in industry as well as in irrigation.

III. ASSESSMENT OF USE AND DEMAND

The particular significance of estimates for water use and prospective demand is that they show the *relative* volumes of use for different purposes.

It is important to recognize that these uses, purposes, and their resulting effects are interwoven regionally and nationally. Any strategy that is devised to satisfy prospective demand must take this into account.

A. Multiple Uses, Purposes and Impacts

The uses that make most demand upon water supply and water-related services are shown in table 4.

TABLE 4. Components and impacts of water use

Components	Common Substitutes	Type Withdrawal	Type In-stream	Type On-site	Impacts Potential quality effect	Impacts Potential consumptive use (percentage consumed)
Drinking	None	x				1-15
Other domestic		x				1-15
Public, urban		x				1-15
Livestock	None	x	x		Organic	1-15
Soil moisture conservation	None			x	Sediment	0-100
Irrigation	None	x			Salt	10-80
Drainage					Salt	0
Wetland habitat	None			x		0-10
Aquatic habitat	None	x	x			0
Navigation	Land transport		x			0-10
Hydropower	Other energy sources		x			0
Mining		x	x			1-5
Manufacturing:						
Cooling (including steam power)	Air	x			Thermal	0-3
Processing	Mechanical	x			Organic, toxic	0-10
Waste disposal	Air and mechanical	x	x		Organic	0
Recreation			x			0
Aesthetic			x			0
Flood loss reduction	Land use		x	x		0

Source: Gilbert F. White, 1976.

All of these uses contribute to the vitality of human settlement, the quality of life, agriculture, industry and the social infrastructure. They vary in the degree to which they are essential to an economy and in the degree to which they affect the human environment.

At the simplest level, uses are single-purpose: providing drinking water, driving a hydroelectric turbine or carrying barges in a canal, to cite a few examples. But increasingly, water uses are combined and multiple. For example, a large proportion of the water distributed to a community is used for washing and for carrying away human and other wastes and may subsequently be used in agriculture;. a storage reservoir for electric power also offers recreation and irrigation facilities; a canal provides wildlife benefits.

It is therefore misleading to think of a cubic metre of water diverted from a stream as serving only one purpose in only one sector of an economy. The technology for achieving multiple benefits has expanded rapidly and this has improved our capability to use, purify and reuse available water supplies.

If we classify water use by withdrawal, on-site and in-stream, as in table 4, and take into account the consumptive or non-consumptive character of each, we then have a better understanding of the effect of water use on the human environment.

Uses which actually withdraw from a water body — drinking water, irrigation, industry, for example — deplete the source unless it is refed by return drainage.

In-stream uses — navigation, hydropower, fisheries, for instance — leave the volume of flow unchanged.

On-site uses — for rain-fed crops or wildlife habitat, for example — may or may not affect the volume of flow.

All these uses, whether consumptive or non-consumptive, may cause a change in water quality. And all may potentially result in a loss of available supply through evaporation, transpiration or diversion, so that there may be a net depletion of a source stream or aquifer. While some uses, such as irrigation or even repeated withdrawal for drinking water, can wholly deplete a stream, other uses like repeated use for thermal cooling, will reduce flow only slightly.

In summary:

(a) Uses vary according to the availability and economic feasibility of substitutes;

(b) Uses are increasingly multiple;

(c) As uses multiply, so do the possibilities of altering water quality;

(d) Consumptive depletion of available supply varies according to use and available technology, and in extreme cases local supply can be completely dissipated.

How societies choose to use water and what technology they apply reflect individual and public attitude in appraising resulting costs and benefits.

B. *Methods of Projecting Water Demand*

The term "water demand" has an economic connotation. It means the amount of water or water-related services that would be used at a given price. But in contrast to most other commodities, there is no easy way to establish reasonable levels of water demand and supply through pricing policies.

It is a major task of local, regional and national water organizations to strike a suitable balance between supply and demand while taking price/demand relationships into account. Fundamental to this process and to the international examination of what needs to be done in managing the world's supply of water is the way in which demand is forecast or projected.

A first step is to estimate current use. The next step in planning for future management or conservation is to estimate how additional or different use will affect future demand and then establish a rational service level. For example, given finite resources, it may be necessary to evaluate whether it is preferable to serve more people at low-service levels (with standpipes and latrines), or alternatively serve less people (with house connexions having unrestricted water use and sewer systems).

In general, demand for water can be projected in aggregate terms. In Hungary, for example, the range of demand was projected to the year 2050 on the basis of historical relationships between *per capita* aggregate use and gross national product.

More detailed studies require examination of each of the categories of use outlined in table 4 at the national level, or even for smaller areas such as basins and sub-basins. To do this, the most rudimentary method is extrapolation of a rate of change observed over a given past time period. This method is widely used and assumes no change in either the socio-economic factors that motivate demand, or in prevailing technologies and policies. Extrapolation therefore rarely yields satisfactory results, except in the short term in some instances and under conditions of abundant supply.

Apart from extrapolation, there are numerous analytical models that examine the factors influencing a particular use and their interrelationships. Demand may thus be related to population, food consumption, industrial activity, technology, costs, political objectives and numerous other variables. Typically, such a projection forecasts the form and size of a future economy, assigns some water requirement per unit of expected output, and revises the expected usage in light of projected costs. These methods vary greatly in their sophistication and in the extent of the required data base. Using them, many projections are made that indicate how much water will be required for particular areas at particular times. The specific method used will depend upon the particular use being studied.

All these projections for cities, basins, nations, continents and the globe need to be interpreted with great care. The data base is often meagre. Frequently assumptions are made about such matters as population, industrial processes or farming practices that may change radically over a period of time. Since these projections do not rule out extrapolation, they help specify the range of uncertainty attached to each assumption. In this respect, they lay the groundwork for informed decisions concerning which policies and technical measures may be most appropriate to guide demand in the future. For this purpose, they are fully useful only when cost/price considerations enter into the analysis. It may, for example, be highly misleading to estimate industrial cooling water withdrawal needs without taking into account the costs of providing increased supplies. In this connexion, one further consideration is the incremental cost of sewer systems and waste disposal/pollution control associated with high levels of water consumption.

The following subsections summarize what is known about total water uses for each component of demand, and indicate the status of projections for future demand. Chapter IV then outlines the chief considerations in supply/demand relationships. Because of gaps in data and incomplete analysis, it is not possible to present a comprehensive global picture of water use and demand. It is practicable, however, to sketch the main features of use and show what information, analysis and judgement would be desirable if we were to make reasonable appraisals of the supply/demand situation for any basin or aquifer.

C. *Domestic Use and Demand*

To a person living in a semi-arid land, domestic water use may mean a few litres a day, mainly for drinking and cooking and excluding requirements for washing and bathing. In small communities in non-industrialized countries, domestic use may, in addition, include bathing and washing needs. In higher income societies, watering of lawns and kitchen gardens is common. In middle- and upper-income sections of large cities, household appliances, swimming pools and the washing of automobiles considerably increase domestic demand. A farming household may also use its supply to water livestock and irrigate a small garden.

Municipal supplies rarely provide water exclusively for drinking and other household uses: they also cater to the needs of commercial districts, small industrial establishments, and public uses such as street cleaning, watering of public gardens and parks, public baths and fountains, and firefighting. Commercial industrial and public uses may claim 5 to 50 per cent of the total pumpage in an urban supply system and may sometimes total several times the household withdrawal.

The quantity of water used in a household is related to the quality of living. For broad purposes, domestic water may be classified as meeting these needs: drinking water for survival; personal hygiene; basic comfort; positive well-being. The total amount used ranges from 3 to 700 litres *per capita* daily. Lawn watering may account for one half of total use in a middle- or upper-income household. As shown in Fig. 2, the range of use is set according to whether the water is carried from the source, provided by a single tap in or near the household, or supplied by multiple taps. Within these limits, the actual volume consumed by households is influenced by income, climate, culture and a variety of other factors, including the efficiency of the delivery system. In some urban areas, as much as one half of the water stored and pumped is lost through leaks in pipes and faucets. In such cases, the true average daily *per capita* consumption is only half the apparent consumption; also, twice as many people might be supplied without increasing the resource if leaks and wastage were controlled.

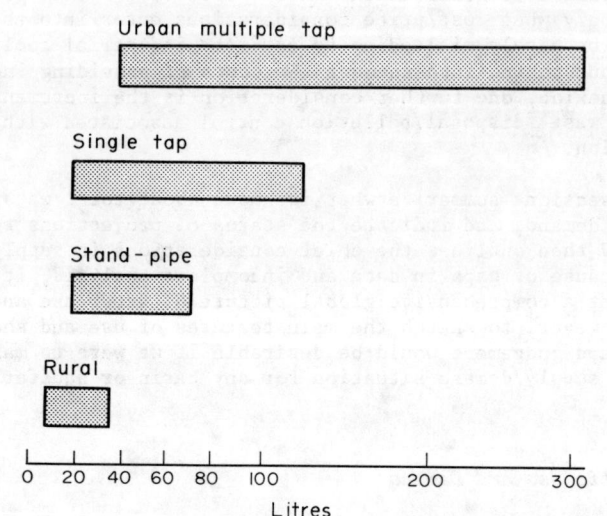

Fig. 2. Range of daily domestic water use *per capita*
Source: A.U. White (1976).

1. *Quality of supply and its effect upon health*

Quality of supply is critically important to human health. Biological pollution through fecal contamination is the cause of morbidity due to water-borne diseases, which as a group rank first among all other kinds of disease in less developed regions. In certain parts of some countries, naturally occurring substances which are deleterious in excessive concentration such as nitrates, fluorides and toxic substances such as arsenic have a strictly local distribution. Pollution of water by indiscriminate discharge of synthetic organic chemicals is cause for grave concern in highly industrialized and developing countries alike. While some of these chemicals are acutely toxic, their effects however can sometimes be remedied. Of greater concern are the long-term teratogenic, mutagenic and carcinogenic effects of pollutants. Their full effect on human health is known only for a few groups of substances.

To protect human health, water used for drinking and for preparing uncooked food should, as a matter of public policy, be free of pathogenic organisms and toxic substances. So that consumers will not use less safe sources, public water supplies should also preferably be attractive to sight and taste. Guidelines for water quality are presented in the WHO publication *International Standards for Drinking Water* (3rd edition).

In connexion with public policy, the optimal requirement for domestic water is that a supply should be available daily and conveniently, at reasonable cost while meeting the criteria mentioned above.

2. Quantity required

The quantity of water required domestically varies with local circumstances, the method of excreta disposals, and is income elastic. It is common to design new community supplies for delivery of an average of 100-350 litres *per capita* for house connexions, and 10-25 litres daily for people using public stand-pipes. In rural areas, the design figures used by government agencies differ according to the likelihood and availability of natural sources. In general, water consumption increases as the standard of living increases.

3. Existing and proposed community water-supply and excreta disposal levels

In 1972 the twenty-fifth World Health Assembly adopted the following targets for community water supplies in developing countries, to be achieved by 1980:

In urban communities:

60 per cent of the population to be served by house connexions

40 per cent of the population to be served by public stand-pipes

In rural areas:

25 per cent of the population to have access to safe water

Bearing in mind prospective population growth, this would mean that the additional people to be served by 1980 as part of the Second United Nations Development Decade would be:

255 million by house connexions

135 million by public stand-pipes

274 million by rural improvements

This would still leave some 822 million people in rural areas without access to safe water.

In 1976, the World Health Organization (WHO) conducted a survey to determine progress achieved in reaching the 1980 targets. The results show that at the end of 1975, the following service levels have been achieved:

In urban communities:

57 per cent of the population is served by house connexions;

20 per cent of the population is served by stand-pipes;

76 per cent of the population (445 million) is adequately served.

In rural areas:

22 per cent of the population (310 million) has reasonable access to safe water.

The total urban and rural populations served are 35 per cent (755 million).

The WHO survey revealed that the following population had excreta disposal facilities, either through public sewers or household systems:

Urban communities	- 75 per cent (435 million)
Rural communities	- 14 per cent (195 million)
Total, urban and rural	- 32 per cent (630 million)

It is evident on the basis of the mid-decade review that there has been an increase not only in the gross number of people provided with water supply and excreta disposal facilities over the five-year period 1971-1975, but also in the percentage of the urban and rural populations served. In other words, progress in the provision of these services has more than kept pace with population growth in the urban and rural sectors. As this survey covered nearly 90 per cent of the total population of the developing countries (excluding China), it would not be unreasonable to assume that this progress applies to the developing countries taken as a whole. However, as the over-all goal for the end of the decade is for over 90 per cent of all urban populations to be supplied with safe water either inside their homes or from public standposts, it can be readily appreciated that in spite of the progress achieved, a major effort is still required to meet that goal. Practically all the data presented are estimates. The bases on which estimates were made vary. Concerning estimates of numbers of people served, countries have better information on community water supply services than on excreta disposal services and have better data on the urban than on the rural situation. The inherent difficulties in accumulating this type of basic information from different sources within a country for use in preparing estimates should serve as a note of caution in interpretation.

The survey also showed regional differences in progress. Taking this into account, member States endorsed at the twenty-ninth World Health Assembly in May 1976 the regional targets proposed by the Director-General of WHO for community water supply and excreta disposal in the developing countries to be strived for as a minimum by the end of the Second United Nations Development Decade and recommended, *inter alia*, that member States establish and periodically review feasible programme targets in community water supply and excreta disposal. If regional targets are to be achieved, it will mean that by 1980:

In urban areas:

    68 per cent of the population to be served by house connexions

    23 per cent of the population to be served by stand-pipes

    38 per cent of the population to be served by public sewers

    56 per cent of the population to be served by household systems

In rural areas:

    36 per cent of the population to have reasonable access to safe water

    24 per cent of the population to have excreta disposal facilities

These targets imply far greater financial resources for improving service levels in urban areas where relatively high levels already exist and further improvements are costly. In view of resource limitations, individual countries may well decide to modify these targets and attempt to provide lower levels of service (stand-pipes instead of house connexions) to a larger number of people.

4. Delay and cost of improving domestic supply and excreta disposal

A unified attack upon problems of providing rural water service has been launched by a consortium of organizations including WHO, the World Bank, United Nations, UNDP, United Nations Children's Fund and the International Development Research Centre. Still, the basic questions raised by this discussion are: Why have improvements in domestic water supply moved so slowly? What can be done to speed them up? Among the reasons often given for the slow pace of development are: shortage of funds; shortage of trained manpower; weakness in national programmes; difficulties in system operation and maintenance; inadequate legal frameworks; insufficient involvement of potential users.

In the WHO survey, the *per capita* cost at 1970 price levels for new community water supplies under government auspices was found to range on the average over large areas from $15* to $55 *per capita* for house connexions, from $9 to $30 for public stand-pipes, and from $6 to $24 for rural supplies. Similar *per capita* costs were used for excreta disposal. Where community participation in projects is substantial, the costs can be reduced. But the total funds required to meet the Second Development Decade are still immense.

Adjusting the above *per capita* cost figures for inflation, WHO estimates that the funds required to meet the revised 1980 targets amount to $12 billion for urban house connexions, $2.5 billion for urban stand-pipes and $6.5 billion for rural water supply. An estimated $13 billion is needed for urban and $2 billion for rural excreta costs.

These estimates are probably far below the actual expenditures which will in fact be required. In this connexion, a recent World Bank calculation of costs to meet 1980 goals for Latin America under the Santiago declaration for both water supply and excreta disposal, placed investment needs at $16 billion over a five-year period. Only about $5 billion of this would be investment for water supply: this reflects both the customary 1 to 2 ratio of *per capita* urban water supply and excreta disposal cost and also the need to accelerate investments in heretofore neglected excreta disposal. This level of investment would be roughly four times the actual expenditure in Latin America for water supply and waste disposal during the first five years of the decade.

The costs quoted in the previous paragraphs are based on very rough approximations and are merely indicative of what will be required. They illustrate, nevertheless, possible cost trends. In addition, they show the options available in making investment decisions. The costliest option is water supply by house connexions and excreta disposal by sewer system. Respective *per capita* costs of these vary from $50 to $100 and from $80 to $200. In contrast, stand-pipes and latrines or pit privies cost from $10 to $35 and $5 to $10 *per capita*, respectively.

Obviously the choice of service level has a significant impact on how many people can be served. In general, it would be preferable to provide low-level service so that the maximum number of people could benefit. Service levels could then be upgraded as investment funds become available and as standards of living increase.

---

* The symbol ($) refers to United States dollars unless otherwise stated.

Even if funds of the above-mentioned magnitude were available, the mounting of construction programmes to meet these goals would place heavy demands upon the existing small pools of trained personnel and equally heavy demands upon the capacity of national and municipal organizations to mobilize the affected population, given lack of information and lack of community concern. The difficulties are especially acute in rural areas and in the expanding shanty towns of tropical cities.

The volume of water needed to meet the required minimum of the Second Development Decade is not large in comparison with available run-off. The populations in need have a supply of a sort, much of it inadequate in volume and virtually all of it subject to some degree of health hazard. The problem is how to arrange for suitable storage, treatment and distribution, at costs that users can afford and by means that are appropriate to local supply and local socio-economic conditions.

D. *Industrial Use and Demand*

The economic development of a country and its applications of technology, influence the use and demand of water for industry to an even greater degree than they influence the use of water for domestic purposes.

Lacking global statistics, industrial use of water as a per cent of total withdrawal can only be outlined in relation to the experience of a few nations. See Fig. 3.

1. *Major industrial uses of water*

The major uses of water in industry are for: cooling; processing; boiler water; and general purposes, including drinking, air conditioning and cleaning. Cooling is the principal purpose of withdrawal and commonly accounts for as much as 60 to 80 per cent of total industrial withdrawal; this is the reason for the heavy use of water by thermal electric power generating plants.

Industry may draw upon saline, as well as fresh, surface and ground supplies. Process water may enter the product itself as in beverages, or alternatively, serve to wash, float or transport products in manufacturing.

A few industries account for two thirds or more of all industrial use. The chief users are primary metals, chemical products, petroleum refining, pulp and paper products and food processing. (See table 5.)

The way in which water intake and waste of these industries may vary for a given unit of volume is presented in table 5. It is not unusual to find some industrial plants withdrawing 5 to 20 times as much water as other plants for the manufacture of the same product. The principal reason for this range is the degree of in-plant recirculation within the plant. The volume of waste load in water is not well assessed, and the figures given in table 5 show only estimated averages for one country.

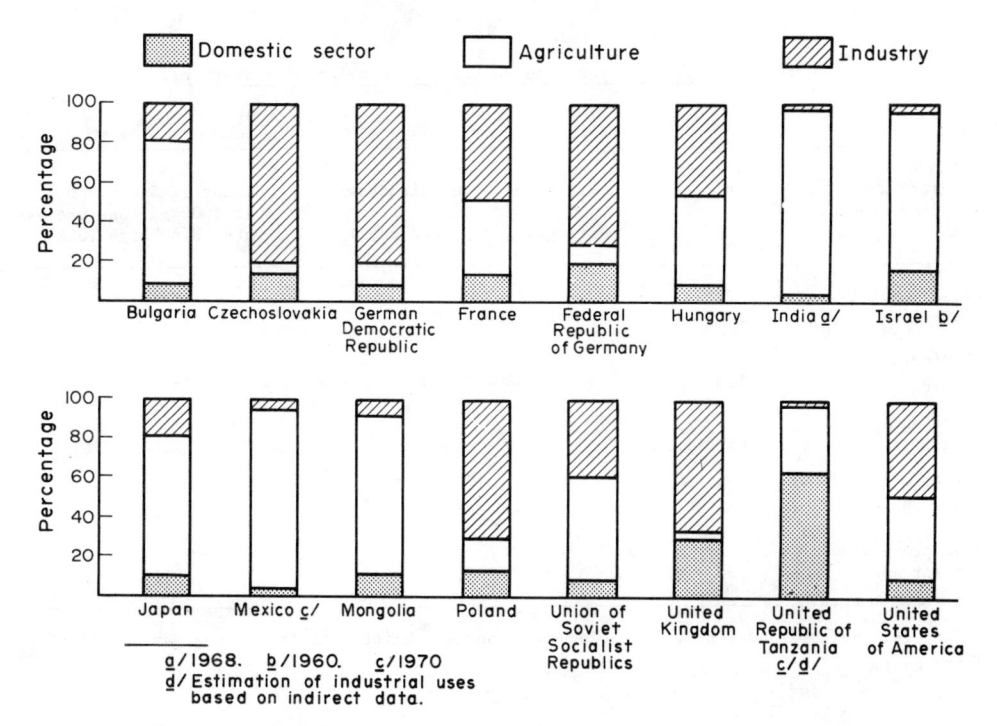

Fig. 3. Distribution of withdrawals among major categories of water uses, selected countries, 1965.

Source: *The Demand for Water: Procedures and Methodologies for Projecting Water Demands in the Context of Regional and National Planning* (UN publication, Sales No. E.76.II.A.1).

2. Consumption and waste

The critical considerations in industrial water use are: how much water is taken in, how much is consumed, and how much and what kind of waste is discharged since this can gravely affect human and environmental health.

Consumptive use rarely exceeds 20 per cent of withdrawal. In the case of steam power generation, consumptive use is less than 2 per cent and has been decreasing steadily during recent decades. The waste discharge affects the quality of the receiving water – the precise effect depending upon flow and quality of the receiving water, its temperature and a variety of other conditions.

As outlined in Fig. 4, once water enters a manufacturing plant, it may be used for one or a combination of purposes. The waste may be treated within the plant or disposed of in a variety of ways. The volume and quality of industrial waste can usually be improved through process design, in-plant recycling and improved plant housekeeping procedures.

TABLE 5. Water intake and waste load in selected industries.

Industry and selected product	Unit	Litres of water withdrawn per unit (range of reported uses)	Pounds of 5-day BOD per 1000 gallons process water discharge (USA)
Primary metals: steel	Ton	8000–61,000	...
Chemical: soap	Ton	960–37,000	16.70
Petroleum: gasolene	Kilolitre	7000–34,000	2.50
Pulp and paper: paperboard	Ton	62,000–376,000	2.21
Food processing: sugar beets	Ton	1800–20,000	9.16

Sources: Wollman and Bonem, 1971; country reports submitted to the United Nations, 1957–1968.

3. *Cost of water and waste disposal*

Cost and convenience are important determinants of what processes are used for water intake, treatment, recirculation and waste discharge. But the cost of water itself usually represents a very small proportion of aggregate industrial costs. For the five most important water-using industries mentioned above, water may represent from 0.005 to 2.58 per cent of total manufacturing costs and rarely exceeds 1 per cent. In many areas, the problem of waste disposal is more limiting to financial and technical growth than the problem of obtaining adequate water supply.

4. *Effects of industrial growth upon water quality and quantity*

Industry is expected to grow at an 8 per cent annual rate in the Second United Nations Development Decade. How this growth will change the use and quality of water will depend upon the cost of obtaining suitable supplies and, above all, the standards Governments set for quality in receiving waters.

Further sophistication in manufacturing techniques will stimulate further measures for quality control and in-plant waste treatment. Such increased sophistication will also undoubtedly multiply the variety of synthetic organics and other effluent wastes. The future demand for water for industry is likely to be affected by competitive agricultural and domestic demands as world population increases.

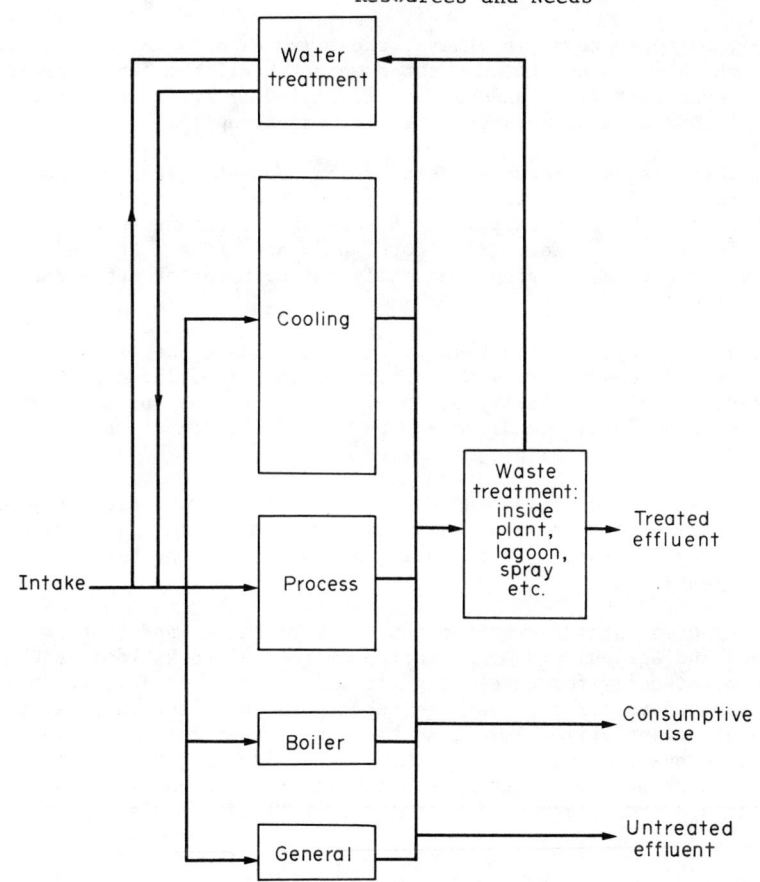

Fig. 4. Flow of water in industrial use.
Source: Modified from Blower and Sewell (1968).

E. *Agricultural Use and Demand*

As world population grows, so does the need for increased food production. A reliable and increased supply of water is essential to sustain this growth. This requires better use of rainfall and better conservation of water for crop and livestock production. Where it is necessary to increase yield from arable land, or to extend agricultural production to marginal or arid land, irrigation is required.

Agriculture is the largest user of water, accounting for some 80 per cent of world consumption, mainly through irrigation. In addition vast areas use rainfall as the principal source of water for crops. Approximately 200 million hectares of land were irrigated in 1970, almost half of this in developing countries where food needs are especially acute.

Because of wide differences in soil, climate, crops and irrigation methods, to mention only a few variables, it is impossible to establish any norm for irrigation water supply. And it is often difficult even to define an "irrigated" area. Levels of water reliability and frequency of flow provide a guaranteed, unrestricted supply in some areas. In others, there may be only an occasional seasonal flooding which in a bad year may not even reach all the land prepared to receive it, although that same land may be classified as irrigated since its productivity depends upon an outside source of water supply.

As a consequence, there is no agreed-upon set of standards to determine how much water is needed for efficient crop production or how much water should in fact be applied. Nor are there comparable data showing the extent to which treated sewage effluent is used for agricultural purposes. (Where treated sewage is used for irrigation, it should normally not be used for crops that are to be consumed raw.)

While it is difficult to define irrigation *per se*, any planned development still requires an ensured controlled water supply to the crop. The quantities and acceptable standards of reliability of supply are determined by local climatic, agronomic and economic conditions, and water requirements are therefore established at the local project level.

The estimates in table 6, land irrigated and harvested in 1970, reflect approximate assessments of irrigation of all sorts. They do not reveal the degree to which the same land may be cropped twice during a year, or may be harvested only in favourable years.

Applying an index of crop intensity as a measure of irrigated land that is harvested, the Food and Agriculture Organization of the United Nations (FAO), calculated the crop intensity for developing economies shown in table 7. These indices, ranging from 65 to 132 per cent are especially important in relation to the proportion of potentially arable land that is already under cultivation. Global statistics, however, do not reflect the wide variations among individual countries, some of which may have little remaining land for expansion and may therefore increase farm production only by increasing yield in existing farmland.

Changes in agriculture may modify crop-water needs. For example, the introduction and expansion of modern crop varieties create a demand for improved water supply both in quantity and in timely application so that the greatest potential of the new crop will be realized while taking into account other related inputs such as fertilizers. Mechanization of agriculture may call for changes in field layouts, planting and harvesting techniques, with resulting influences on the methods and timing of irrigation patterns of water demand, and most important, total water use. Such use could either increase so as to support intensified cultivation, remain unchanged, or even decline through better water management. Improved technologies for the reclamation, re-use and recycling of water may also reduce demands for new sources to some extent. An important concept in water management for the future is the increasing of crop production with poorer quality water, thus making use of a resource previously rejected as unsuitable.

To arrive at the estimates of gross water demand presented in table 6, FAO assumed the demand to be 700 millimetres of water per crop season where the staple food is a dry-foot cereal and 1500 millimetres where it is rice. These values are presumed to be the total quantity needed by the crop, whether supplied from rainfall or irrigation, with typical losses associated with storage, conveyance and application taken into account. Still, part of the water lost in application in one area may well become a source of supply elsewhere through seepage, return flow and ground-water recharge. For this reason, FAO

TABLE 6. Estimated Irrigated Harvested Areas and Gross Water Demand, 1970

Region	Irrigated harvested area (millions of hectares)	Gross water demand (billions* of cubic metres)
Africa (excluding Egypt, Libyan Arab Republic, Sudan)	2	14
Latin America and Caribbean	8	59
Near East (including Egypt, Libyan Arab Republic, Sudan)	16	109
Asia (excluding China and USSR)	75	899
Asia (China and other centrally planned countries)	78	1167
USSR and Eastern Europe	14	95
North America, Australia and Oceania, Western Europe	33	228
	226	2571

Source: FAO report for the World Food Conference, 1974.

* The term "billion" means a thousand million.

TABLE 7. Cropping Intensity of Irrigated Land and Cultivation of Potentially Arable Land in Developing Market Economies.

Region	Irrigated land cropping intensity (percentage)	Potentially arable land under cultivation (percentage)	Irrigated land (millions of hectares)
Africa	98	44	02
Latin America	82	28	10
Near East	65	89	24
Far East	132	84	57

Sources: Food and Agriculture Organization of the United Nations, *Indicative World Plan for Agriculture* and the report to the World Food Conference, 1974.

notes that the totals given in this estimate of 2570 x 10^9 cubic metres, probably greatly exceed the actual use of water by the crop. Other recent estimates have placed projected global irrigation use as low as 1400 x 10^9 cubic metres for 1967 (Holy 1971), and as high as 2300 x 10^9 cubic metres for 1965 (Lvovich 1973).

From a technical standpoint, it is questionable whether the present-day demand for irrigation truly represents a sound starting point for future projections. Irrigation efficiencies are often so low as to be harmful as well as wasteful, and current irrigation water use does not therefore necessarily reflect real water needs. To project water demand by extrapolating past usage for new land is to ignore the opportunities for increased efficiency of use.

Improved water-application efficiency, better over-all water management and the rehabilitation of outmoded water schemes may rapidly achieve local savings of water. However, no general criteria can be formulated to evaluate such local benefits: a loss of water from one project may constitute a source of supply to a downstream user. Only a basin-wide hydrological and economic analysis will identify when savings arising from increased local efficiency are in fact providing a real asset for expanded use.

A review of experience at the basin or project level indicates two widespread and counter-balancing trends in irrigation use.

In some areas, a wise selection of the crops to be produced, better canal linings, better on-farm management, the introduction of spray or trickle application techniques, revision of water-allocation practices and readjustment of water rights have all helped to improve the efficiency of water use. (At the same time, it is not uncommon to find that 70 to 80 per cent of the water delivered to a canal system does not reach the crops. And while the average water consumption per hectare has been decreasing in recent years, this decrease is a very slow process in many areas.)

But in other areas, irrigation schemes are deteriorating through reductions in productivity or outright abandonment of land because of water-logging, salinization and alkalinization, unsuitable drainage and over-application or under-application of water. Return flows may become so salty, as in the lower Colorado, that downstream irrigators must have the waters desalted to render them usable.

In still other areas, urbanization destroys productive land as fast as new projects are built. In upstream locations, the effect of increased on-site use of precipitation is a reduction in downstream flow.

Proper assessment of the global situation must await the completion of the FAO Perspective Study for World Agriculture Development and the proposed World Survey of Water Resources and Irrigation. The magnitude of demand for irrigated land in the near future has been outlined in the Indicative World Plan for Agriculture, in which the over-all objective is to increase the 1970 harvested area by 43 per cent by 1985 in the developing countries.

Other essential agriculture needs, including rural domestic uses, make relatively small demands on over-all water resources. Water demand for livestock, for example, is estimated at about 62 x 10^9 cubic metres per year for 1700 million animal units, and this allows 100 litres per day per animal unit to cover all water needs. Fisheries represent a small volumetric use which is highly remunerative in yield per unit of water consumed.

Roughly three-quarters of the land and water development costs projected in the Indicative World Plan are for irrigation and associated drainage, but the Plan also stresses the great importance of seeds, fertilizers, crop protection, soil conservation, land reform, mechanization, educational assistance, credit, marketing and trade policies.

The cost of irrigation works and associated drainage varies with local conditions. Per hectare costs are mounting progressively as readily accessible soil and water approach full development. Planning and execution time will depend upon the difficulties presented by any particular scheme.

It has become evident that if an irrigation project is to achieve its aims of improving agricultural production and livelihood without environmental deterioration, the engineering works must be accompanied by appropriate credit, transport, housing and related activities. What is more, new irrigation planning is increasingly obliged to find means of developing the water resources of an entire basin or management area so that they may serve multiple purposes, including industry and hydroelectric power.

F. *Hydroelectric Power*

Hydroelectric power generation can be combined with numerous other instream uses. Usually it is organized as part of energy systems that utilize thermal generation.

We can estimate the theoretical potential of falling water to produce electricity, either on the basis of average stream flow (the river gradient) or on the basis of an assured amount being available for some portion of time. This latter amount will vary according to the seasonal character of run-off.

The installed capacity to capture hydroenergy is concentrated for the most part in Europe (including the USSR), North America, Japan, China, India and Brazil. In some countries (Brazil, Canada, Morocco, Norway and Uganda, for example), hydropower accounts for as much as 80 to 90 per cent of all power generated. Elsewhere, the installations may be tied in with thermal-generating units, and are often reserved to meet peak demand. Hydropower provides about half of electric power production in Japan, and about 15 per cent in the United States.

Often hydroelectric storage facilities are also used for irrigation programmes, navigation, domestic water supply or aquatic habitat. Thus, the development of hydroelectric power is often linked to multipurpose programmes. Hydroelectricity plays a key role in the development of the Dez, São Francisco and Volga basins.

Construction costs per unit of generating capacity have tended to rise as the most promising sites have been exploited. But with the recent rise in the cost of other energy producing materials, many sites that were formerly regarded as economically unfeasible for development, may now become economically viable.

The growing industrialization of the developing countries will increase the demand for electric power, and this will require a careful scrutiny and evaluation of remaining hydro-sites.

TABLE 8. Continental Totals of Hydraulic Energy Resources and Current Use.

Continent	Potential available resources 95 per cent of time (thousands of kilowatts)	Potential output 95 per cent of time (millions of kilowatt hrs per year)	Current installed capacity (thousands of kilowatts)	Current annual production (millions of kilowatt hrs per year)
Africa	145,218	1,161,741	8,154	30,168
Asia	139,288	1,114,305	47,118	198,433
Europe (including USSR)	102,961	827,676	135,498	505,317
North America	72,135	577,086	90,210	453,334
South America	81,221	649,763	18,773	91,415
Oceania	12,987	103,897	7,609	28,897
World Total	553,810	4,434,468	307,362	1,307,564

Source: United States National Committee of the World Energy Conference, *Survey of Energy Resources, 1974.*

Not only has the competitive position of hydroelectric power been enhanced by recent increases in the cost of fossil fuels but the fact that it does not produce organic or heat pollution commends it in areas where water quality is threatened.

While the storage capacity of some reservoirs is threatened by silting and the permanence of supply may be dependent upon the preservation of appropriate land use and contingent on upstream development, the relative permanence of the water supply places hydro-projects in a unique position among potential energy sources.

It has been pointed out that hydroelectric power is often combined with other in-stream uses. While some of the uses of a multipurpose project may be complementary, others may in fact be competitive. The intake for a drinking-water supply, for instance, or the diversion structure for an irrigated system can often be located downstream from the hydro-station so that the energy in the water can first be used to generate electricity. On the other hand, the provision for flood control in a reservoir usually means reserving a considerable amount of storage to lop off flood peaks. This reduces the gross head on the turbine and hence reduces the power output.

Not all the theoretical hydro-potential of a river basin can necessarily be developed unless the site is suitable for dam construction, i.e. sound foundations and abutments that are reasonably impervious to seepage; further, the reservoir perimeter must be reasonably free from low areas which would allow overflowing to other drainage basins. Also of great importance is the need to proportion the size of the hydro-development and its generating capacity to the size of the power system it will feed. For an electrical system of any given size, the increment of new capacity must lie within a given range if it is to be economically feasible.

Ideally, the exploitation of any source of energy should be based upon an analysis of all alternative sources so that each may be given a priority for development. Development of hydroelectric power should therefore be analysed in the context of a country's total energy resources. Such analysis not only requires the least cost solution in meeting energy needs, but also that these needs should be evaluated in terms of their net value to the society as a whole. In practice, this would require that pricing of basic fuels should also be based upon their true economic costs.

Once priorities for the development of various types of energy have been established, and the role of electric power in meeting the country's needs has been determined, the next step in planning is to formulate the most efficient mix of investment in hydro, conventional thermal, nuclear and so forth. Where appropriate, a distinction is made between time-of-day and seasonal variations in production and consumption so that the incremental costs of supplying power are reflected in pricing policy. This means that data on hydro potential only has value when viewed in the light of its actual costs and benefits. If alternative forms of generation of electric power are cheaper, or if for any reason demand in a particular country or region does not justify its exploitation in the foreseeable future, the value of data on potential hydro resources is correspondingly reduced.

G. *Water-borne Transportation*

Inland waterways make use of natural streams and lakes or artificial channels. In such great inland water systems as the Rhine, Seine, Danube, Elbe, Nile, Volga-Don, Ganges-Brahmaputra and the Mississippi, storage reservoir evaporation, maintenance of low-water flows and lock operation make the most demand on the resource.

Barges carrying as much as 3000 tons with drafts of 2.5 metres are found on European waterways, and drafts of up to 3-4 metres in North America.

To the extent that regulation of dry season flow is required for minimum operating depths, navigation channels compete with other uses. Their design and operation, however, can be made compatible with the competing demands of hydroelectricity, domestic water supply, irrigation, recreation and waste disposal.

Advances in the design of locks, lifts and inclined planes have reduced the amount of water required to elevate or lower water craft. Further, improvements in the design of barges enable larger cargoes to be handled at lower cost.

These technical improvements have, in themselves, improved the competitive position of water transport *vis-à-vis* road and rail. In addition, two other factors have led to an increased interest, if not a renaissance, in water transport in certain regions. First, recent sharp inceases in energy costs have enhanced the physical efficiency of water as a means of transporting petroleum, coal, minerals, metals, grain and other bulk products. Secondly, the relatively low levels of air, water and noise pollution inherent in water transport make it possible to combine navigation with multipurpose water management schemes involving wildlife conservation and water recreation facilities. As a result, there is a renewed and growing regional and interregional interest in water-borne transportation.

H. *On-site Uses*

Streams and lakes are used for flood conveyance, inland fisheries and recreation as well as for hydroelectric power and navigation.

Fisheries and recreation uses are highly dependent upon the physical, bacteriological and chemical quality of water. In turn, water quality is affected by both point discharges from domestic, industrial and irrigation users, and by non-point flows from forests, fields and grazing lands.

1. *Flooding conveyance*

A natural function of all stream valleys is to carry the peak discharges that occur seasonally or at rare intervals. All forms of water management must allow for these flood flows.

Where the inundated land is potentially useful for crops, transport or city purposes, communities have the option of:

    (a) Accepting occasional or periodic loss of property and life;

    (b) Trying to control flood flows by engineering works;

    (c) Reducing flows by upstream land treatment;

    (d) Modifying building and land use to reduce vulnerability to loss;

    (e) Sharing the burden of flooding through relief and insurance schemes.

On a world scale, the average annual *per capita* property damage from flood is estimated to be increasing, as is vulnerability to catastrophic damage caused by exceedingly rare floods with a probable recurrence of, say, 100 to 1000 years. Urbanization generally increases peak flows. And poor use of land has effects of even greater magnitude throughout the developing world.

Engineering works for power, irrigation, navigation and other purposes, can in some places be combined with flood control. Warning systems, building design, land use plans and regulations can be integrated to reduce vulnerability to loss.

2. *Inland fisheries*

About 13 per cent of the total world fish catch (63×10^9 metric tons) is drawn from fresh water. Unlike marine fisheries, which have shown marked declines in catch and over-fishing of table-grade fish since 1970, fresh-water stocks are stable or increasing.

The demand for fish as a food supply is intensified by the shortage of other sources of animal proteins, minerals and vitamins. Fresh-water fish production thus plays a small, yet significant, role in helping meet increasing food needs. In multiple-purpose water planning, provision for fish production is of growing importance.

3. Recreational uses

Streams and lakes, both natural and man-made, are often used for recreational fishing and water sports. The aesthetic use of water is a consideration here, too. Inadequate treatment of municipal and industrial wastes before discharge may diminish the attractiveness, and even the safety, of natural waters for recreational use. Though impoundments and channel works can destroy valuable aquatic habitat, with proper foresight they can also provide new habitat. Fisheries, navigation and recreational facilities can all, in favourable circumstances, be developed in conjunction with hydroelectric power.

4. Water quality

In industrialized countries, one important objective of water pollution abatement is to make waters safe for fishing, wildlife, sports and other water-based recreation.

This concern is related to the protection of health from pollution and leads directly to an assessment of the effects of on-site uses upstream.

The flow of erosion products from grazing lands, cultivated lands, forests and mines threatens the storage capacity of reservoirs by silting and reduces recreational activity and fishing by increasing turbidity. These effects can be countered by soil and forest conservation programmes. At the same time, nutrients from fertilized fields encourage the growth of algae in receiving waters, and the wide use of pesticides, herbicides and fungicides contributes toxic substances. The intense utilization of precipitation in fields or shifts in forestation and farming practices (including the construction of small reservoirs) may reduce run-off. In these ways, on-site uses of water may exacerbate problems of pollution.

Statistics presenting the extent of different on-site uses on a comparable basis are unavailable. However, on-site uses are increasing and are having greater effect on the suitability of water for downstream use.

I. Summary

Domestic water supply is hazardous to the health of at least one quarter of the world's population. To achieve minimum degrees of safety in potable water supply for the present and prospective population will require major increases in quantity and great improvement in the quality of water supply. The most urgent needs are in rural areas and in the low-income sections of tropical and semi-tropical cities.

Industrial demand, chiefly for cooling and processing in a few industries, is currently satisfied by methods which vary tremendously in volume of water withdrawn and in amount of waste returned to ground, stream or lake. As demand grows with the expansion of manufacturing, the extent to which the volume of effluent waste will vary and the quality of water deteriorate or improve will be governed by the techniques adopted for in-plant processes and waste treatment.

Irrigation demand, the largest consumptive use, is destined to increase in response to the imperative need to increase food production, both nationally and globally. Although efficiency in the use of water for crops is improving to some degree in some areas and although cropping intensity is rising, albeit slowly, water losses are still large and much irrigated land is deteriorating. Meeting new demands will involve more costly projects, greater attention to auxiliary services, and intensified competition for available run-off. It may also require locating population where water supply is more readily available.

In-stream uses will be affected by changes in water flow and quality. On-site uses are expanding, with a consequent reduction in downstream flows.

Whether at the metropolitan, basin, national or international level, these shifting demands on finite supply will only be satisfied by improved water management programmes where the demand/supply relationship and the administrative and legal structure will influence the allocation of water and the choice of technology.

IV. DEMAND/SUPPLY RELATIONSHIPS

Throughout the world, the essential water problem is how best to reconcile increasing use of a fixed supply with the needs and constraints of human society, in a way that will maintain a stable environment. Three characteristic situations emerge in this evolving relationship between constant water supply and dynamic demand.

At one extreme are the regions, countries or parts of countries with a large natural supply and a relatively low level of demand which can be satisfied without regulation of water resources.

At the other extreme are areas with scarce supply and relatively high levels of demand which are satisfied only through complete regulation of water resources.

In between, are areas where demands for water are satisfied through partial regulation of flow and quality.

In those situations where no interference in water flow is required, water management usually proceeds on a project-by-project basis within a local framework. In the intermediate situation of partial regulation, there are two principal alternatives for balancing supply and demand: increase availability of supplies, or alternatively, decrease net demand by making more efficient use of supplies at hand. In situations of complete regulation, only the demand management option is available and this may call for changes in the location of production or in the mix of products.

This latter situation develops over different periods of time depending upon the whole range of factors affecting demand/supply relationships. In the Tisza River basin (a 156,000 sq km subbasin of the Danube shared by five countries), water management began about 130 years ago and is expected to reach complete regulation in about 60 to 80 years. The Salt River basin (32,000 sq km in the United States) developed complete regulation over a 60-year period. For many areas, long-range equilibrium of demand and supply can be achieved without planning for complete regulation in the short term.

The process of projecting the relationship between supply and demand normally requires a careful examination of alternative development patterns and policies and the likely consequences of each. In addition to the basic requirements for domestic and municipal water, the projection takes into account the desired or possible activities that might require water and the likely water demand for each unit of output. Inevitably, this requires knowledge and experience from many areas: socio-economic, financial, technological, legal and administrative.

Demand/supply management presents particular difficulties in arid and semi-arid lands. The population in these regions is confronted with over-grazed and sometimes parched or even sterile pastureland; a degraded, sparse and vanishing forest; and a precarious agriculture subject to uncertain rainfalls and river flooding. These conditions are frequently exacerbated by the drying-up of surface water supplies between seasons; the problems are further compounded in cold desert regions.

In many arid areas the Sahel countries, for example, a relatively large water potential is often, in fact, available for development. The real problem, therefore, is not the lack of water resources, but rather the lack of an integrated water management policy that will help alleviate the current tragic conditions and also prevent further desertification.

Any policy for such regions must not pay heed only to the uneven distribution of rainfall and water resources over space and time; the cost of water structures and the relatively high cost of ground water exploration and development must also be taken into account. Moreover, systematic training of technicians is required to cope with operation and maintenance functions over areas with scattered population. As a result, the investment required to develop available resources in turn requires a careful appraisal of the social and economic benefits of future water use projects.

A. *Socio-economic Considerations*

Certain socio-economic questions are basic to the water demand/supply relationship: What are the social benefits of various demands for water and water-related services? How do these benefits compare with the social and economic costs of providing an acceptable level of supply and water-related services? Are the required funds obtainable considering other demands for investment and services in other sectors of the economy?

Optimal demand/supply relationships are often judged on monetary criteria alone. But non-monetary considerations also influence decisions about the appropriate level of water resource development when national goals include such objectives as income redistribution, improvement of public health standards and the general quality of living, income stability for small farmers, and environmental protection and improvement.

As a result, after water demands have been estimated and compared with the costs of supply, those responsible for making investment decision about water supply facilities and production facilities that use water, may well modify the initial projections. For example, plans for type and level of service for a community or district may be adjusted so as to improve a well or spring rather than providing house connexions or stand pipes.

Normally. the basic pattern of a nation's growth is not, except for agriculture, dominated by the availability or the lack of water. The distribution of activities among sub-basins or basins and the technology of water use may, however, be acutely affected by the level of water supply. This intensifies as the marginal costs of water, both for quality and quantity, increase — a common tendency as cheaper supplies are claimed, waste loads increase, and better quality is desired.

Policies for agricultural production, price controls, international trade, urban improvement or similar aims, may be reinforced or counteracted by investments in the water resources sector.

B. *Financial Considerations*

Although pricing is a powerful instrument for controlling demand/supply relationships, it has rarely been used in water management. This situation may change since a gradual shift from supply management to demand management is under way in many parts of the world as a result of rapidly increasing costs of supply.

The way in which water is traditionally priced by a utility in industrialized societies — price per unit of water declining as gross use increases — can result through time in significant over-investment in water supply. Many water utilities now realize that larger consumers should pay the same price per unit for their incremental consumption as small consumers. They also realize that the price charged should reflect the investment cost of expanding the system capacity through time. If consumers are charged a price which reflects this cost, it is more likely that water-saving and water-using technology will be adopted.

C. *Technological and Environmental Considerations*

Every technological change has some impact on the environment and each change may have potential costs or benefits. Any projection of demand/supply relationships must allow for likely technological change, and research that fosters desirable new technologies should be built into the planning process.

1. *Effects of water and non-water technologies on water supply and demand*

Technological developments may contribute to better conservation of existing sources of water supply (e.g. evaporation reduction, phreatotype control, and surface water harvesting). Some may also open up new sources of supply (e.g. desalination of sea and brackish water, precipitation increase through cloud seeding, fog drip augmentation, iceberg towing). These technologies become especially relevant as a society approaches or reaches complete regulation of a region's natural supply. In these conditions, improved and usually more expensive water-use technologies are also available for achieving a balanced demand/supply relationship (e.g. advanced waste treatment for recycling and reuse, greenhouse irrigation, replacement of unlined canals by lined channels or pipelines for water conveyance).

Non-water technologies can also affect the water demand/supply relationship. Some of these exogenous technologies tend to increase future demand for water (e.g. gas production from coal, transport of solids by water slurry pipeline). Some tend to decrease further water demands (e.g. genetic development of plants to withstand drought and salinity, bioprocessing to provide food, electric power generation by use of wind and water power, cooling systems using air). The effects of others depend on local conditions (e.g. use of geothermal energy, vegetation management, oil shale conversion to liquid fuels, conversion of solar energy to heat and power).

2. *Effects of technology on health and ecology*

All water management technologies are subject to ecological constraints. Emphasis on water quality varies from country to country, and even among uses and regions within a country. Maintenance of health is, of course, a paramount concern. But the establishment of appropriate standards for limiting particular substances in water is inhibited in many instances by lack of knowledge of the effects of a particular substance on humans and other organisms in the environment. Efforts are made to regulate the discharge of poisonous industrial wastes, since many are amenable neither to waste treatment nor to water treatment, except at inordinately high cost. The "proper" level of water quality should be determined for each watercourse, depending upon the concurrent or sequential uses to which it is put. Whether effluent control policy standards should be uniform within a basin, within a country or within a multinational region will depend upon development objectives and environmental policies. For example, one basin or sub-basin may be given special status — high quality or low quality — and effluent standards applicable to industries and communities in that basin may be different from those of neighbouring basins.

3. *Effects of water management on the environment*

When stream flow regulation converts rivers to lakes or reservoirs, scenic values are changed. Also, reservoirs substantially increase evaporation from river systems, change water temperature, alter erosion around reservoir banks and trap sediment. If the full consequences of a new reservoir are to be weighed, they must place a socio-economic value on the resulting displacement of people, communicable disease hazards, the inundation of farm land, the enhanced potential for fish production and the modification of wildlife and agricultural production that was dependent on the previously existing régime. Further, important ecological effects will often result from the recreational and urban developments that often follow the construction of a reservoir system.

Large-scale drainage and irrigation projects may modify the physical environment, and generate changes in climate, soil and vegetation and, in ground and surface-water levels. A social environment may often be transformed from a rural to an urban-industrial economic system with numerous secondary environmental and social effects.

Unwise short-term decisions about river regulation may jeopardize long-term possibilities for sound development. The record of water development shows that the advances and consequences of technology can only be ignored at great potential cost to the community. At the same time, the record also shows that with proper foresight, environmental improvement can be one of the multiple objectives of water resource planning and management. Environmental policies must therefore be built into the planning of any water management development programme.

D. *Administrative and legal considerations*

Administrative and legal structures greatly influence water balance efficiency and under conditions of scarce supply offer important mechanisms for regulating a balanced demand/supply relationship.

As demand intensifies, large-scale regional water supply systems are often developed by the integration of several smaller river basins with the groundwater system. This tends both to strengthen national management agencies, and to establish or modify the structure of river basin or other commissions or committees.

Whenever large river basins are shared by two or more countries, the tendency towards interrelation encourages international basin management and development. Many international agreements have been signed during the past decades. But for a large number of rivers, either no agreement has yet been reached, even after many years of negotiation in some instances, or the agreements reached have little substance and prove to be ineffective in the solving of difficult problems such as pollution control and the development of large-scale facilities.

Through the powerful tools of socio-economic and monetary policy, Governments can, in effect, control the demand for and the supply of water. The form of action any Government will take in managing water resources will generally reflect the availability of financial resources, cultural and political traditions, and the priority given to water development and preservation.

V. CONCLUSION

This paper has described a condition where the global stock of water is fixed, and postulated an accelerating future demand. It is tempting in such circumstances to extrapolate demand curves for future times when they might outstrip supply. But there is little help in such an exercise.

To be sure, water demand has already exceeded supply in some areas. And there is no question that demand will have to be curbed in some instances in the near future, unless available supplies can be inceased and water management radically improved.

Rather than extrapolating from present data on the presumption that current conditions will persist, it might prove more salutary and realistic to focus attention on alternative and improved methods that will correct current carelessness or profligate practice. The crucial question is how to implement effective and socially acceptable demand management procedures before they are dictated by shortages.

Further, the basic data about water supply and its rational use is inadequate for large sectors of the land surface. Decisions about future management for such areas are riddled with uncertainty and frustrated by large margins of error in data derived from inadequate observation networks and equally inadequate modes of analysis. Also, the gap between scientific knowledge and its application is vast and widening in most parts of the world.

The opportunities for radical improvement in the socio-economic, financial, technological, administrative and legal conditions that influence present circumstances are immense. It should therefore not be taken for granted that any sector of the world's population need drink contaminated water, that industry need continue its present pattern of largely unregulated water use and discharge, that agriculture cannot alter its current pattern of irrigation loss and misuse of water, or that productive soils need be destroyed and aquifers exhausted beyond our ability to replenish them in our own lifetime.

Finally, it must be stressed that the urgent need in many areas is a matter not so much of devising new management methods, but of putting to use the technology and institutional devices which are available now. Subsequent papers will discuss how this might best be accomplished under different physical and socio-economic conditions.*

---

*These papers are included in *Water Development and Management*, edited by Asit K. Biswas, Pergamon Press, Oxford, 1978.

Policy Options

INTRODUCTION

This document is the third basic paper prepared for the United Nations Water Conference. It comes under topic III of the provisional agenda approved for the Conference by the Economic and Social Council. The first paper deals with resources and needs and analyses present-day trends in supply and demand. In addition, it reviews the general situation and shows that in certain regions the water problem may assume quite serious proportions if it is not corrected.

The second paper* comes under topic II of the provisional agenda. It deals with the potential and limitations of technology and emphasizes the need for strenuous efforts to improve present utilization of available technologies and to adapt techniques of a type and scale appropriate for developing countries, in view of their manpower needs and their economic and social conditions. With regard to supply, it does not appear that revolutionary developments are likely to take place in existing technology.

I. NEED FOR A WATER POLICY

Before discussing the reasons why a water policy is needed and the alternatives that are available, it would be useful to recall a number of fundamental considerations. The traditional political and administrative organization of a country is based on the identification of the different functions to be carried out for the development of certain economic or social activities, for the exercise of options or for the achievement of a synthesis (justice, finance).

Generally speaking, specific and well-defined human preoccupations are used as a criterion, and it is only recently that ministries and public organizations have appeared that are more concerned with defending broader ideas or objectives already being dealt with by several ministries - the protection of the environment, for example, or of natural resources. Such ministries and organizations often find it difficult to gain a foothold in the existing system.

Water is a universal topic that involves almost the entire population and all ministries; it is a subject that gives rise to numerous practical activities and legal texts. It might therefore be asked why questions of water reform are constantly being discussed.

A. *Omnipresence of Water*

Water is everywhere, but it is limited in quantity and quality. It is everywhere, but it is constantly in motion, passing from one state to another and from one place to another.

Water problems vary enormously from one region to another, from one season to another and from one year to another. Water shortages have always existed in desert areas, whereas it is only more recently that they have occurred in temperate regions. Such climatic extremes have nevertheless brought about tragic consequences since time immemorial.

---

* See *Water Development and Management*, edited by Asit K. Biswas, Pergamon Press, Oxford, 1978.

B. Multiplicity of Uses

The uses of water are countless but may be grouped under two main headings. Firstly, water is an integral part of a certain number of entities, whether mineral, vegetable or animal. Secondly, it serves as a vehicle in almost all the uses it is put to by man — for personal or household cleanliness, for cooling automobile or factory motors, or for extracting useful substances contained in minerals or other products.

C. Variability of Quality

The quality of water varies greatly. When water is used as a vehicle it can easily absorb all kinds of products either in dissolved or suspended form.

Nature has built the world in this manner, and man has merely imitated it in his industrial and social uses. However, nature is equipped with regenerating processes so that, as long as population density is not too great, natural self-purification is able to maintain a biologically living and healthy environment. Nevertheless, urbanization, industrialization, expansion of the use of synthetic products and destruction of the living environment by ruthless interference have entirely upset this balance with the result that the power of self-purification of waterways is no longer sufficient; rivers have died and pollution has come into being.

Even here we are faced with a contradiction, since most of the time, as we have seen, water is used exclusively for disposing of waste products, which automatically alters its quality and makes it unfit for other uses. To prohibit waste disposal, however, would in fact prohibit all water use.

In certain regions the harmful effects of water assume catastrophic proportions. Cyclones, floods, soil erosion and drought are some of the so-called natural calamities. A large number of measures must be taken to protect man from such calamities, measures that sometimes run counter to certain soil or water uses and to other imperatives of national policy.

D. Multiplication of Conflicts

Water is thus the source of innumerable conflicts that may arise at every turn. For example, when a new well dries up a neighbour's well; a stable pollutes a neighbouring source of water; there is not enough water in the dry season in a given region; a city or factories pollute the water downstream; an underground sheet of water is no longer fed because a canal has been dug that diverts the water from its natural bed; the establishment of factories and their industrial uses spoils the shores of a river and prevents fishing, bathing and recreation; a large metropolis obtains its water supply from increasingly further distances and robs the resources of neighbouring rural regions, and at the same time the impermeability of its soil causes more frequent flooding; and even the biological life of the sea is threatened by polluted rivers, by port areas or by large industries established on its coasts.

In all places and at all times large or small-scale conflicts set neighbours or the members of the same profession against one another and set cities against rural areas, industrialists against fishermen, agriculture against electrification and upstream areas against downstream areas.

E. *Role of the Public Authorities or of the Community*

The role of public Powers is to settle such conflicts. The usual means of settling conflicts in human societies is to resort to the arbitration of a wise man or to the courts. The same has been true historically with regard to water, as evidenced by the famous water court in Valencia, Spain, and the renowned Kelian Subak in Bali.

However, when conflicts become extremely numerous and involve forces as powerful and necessary as the development of agriculture, cities, industry and recreation, flood protection or the development of mountain areas and consequently require enormous investment for their satisfactory solution, simple arbitration is no longer sufficient. The public authorities should therefore promote a positive and cohesive policy for developing water resources that will in turn make it possible to develop all the components of national life both in their own right and in respect for others.

This gives rise to the need for direct governmental intervention, whose objectives and means will now be analysed.

II. OBJECTIVES OF A WATER POLICY AND PHYSICAL PLANNING

A. *Objectives of Economic and Social Forces with Regard to Water*

A Government, faced with the problems which arise for its people, first sets very broad objectives of economic development, social progress and interregional balance. These objectives are achieved by very varied means such as intensification of agriculture, establishment of industries, promotion of tourism, growth of cities, modernization of rural areas and so on.

These economic forces use water and then, after use, discharge it as waste. Traditionally, they tend to regard water as a gift from heaven and hardly give any thought either to the quantity used or to the quality of their discharges.

These forces would suggest, explicitly or implicitly, that an adequate supply of clean water in rivers and lakes does not entail any economic cost.

Experience has long showed that, to the extent that "needs" exceed "available resources", far-reaching and costly collective actions are essential to ensure a balance in the water system at all times.

These collective actions are not the only ones possible and the range of technical means available to ensure stability will first be briefly discussed.

B. *Technical means of Ensuring Stability*

Quite briefly, these technical means can be applied to achieve the following:

Increase of resources

This can be done by the following means: regularization over a period of time (dams); intra-basin and inter-basin transport; combination of the use of surface water and ground water; planning of vegetation cover; recycling of water after first use; more sophisticated techniques such as desalination of sea water, artificial rainfall, control of evaporation and so on; reduction of "needs".

The concept of need of water for a given use has only a relative value and experience shows that in order to fulfil a given economic function, the flow of water to be drawn off in nature can vary greatly depending on the scarcity of supply and the acceptable costs within the system which carries out that function.

This is true regardless of whether we are producing steel, beer or rice, cooling generating stations, or transporting merchandise, because in all cases the amount of water to be incorporated in the product is infinitesimal in relation to that used to dissolve or discharge useless by-products to generate heat, or to carry ships. The technology exists to reduce considerably these quantities of water by recycling after purification and, in some cases, water can even be dispensed with, for example, in air cooling or road transport.

Purification of discharges

If, at the end of a given industrial process, in addition to the finished product, there are a number of useless elements which must be thrown out, it is quite possible to extract these elements from the "used" water in which they are found before reincorporating that water into the natural cycle. These purification techniques exist and are being improved daily. Of course, they entail costs, sometimes considerable, but the limitations are economic and not technical.

Reduction of water damage

Floods and cyclones are among the major scourges of mankind which has always sought protection from them by evacuating threatened areas and withdrawing into zones outside the area affected by the torrent.

The means to be used and the economic and social consequences of these means are obviously of far different significance. Thus, a technical solution may be found for any water problem affecting the economic and social development of a country but the difficulty arises from the fact that, depending on the method selected, the cost will vary greatly and, above all, the implementation and financing will be the task of different bodies.

Generally speaking, public agencies have the responsibility of increasing supply to meet increased demand or to dilute pollutants, undertaking projects for protection against the harmful effects of water or digging navigational canals. The Government must, in matters relating to water as elsewhere, define its policy and establish the machinery that will permit the optimum selection to be made. Before giving consideration to such machinery, however, it is still important to define the areas where governmental choices are to be made. For clarity in this report, a distinction will be made between "internal" and "external" options in matters relating to water.

C. Internal Options in Matters Relating to Water

Water is to be found on the earth in four forms: atmospheric water, surface water, ground water and the sea. Any decision taken in the economic field leads to modification of the following fundamental elements, which may be regarded as "internal" in matters relating to water, as opposed to use-related elements:

For atmospheric water: modification of the natural cycle; protection or planning of catchment areas.

For surface water: minimum flows; water quality; extent of flood areas; harmful effects of water.

For ground water: level of stability; degree of contamination.

For the sea: degree of pollution.

This breakdown of the internal elements is essential for two reasons; decisions on the limits to be respected in each case depend on development programmes, the needs which they imply and the available means, in other words, "external" elements; real decisions are rarely taken, even today, by making explicit reference to these limits.

Atmospheric water

It is increasingly clear that it is possible to modify the presence of the renewing cycle of fresh water by influencing the atmospheric phase of the water cycle. Artificial manipulation of the weather is rich in technical promise. Precipitation can be induced at times and in places where it would not occur (at least not in the same degree) under natural conditions. It is possible to prevent hail and to moderate storms by using certain techniques. Consideration is even being given to modifying the climate and, in particular, making permanent and substantial climatic changes. All these technical means, however, are at the research stage and a water policy must take into account only the facts which have been unequivocally established by science.

Surface water

(a) *Minimum flows*. There are several elements which affect the selection of minimum flow: protection of the living environment and the physical balance (erosion); utilization for leisure (sports, fishing) or navigation; aesthetic character of sites; need to replenish ground water; needs expressed downstream from the segment considered. The concept of level is thus added to that of flow. Since minimum flow is supposedly fixed as a result of all these considerations, only the surplus can be allocated to net riparian consumption, since the draw-offs that are immediately returned to the river are limited only in quality. The *a priori* setting of such minimum flows is of extreme complexity in view of a number of factors involved and can lead to very serious conflicts between different zones in the same basin; however, the fact remains that in one manner or another these flows evolve in terms of each decision and the problem cannot be avoided.

(b) *Water quality*. As far as principles are concerned, it would seem that it would not be too difficult to reach agreement in this field. To transform rivers into sewers can hardly be said to be one of the aims of modern civilization.

What must be done, on the contrary, is to establish a minimum quality standard which must be respected for each river. This is where the difficulties start. Choices have to be made and the limits of pollution have to be defined according to the places, the pollutants and the utilizations.

On the basis of this hypothesis, oligotropic lakes should be specially protected so as to prevent them from getting choked up, a problem that can be solved only with difficulty. Or would it be better to abandon the idea of quality targets and only set standards for the discharge of waste for each use, standards which could be identical for all identical uses? Whether it is considered as an objective or as a consequence, the quality of the water of a river or a lake at each point is a fact, and it would certainly be better to come to a clear decision about what is wanted.

(c) *Harmful effects of water*. In defining a water policy, there will be many options also with regard to the control of the harmful effects of water. These effects are related, *inter alia*, to floods, the submersion and deterioration of the banks, soil erosion, the environment and salination. In the case of flooding, for instance, a choice must be made between constructing protective works which are increasingly expensive depending on the area to be protected and the frequency of the risks against which protection is sought, on the one hand, and abandoning some forms at least of land use where protection would be too expensive or would involve damage to other parts of the basin, on the other hand. Such a choice goes well beyond the problem of water itself and it is one of the examples which shows very clearly the relationship between water policy and physical planning.

Underground water

Underground water is of special interest because of the regular flow it provides and the quality of the water in many cases. Here again, it is not possible to draw off unlimited amounts and, if the reserves are not to be exhausted, the maximum flows to be drawn off must be established, bearing in mind the natural or artificial replenishment of the reserves. As all movements involving underground water are extremely slow, pollution appears only insidiously, but when it has occurred it is very often irreparable on the human scale of time. Such water must therefore be vigilantly protected.

Something that must be emphasized here is the problem of the intrusion of sea water into the water-bearing strata along coasts. Over-exploitation of underground water located near the sea may create a disequilibrium which results in the infiltration of sea water into the underground reserves, making the water unusable.

The sea

The sea is the collector of all water that runs off the surface of the earth and it therefore receives also all the wastes discharged into rivers and lakes and on its own shores. There are therefore certain differences which distinguish it from running water and which are due to its role as a collector: microbiological pollution, the discharge of stable and toxic substances which are concentrated along the trophic chains and accumulate in the sea and in lakes; they become more dangerous with time and may cause irreparable harm to the flora and fauna and eventually to man.

The definition of an objective for a given *milieu* - quality, for instance - is a policy decision based on objective data (the natural quality of the water, its present quality, the cost of reducing pollution, the quality level required for certain uses) and it must also comprise many subjective factors, such as the uncertainties of science, aesthetic considerations and irrational attitudes on the part of the public. Thus, there is an infinite variety of possible procedures for establishing such objectives. On the other hand, a policy of water management according to quality objectives has no meaning unless it is closely linked to physical planning and is applied in a coherent manner within a single hydrographic basin.

Many conflicts may arise in this connexion, and they will be all the more serious the more the different parts of the area concerned come under many different political and administrative authorities and the more independent they are of each other.

D. *External Options: Water and Physical Planning*

The internal options described above form the basis on which a coherent water policy may be built. In practice, the practical programmes give prominence essentially to the satisfaction of the growing needs of the developing sectors, i.e.:

Water supply for towns and rural communities;

Irrigation;

Drainage of swampy or floodable areas;

A great diversity of industries, navigation, production of hydroelectric and thermal energy;

Satisfaction of needs in the area of sports, recreation and relaxation.

The usual approach to these problems, at least in regions which are rich in water resources, is to find as it were, *a posteriori* solutions. A town that is expanding, an agricultural area that is being modernized, an industrial complex that is developing, all seek the nearest water resources and carry out whatever works seem the most appropriate, perhaps with financial assistance requested from the public authorities.

When, on the contrary, what is envisaged is the deliberate development of a region or a country, the first thing to take into account, before taking any action, is what the different development sectors want from the country's resources, including its water resources. It is usually necessary to modify the initial projects to allow for the constraints imposed by water and to orient the choices on the internal options relating to water in directions which were not originally foreseen. The actual scheme for physical planning that is finally reached in this way includes the problem of water and takes account of its regional characteristics, but at the same time imposes its own guidelines.

This idea of combining physical planning with the planning of water resources is really somewhat idealistic but this is a goal that should be sought. One of the most pragmatic ways of avoiding too many mistakes while permitting a constant adaptation to human and material changes is to draw up several alternative schemes, and measure the consequences, advantages and disadvantages of each one; in this way the repercussions of every day decisions may be correctly assessed.

E. Conclusion

Finally, what may the objectives of a water policy be? They will be set down here in a style which is deliberately telegraphic but which is intended to combine all the concerns that have been expressed.

To ensure, on a continuing basis, a balance between the supply of water and the demand for it, for all uses, by dual action: improvement of the resources and adaptation of its uses;

When necessary, to direct economic and social activities towards the optimum use of water and other resources;

To provide the country with clean rivers and clean underground water and to ensure that the quality of the coastal sea water is satisfactory.

"By what means can this be achieved?" will be the subject of the next section.

III. MAIN OVER-ALL OPTIONS AND MEANS OF ACHIEVING THEM

The heart of the issue

This chapter takes us to the heart of item 3 of the provisional agenda for the Conference. Its aim is to invite discussion not to lay down precepts. Thus it contains a series of open choices rather than definitive answers. These choices are by no means exhaustive, since the subject is too vast; nor are they perfectly adapted to world problems which are too varied. This chapter is simply an effort to present options which require a decision at the highest legislative and executive levels of the State and which will influence over-all water policy.

A. Inventory and Collection of Data

An inventory of information on water and the collection of basic data are prerequisites in the formulation of water policy and an integral part of that policy.

Available documentation, particularly with regard to urgent decisions, is often limited, incomplete and heterogeneous. According to over-all statistics recently collected by the World Meteorological Organization and submitted to the Conference, there are many important gaps in the measuring stations network, particularly in the developing countries. Consequently, it should be recognized that data are still very fragmentary in vast areas of the globe and in all countries. In particular, little is known about dry periods, although it is essential to be able to forecast such periods in order to establish a balance between the supply of and demand for water and determine the extent to which it is possible to draw on underground sources over a long period without exhausting them. Finally, in most countries, with certain very recent exceptions, virtually nothing is known about water uses or the quality of surface water. Thus, strenuous efforts are required in order to elaborate a sensible water policy.

Many bodies collect data which is useful in the preparation of water policy. Such bodies consist mainly of meteorological and hydrological services but also include electricity-generating stations, navigation services, ministries of agriculture and other public and private bodies. The task of making the complex structure work is complicated by the fact that these bodies also use the data, value their prerogatives, and regard the possession of data as one of the bases of their power.

Thus, it is imperative to improve the system of gathering and processing basic data. In the case of decisions relating to water policy, there is an obvious need for all available data, not only that which relates to the quantity and quality of water but also economic data (amount of investment, costs, etc.), legal data, (legal documents relating to water such as utilization statements, licence registration, etc.) and other data. However, although this information may be gathered in a relatively short time, hydrological and meteorological data, which is perhaps the most useful, requires long years of observation. Those responsible for water policy do not always realize that it is absolutely impossible to base decisions on only one or two years' observation of a hydrological system, particularly in highly variable climates, since such a short series of data is susceptible to an error factor of up to several hundreds per cent. Lack of data or imprecise data create great uncertainty and unnecessary risks with regard to the necessity, profitability or legality of certain projects or with regard to the date on which they will be necessary or profitable. Nobody would dream of putting an oil-field into operation without having very definite information concerning its capacity. Unfortunately, such things are daily practice with regard to water. In developing countries, particularly those in tropical regions where life is closely linked to natural conditions, efforts to prepare inventories are even more important than elsewhere.

In the limited sphere of inventory problems, the interplay of the different forces affecting water and the outlines of the main structural options open to Governments become clearly visible. Inventories and basic data must therefore be overhauled. It is often necessary to establish co-ordination between different bodies dealing with the problem and to ensure that the co-ordinating body has sufficient power to define methods, allocate tasks, control implementation and ensure adequate distribution of results. In the first instance, in view of the requirements in the field of long-term observation of hydrological systems, each Government should ensure that the services responsible for hydrological and meteorological observation networks work efficiently.* Within the framework of a water policy, the structure of such services should correspond to the requirements of all users of the data and not just of one particular user or a single economic sector, however important.

B. *Formulation of a Water Policy*

All Governments should formulate water policies. All water policies should be based on sectoral policies linked to the different activities in respect of use, conservation and development of water resources or applied to different geogra-

---

* More details about statistics on networks and organizations of these services will be found in the supporting document on the subject.

phical areas. The problem is particularly acute in big countries with marked climatic variations and highly dissimilar economic development regions and even different populations.

In countries with a federal structure, this question has a bearing on the definition of the respective roles of States and the Federation with regard to water and, in other countries, on regional rights and availability.

On the other hand, choosing and maintaining future lines of action is the essence of any water policy. Frequent changes of policy are equivalent to no policy. However, it must be recognized that we live in an era of rapid change. Policies should be adapted to local conditions and there should be room for a certain amount of flexibility to cope with changes in the nature of problems and in customs.

The objectives of water policies vary widely and each country should formulate its own. However, the main objectives should include optimum utilization, conservation and management of available water resources, maximization of the benefits deriving from water conservation and utilization, valuation of water, and the satisfaction of present and future water requirements for all purposes, in the light of water availability, population increases and advances in technology.

With regard to content, an over-all water policy might include, *inter alia*, the following: the integrated management of land and water; the establishment and fulfilment of priorities in the different fields of utilization (domestic, agricultural, etc.); the adoption of measures to forestall and counteract the harmful effects of water (flooding, drought, soil erosion, spread of disease) and to control the quality of water so as to protect the environment and public health; and the adoption of guidelines concerning the economic and financial implications (prices, costs, reimbursements, subsidies and exemptions), the education of and participation by the public, and international co-operation. Certain countries have also stated that they will take account of the effects which their national water policies might have on other countries.

Institutional, economic, financial, technical and legal machinery should be established in order to implement water policy.

In most countries of the world, water problems have been tackled as a result of difficulties encountered by the different categories of users; legislation, administrative structures and financing have been based on this concept. Fears of future shortages under present operating conditions have prompted a number of countries to adopt a water management policy.

It is generally considered that the difficulties of formulating and implementing a water policy are derived mainly from increased living standards, the demographic explosion and the persistence of poor social attitudes where water is concerned. However, these three main causes cannot fully explain the increase in water problems. In seeking other explanations for the rapid and recent deterioration in the water situation, many specialists, including Barry Commoner and Philip Saint-Marc, have finally blamed the poor application of certain technologies.

Those responsible for water policy will evaluate new technologies and decide which of them should be encouraged and which should be limited and even eliminated. They will exercise this discretion in the light of fixed objectives.

Society has always had to judge science and technology on the basis of criteria other than purely scientific ones and in the light of cultural, social or political values. The importance of environmental protection is becoming more and more apparent. Evaluation of technology has become a highly topical issue and the fact that technology can provide a solution to certain difficult water problems is no longer regarded as the ultimate test of its acceptability. New technology must now pass other tests: economic (reasonable cost), ecological (no effects on the environment), social and even cultural tests. In addition to being proved effective from the point of view of quality, it must prove that its effects on the environment are beneficial.

C. Water Policy and Water Planning

While the purpose of a water policy may succinctly be stated as the achievement of maximum benefit from water resources development and conservation, one or more of the following goals generally constitutes the underlying objective of water resource development: (a) to increase the national or regional income; (b) to redistribute income among regions; (c) to redistribute income among various social groups; (d) to improve environmental quality. Water resource planning is an input into the general process of policy-making. Broadly speaking, it constitutes the link between the formation of the goals which society seeks to attain on the one hand, and the selection of the best means of attaining them on the other. The two processes are closely interrelated.

The actual role played by the planner in the policy-making process varies considerably from one country to another. In some cases, planners act mainly in the capacity of analysts and technical advisers, and there is a reasonably sharp division between the planning and policy-making functions. In other cases, as for many developing countries, considerable reliance is placed on planners not only to recommend solutions to problems but to identify goals and participate actively in the final decision concerning the action which should be taken. Although there is doubtless considerable merit in having the planning function closely linked to the policy-making function, there is a possibility that, in such cases, goals may to some extent reflect agency traditions and professional training. The same may be true of the means selected for dealing with the problems identified.

A series of questions which may help to identify the extent to which a plan truly reflects problems and new social values can be summarized as follows:

   (a) Whether the goals accurately reflect current social values;

   (b) Whether the problems identified by the planners are the same as those which are perceived by the public or other agencies;

   (c) Whether the range of choice embraces alternatives beyond those which have been used in the past by the agency involved;

   (d) Whether the weight attached by the planners to particular criteria for evaluation accurately reflects public preferences;

   (e) Whether there is evidence to suggest that the recommended policy has been successful in the past, and whether it will not have ecologically disastrous or publicly undesirable side-effects. Where such questions can be answered positively it is likely that the administrative framework has been flexible enough to respond to the new challenges of water resource planning. Where there is some doubt, it is possible that further adjustments may be needed.

As the rule to be followed is that of adapting water policy to the individual circumstances of each country, it is merely a basic precaution to be wary of global solutions. A study of the different programmes or efforts which have been devoted to developing water resources over the last 30 years indicates that the results obtained in the least developed countries have been rather poor. Water policy has failed to make the expected contribution to the struggle against those countries' most serious socio-economic problems, namely, unemployment and underemployment, malnutrition, uncontrolled urbanization and unacceptable sanitary conditions. The disappointing results of development efforts in those countries are apparently sometimes linked to the rather arbitrary application in developing countries of methods which have proved successful in the industrialized countries.

One cannot overemphasize the basic differences between industrialized and developing countries, differences which mean that any automatic transfer of solutions is bound to bring failure. The developing countries differ from the developed countries on points which are fundamental to water management in particular.

Firstly, in the industrialized countries individuals and institutions apparently adapt almost spontaneously to new means of production (for instance, new irrigation techniques), because of existing communications networks and already-established institutions. Secondly, the industrialized countries are societies which are economically homogeneous, while the developing countries are economically heterogeneous, with different economies existing side by side (modern sector and traditional sector). Furthermore, the main objectives of most developing countries must be defined in accordance with an integrated and intersectoral approach, while the industrialized countries have sometimes been able to determine their objectives project by project, or sector by sector. Finally, foreign currency, capital and skilled manpower resources are generally scarce in the developing countries. These differences, which have a bearing on the nature and the extent of the problems involved, take on special significance in the selection of a water policy. The tools available and, above all, the solutions which they provide, must be used in very different ways according to the individual circumstances of each country.

D. *Physical Planning*

Planning is an important stage in water policy.

The volume of investment required for hydraulic works, which can seldom be completed quickly (dams, canals, water-treatment plants), and the long lifespan of water-using installations (irrigation systems, factories, urban networks, electric power stations) call for extremely careful planning, and for strict execution of plans once they have been adopted. However, because of the immense difficulty in forecasting future developments, even over the relatively short term, and the need to leave room for innovation, for the reciprocal influence of economic forces and for the development of international trade flows, all data and planning, while being as detailed as possible, must be extremely flexible.

National development plans should include a national water plan (water master plan). The national development plan would place each development option in its proper perspective in relation to the total needs of the population, by specifying time-limits, guidelines and priorities for detailed plans and for the preparation of sectoral projects. Such planning generally involves identifying the problem, defining objectives, proposing different plans, evaluating those plans and selecting one of them on the basis of the objectives to be met (economic development, regional development, social welfare, environmental protection), executing the plan, making a critical analysis of the results and, where necessary, correcting the plan. There can be no doubt that only a plan which is based on an accurate compilation of information and water resources can be realistic and thus have positive results.

A water master plan could take into account such elements as available land and water resources which are likely to meet household, agricultural, industrial, commercial, energy etc., needs; measures required to anticipate and minimize such harmful effects of water as floods, drought, salinization and soil erosion; measures to be taken to protect water quality, namely the prevention of pollution and water-borne diseases, etc.

Detailed feasibility studies and preliminary studies for specific projects should follow as closely as possible the programmes, objectives and priorities established by the plans for the drainage basin or region in question. Specific plans generally include technical feasibility studies, financial justifications, cost estimates, and the time-table for their implementation. Analysis of legal constraints is always required.

The water administration may then act, if necessary, on the basis of the national water policy and the water master plan, to approve projects for water use or conservation.

In the planning exercise, it is advisable to ensure that each element has been the subject of a comparative analysis of advantages and drawbacks, of a cost-benefit analysis which includes analysis of both the economic and social advantages and the benefits for environmental protection and resource protection. However, it must be acknowledged that such a diversified planning procedure requires more and better information than many countries possess, and also a considerable amount of time, which may delay the selection of the plan and thus threaten the economic profitability of a project.

Generally speaking, a plan is never fully completed. A possible solution might be to establish such guidelines as: rational use, State control, system of user permits, etc., or to establish goals and proceed directly with development on the basis of available knowledge, on the understanding that any activity can be changed to bring it into line with the planning exercise as it progresses.

Finally, one of the most important areas of future research is the perfecting of multiple-objective planning techniques. An exchange of information on those techniques among States would be most valuable.

In many countries, the drainage basin has been regarded as the ideal unit for land and water planning. Sometimes, as in the case of inter-basin water transfers, regional planning may yield better results. Such basin or regional plans should be formulated within the framework of the national water master plan and allow for current needs and final objectives. Resource planning must obviously include planning to meet certain needs (food production, energy production, public health protection, etc.).

The distinction which has to be made between the geographical unit which is suitable for water planning and exploitation and that which is suitable for physical planning or for development in general becomes really important in certain specific cases. This is true for instance, of certain federal States and also in situations where it is more profitable to treat several small basins as one unit, where one basin is particularly extensive or, finally, where political and constitutional constraints make it very difficult for the basin to exist as a single, separate unit. In recent years, the growth of major urban centres has shown that such centres constitute more appropriate planning units than the basin to which they belong. The concept of drainage basin* as a planning unit cannot therefore be an absolute, and must in many situations be reduced or expanded in the light of individual circumstances and needs.

E. Forces Involved

It is useful to summarize briefly the different forces involved in water problems. They include the following: individuals, associations and companies who may use and discard water, build wells, install pumps, establish themselves in areas where flooding rarely occurs or use rises and falls in the water level for agricultural production; communities which install water supply and sewage systems, which make the soil impermeable or block the advance of floods; industries and industrial complexes, which use or pollute water on a large scale; energy producers, who build dams and sometimes harness entire rivers to meet their needs, or who heat up river water to cool the engines in their power stations; agricultural, irrigation or drainage complexes; complexes which provide protection against water; shipping organizations, canal and dam builders; organizations dealing with broader issues, such as regional development, and which take action with regard to water; national civil service departments, each of them responsible for promoting the progress of a given sector of the economy, and which often espouse the cause of those under their administration; finally, public opinion which, although divided and fickle, is powerful and whose support is vital.

F. Institutional Options

The institutional framework may be studied according to the functions of these institutions and the geographical area which they administer.

A national administration can and must intervene in water-related issues chiefly with the aim of:

> Keeping abreast of developments regarding resources, consumption, effluents and floods and maintaining an up-to-date inventory of the situation;
>
> Anticipating future developments, evaluating the consequences of various

---

* An international drainage basin is a geographical area extending over two or more States and determined by the limits of the area fed by the surface-and ground-water system flowing into a single river mouth.

alternatives, and formulating a water policy;

Supervising implementation of these decisions, co-ordinating, and occasionally settling disputes;

Intervening at times directly in certain works or programmes, for example through administrative or semi-public bodies established for exploiting a region or basin.

The geographical basis of management may be international, regional, basin-wide, sub-basin-wide, local or project-related; political options should define clearly the various functions and relative powers at each administrative or management level.

At the national level, it is usually found that a number of ministers have responsibility for one aspect or another of water-related problems. There is a great temptation therefore to create new super-agencies to develop and/or implement a coherent water policy. Since water is one of the natural resources and since exploitation and conservation of all natural resources have a certain number of common characteristics, there is also a great temptation to establish a super-agency for natural resources or the environment.

All actions require an authority which can decide on the line to follow and to ensure that its decisions are respected and implemented. The water sector is no exception to the rule and the choice of an agency to wield this authority is extremely important. The choice will, of course, depend on the solutions adopted to the above-mentioned geographical problems, on the general political structure of the country and the organization of its Government, and on the functions of the authority.

At the highest government level, the question is especially delicate. A search for the best theoretical division of ministerial competence reveals very quickly that there are many possible options, some respecting the unity of one problem, some another. The responsibilities of each and the external restrictions to which it is subject must be clearly defined, bearing in mind the nature of the problem.

In water-related issues, it is clear that the various ministries (of agriculture, industry etc.....), which are responsible for an activity using water, must pay special attention to the "water" aspect of their problems (irrigation development, etc.....) and participate fully in the elaboration of a general policy on resource management. Also, it is clearly indispensable to initiate a dialogue between these users and those responsible for the resource which must be protected by an "awareness". But who should hold the authority? To avoid proliferation of machinery, it seems logical to vest the authority for water problems in a special minister.

The choice of minister depends on governmental organization and the major problems in the country. It may be possible to entrust this role to one of the ministers responsible for a water-related sector, such as the Minister of Agriculture, especially in predominantly rural countries. But there is the risk of conflict of interest, even in cases of the greatest integrity, when the same minister manages resources and user activities also fall within his competence.

Where there is a minister responsible for regional development or physical planning, authority on water problems may be entrusted to him.

Where a ministry for natural resources or for the environment is set up, it may also be logical to include water-related issues. The affinities between water and the other natural resources must, however, be taken into account, in relation to requirements, at various stages in the life of a country. If a ministry for physical planning and a ministry for the environment are both set up, the prime minister will decide between the two.

In any event, a water policy is so closely linked to land utilization and, more generally, to physical planning that there must be close organic links between the agencies responsible for these activities in order to avoid new sources of dispute.

The powers of a "new" minister for water are also of crucial importance. Most of the time, as we have seen, the various ministries have a share of the power in managing the resource. The question is whether each ministry should retain that proportion of power and the "new" minister should merely co-ordinate, or whether he should be given all the power. Given that power, should he retain all of it, or part of it, or delegate it, under his responsibility, to the "former" ministries.

In any institutional analysis and review, all options should tend to ensure that the institutional and administrative framework can co-ordinate or prepare an over-all water policy, and ensure rapid and effective implementation at all levels.

Below the national level, there is what might be called the "intermediate" level which covers inter-State (in federal countries), regional, provincial or basin levels, according to the country involved.

At the level of the provinces or States of a federation, problems vary enormously according to the political organization of the country. Options at national level may serve as a guide for the allocation of responsibilities and the determination of their size at the provincial or State level.

At the level of the basin, or any other geographical planning unit, similar problems arise but sometimes in different terms. It is generally recognized that the powers of a basin organization are of prime importance. Data collection and physical planning would seem to be the minimum acceptable for this geographical level. At international levels, certain bodies are responsible for these tasks for a particular international basin.

Another question is whether water management agencies should be purely technical or whether they should be directly concerned with policy-making. Where water management is often integrated into local or regional development structures it is possible that the water agency has only policy-making power.

There are two major hazards in water administration, which, as we have seen, is a sphere *par excellence* for real and profound disputes:

Paralysis and disorder in co-ordination because of the impossibility of coherent decisions owing to the number and incompatibility of the forces concerned.

The absence of contact with the real situation where there is a structure specially for water management, which is apparently effective but would not be if it were isolated from the active elements of the country.

Like the law which created them, the administrative institutions responsible for applying legal texts, decisions and recognized customs, are an essential element in the success of water resource management. Interactions between the law and the administration are innumerable; the good qualities of the administration benefit the law and the defects of the law are harmful to the administration. The effectiveness of a water law will depend on the administration and the power of the administration responsible for water resources will depend on the water law. There can be no effective regulation of water pollution, for example, if the inertia or weakness of the administration results in measures not being implemented; nor can there be good water management if the law leaves it in the hands of institutions which are divided, dispersed or even in competition.

It is tempting to think that, to be effective, the administrative machinery should be consolidated in a single central administration, a sort of ministry or national water agency. In fact, the important thing is to have coherent administration of the resource. This coherence has been achieved in some countries recently by the creation of a ministry of water or of the environment. In other countries, the same result may be obtained at much lower cost by the institution of interministerial co-ordinating machinery. The creation of a single authority may thus be an unnecessary, or even harmful, reform, when it disbands good work teams or requires reorganization which is ruinous to the State machinery. Nor is centralization necessary; it is sometimes even a serious obstacle to certain policy options which go beyond water management or to the organization of public participation in decision-making.

There seems to be no miracle solution but it is very useful to study the validity of various options.

G. Co-Ordination

Some countries believe that co-ordination will in itself solve the institutional water problem caused by the opposition between diversity of uses, and the historic division of management responsibilities on the one hand, and the unity of the resource on the other.

There is no doubt that, because of the many interrelated problems, water management requires close co-ordination at all levels. The idea of co-ordination need not be limited only to the preparatory stages but must apply also at the decision stage. A responsible minister would preside over a committee and arbitrate in case of disagreement.

It may be asked whether the committee's meetings should be limited only to governmental bodies. Undoubtedly, the answer would be yes where decision-making is concerned. But in the preparatory work, there may be great advantages in consulting the active elements affected by the decisions.

There are many other questions with regard to the organization of this co-ordination. They concern especially the geographic level at which it should be conducted. In addition, co-ordination is not concerned only with user-resource relations but also inter-State and interbasin relations and those between member States of certain federations. Similar problems arise when general development is prepared, planned and at least partly carried out at the level of autonomous regions. The choice of the power-holding body is more difficult when the representatives of States or provinces are usually elected. Decisions may then be taken by vote, possibly with recourse to arbitration by the minister in unitarian countries. Where the structure is federal, problems may be even more thorny and concern the respective powers of States and the federation. To solve specific water management problems, intense co-operation or arbitration authority is necessary.

In the choice of bodies participating in co-ordination work, preoccupation with the environment may, in some industrialized countries, assume particular significance. It is important to analyse the possible mode of association and the methods of evaluation to be adopted in the face of options based largely on economic considerations or relating to subjects which do not easily lend themselves to financial quantification.

Research is under way but we must not deceive ourselves into thinking that any procedure, no matter how sophisticated, can take the place of quantifiable data.

H. *Participation*

Co-ordination and co-operation are closely linked to participation. To co-ordinate the work of several bodies is to encourage them to participate in a collective task and to enlist the co-operation of several provinces or States is to invite them to participate in a joint effort. The full extent of this notion of participation is involved where users have to be persuaded to take part in decisions concerning water policies. The organization of this popular participation must go hand in hand with an education and training programme, which is the long-term guarantee of any policy. Participation usually has most significance at local levels.

The problem is how to associate the active bodies concerned with water problems at the various co-ordination levels. It is easy to see that different categories of water users must participate in formulating water policy at all levels, but not so easy to see who represents these users and the public in general.

There is a problem as to whether representatives of user associations or professional groups or unions should be associated at the same level as ministries or at a more consultative level. The representatives of environmental protection bodies could also be included in this popular participation.

Problems concerning participation of active elements become increasingly important as the problems become increasingly down-to-earth rather than theoretical, as for example in the case of irrigators' associations.

Since any implementation of a water policy affects all individuals, it seems essential that the State should guarantee their co-operation so that they can be fully aware of the facts underlying the decisions taken.

I. *Options and Economic and Financial Mechanisms*

The formulation and implementation of a water policy also requires options relating to the economic and financial aspects of water management.

Policy Options

There is a wide variety of doctrines concerning the optimum management of a country's economy. Until quite recently, they have accorded scant attention to water problems. For some time now, however, numerous studies and some experiments have been carried out.

In market-economy countries, efforts have been made to determine the possibilities and the limits of incremental pricing applied to drinking water and energy, and possibly also to agriculture, combating pollution and the like. The concern has been generally to decentralize to the maximum extent the choice of investments in order to reduce their amount.

In planned-economy countries, more thought has been given to methods of planning, and the concepts of cost to the economy and pricing have been divorced.

Nevertheless, in some cases, these countries have studied and even established financial systems for encouraging the decentralized economic agents to make investments which are favoured by the central authorities but not solely determined or regulated by them.

Matters involving the economic and financial aspects of water management include firstly the criteria and the procedures for assessing projects and weighing their merits. In that connexion, the cost/benefit ratio of a project is a factor taken into account. In countries where there is a manpower surplus, for example, the undertaking of a project creates work, the value of which could be identified among the benefits. In the case of multi-purpose projects, the cost must be distributed equitably among the various purposes in order to assess their respective merits. In general, while in the industrialized countries the choice between various solutions may be based entirely on cost/benefit considerations in respect of specific and clearly defined projects, in the developing countries the choice must take into account social factors (overpopulation, poverty, level of living, health) and above all the fact that water becomes an instrument of economic development at the national or regional level. Accordingly, water's contribution to the solution of such specific problems as food production, health and social welfare must be determined. If the price of water is considered as a means of promoting the development process, it is necessary to be certain that this price will be able to:

(1) Ensure effective utilization and distribution of water;

(2) Meet specific criteria for controlling demand as a function of current and future supply;

(3) Promote the achievement of the country's economic objectives, especially in the agricultural sector.

The water manager cannot remain indifferent in the face of the multiplication of unfounded needs when essential needs suffer as a result. Managing demand for water therefore has become the cornerstone of a modern water policy. In managing demand, economic and financial mechanisms seem to be of unequalled effectiveness.

Most water-related projects require very considerable investments to cover the high costs of exploration, exploitation, distribution and other management operations. When the user or beneficiary of management measures does not bear the cost of use or protection, the State or other members of the community must bear the cost either through taxation or other means.

Given the fact that prices influence use and, therefore, investment, one must consider the following criteria when evaluating policies from a purely economic point of view.

(1) *Allocative efficiency*. This deals with the issue of equating incremental benefits and incremental costs. The pricing policy that accomplishes this objective is one in which the price charged is equated to the incremental cost. The general policy implication of this rule is that water users should not be subsidized, but rather that they should pay the full incremental costs of the water they consume. If subsidies exist, water prices are too low and water is over-used at levels at which incremental costs exceed incremental benefits. On the other hand, water supplies should not be used as "taxing authorities", in other words, prices charged should not exceed incremental costs. If they do, water will be under-used.

(2) *Administrative costs*. Any system of measuring water use and charging a price that reflects incremental costs involves some administrative costs. In evaluating a pricing structure, one must evaluate these costs to ensure that they do not exceed the allocative efficiency gains made by selling at prices equated to incremental costs. Here again the allocative efficiency rule applies — one should continue to refine a pricing structure up to the point where incremental benefits derived from the refinement are equated to the incremental costs associated with making the refinement.

(3) *Equity*. Any pricing structure should be based upon a principle of equity. There are two basic principles that can be used. The first is referred to as the "ability to pay" principle. If strictly applied, this principle would charge high prices to those with high incomes and low prices to those with low incomes. It is clear that this principle is not consistent with the principle of allocative efficiency and the efficient use of water resources. Thus, in the developing countries in particular, it may be felt that equity considerations should be taken into account only in the case of domestic consumption. They should not influence the pricing of water supplied as a factor of production. If they do, the related consequences should be taken into account in the planning process. The reasons are clear:

(a) Subsidizing some level of *per capita* consumption is intended to assure a certain minimum level of personal and domestic water consumption which is regarded as desirable for social and health reasons. A direct subsidy to income would be ineffective for this purpose.

(b) Subsidizing water used in production leads to an insufficient allocation of supply and in addition is a very inefficient way of subsidizing the income of low-income producers.

The second principle which is consistent with allocative efficiency is the "benefit principle of taxation". This principle states that the beneficiaries of water resources projects (those who also impose the incremental costs on the system) should pay in proportion to the benefit received.

Incremental pricing has generally proved to be the most effective policy and is most in keeping with the concern for sound water management. It would, of course, be unthinkable to generalize regarding the applicability of a pricing system for

water based on the incremental cost. It is nevertheless true — and this is the
essential point of this section — that every official must be aware of the cost
of his policy. In choosing and implementing a water policy, price and other
economic criteria, better than any other indicators, enable the official to
become aware of the consequences and effects of various solutions.

J. Water Law*

Policy decisions cannot be implemented successfully unless there is an adequate
water legislation. Based upon the decisions made by the planner, water legislation has the purpose of ensuring, as far as possible, the most economic and
equitable use of available water resources.

Water legislation, in turn, is strongly influenced by the legal system followed
by each State and care should be exercised, in considering legal provisions affecting water, not to introduce concepts which do not comply with the over-all
legal, philosophical, sociological and religious character of any particular
country or region.

The philosophy of water legislation could take into consideration the availability of water in a country, basin or region; the environmental consequences
of water use, particularly on the ecosystem and other resources; existing uses
of water and the amount used, by whom and for what purpose; the cost of different sources of water; present and future water requirements of the country
or region; and government water policies, including water planning.

Water law is the ultimate means of implementing and enforcing water resources
policies. In many countries, legal provisions directly or indirectly affecting
water resources are scattered throughout numerous texts, which are often fragmented, confused, and anachronistic. This is the result of historical developments which necessitated the enactment of legal provisions to regulate specific
water problems as they arose. As a consequence, in many countries water legislation is not adequate to allow easy implementation of water policy decisions.

Although it may not be possible to formulate clear-cut indications regarding
sound water legislation, mention could be made of the following subjects: definition of water policy objectives; ownership of other judicial status of water
resources; mode of acquisition of the right to use water and limitation thereof;
order of priorities (between uses and areas); terms and conditions for the various beneficial uses (domestic, municipal, agricultural, fishing, hydropower,
industrial and mining, transport, recreational); provisions for controlling harmful events (floods, droughts, soil erosion, etc.....) and the quality of water
(pollution, health and environmental preservation); special regimes regulating
ground and atmospheric waters and coastal areas; measures to protect waterworks
and structures as well as for declaring water resources development or conservation zones or areas, water rates and fees, financial contributions, special
development agencies, implementation and enforcement of water legislation, including "water justice". Finally, water legislation is also the means through
which it is possible to spell out the respective responsibilities and powers
of government, ministries, agencies and institutions, with regard to the functions to be performed (policy making, planning, co-ordination, executing and
operational) and the level of authority involved (national, basic, regional);
of particular importance is the inclusion of the role of water users association

---

*See *Water Development and Management*, edited by Asit K. Biswas, Pergamon
Press, Oxford, 1978.

in the administration of water.

It is the legal framework of each State which can determine the type and form of the legal enactment (code, act, regulation, ordinance). Some States have adopted the legislative technique of promulgating a consolidated water act or code containing basic principles and leaving it to subsidiary or subordinate legislation — not requiring parliamentary approval — to regulate provisions of detail or of a less permanent nature. Other countries have, on the contrary, included in one single text all the provisions relating to water.

One thing which seems to be required in many countries is to co-ordinate and consolidate the existing sectoral legislation on water resources conservation, development and utilization.

As far as options for national water legislation are concerned, the International Association for Water Law (AIDA), during its Caracas meeting in February 1975, has proposed a set of recommendations which are to be circulated at the United Nations Water Conference together with a supporting document.*

K. Conclusion

Fundamental political options and the means which can be employed

While the means to be employed depend, as has been seen, on the objective situation with regard to a region's water and its development prospects, they also depend on the fundamental political options chosen by each country.

There are many different political systems in the world and, hence, many different means employed by Governments to ensure that the efforts of the various economic agents converge on the goals pursued. Historical traditions, ancestral customs, political boundaries, the area of territories, the federal or unitary nature of the State, the desire to decentralize decisions or the pursuit of centralized planning, all these are general political factors which have a profound influence on the means employed, even when the specific problems faced are the same.

As regards legal principles, the options range from allowing private rights of water use to nationalization by the State of all water sources. However, the authorities must always intervene in individual cases whenever a general problem arises.

On the financial level, countries are often motivated by the desire to decentralize decision-making by providing each economic agent with information enabling it to exercise its own choice in pricing items, including, as has been seen, water or pollution. Conversely, some countries make centralized choices based on economic data such as the prices laid down in the plan, and determine prices on the basis of a wide variety of considerations, such as those of a social nature.

Administrative structures also vary tremendously even though in the various political systems similarities can be perceived among specialists as regards some institutional patterns such as basin organizations as a result of the very strong pressures of realities.

---

*See *Water Development and Management*, edited by Asit K. Biswas, Pergamon Press, Oxford, 1978.

Policy Options

The synthesis specific to each country

Of course it is for each country to make its own synthesis of its objective water situation, its general policy options, man's experience in water management and the goals assigned to its people for the future.

Before taking up the questions of administration, law and finance respectively, we would stress once again two fundamental ideas:

The means employed must be suited to the real nature of the water problem and not to the appearances, which so far have too often been the only elements taken into account; these means must ensure a close and daily link between water management and the management of the rest of the country's economy.

Options for international action

Two main categories of problems arise, one relating to the co-ordination of national policies, and the second to inter-State co-operation in the field of international water resources.

The first of the two sets of problems may be solved either by enacting parallel national legislations or by harmonizing them. Thus, a State may declare that it will take into account the effects of its national water policy on other countries, or may undertake an exchange of information on matters relating to water. Another question of concern to industrialized countries involves the acceptance by a group of States of common affluent standards for controlling water pollution and avoiding unfair competition.

The other category of problems concerns waters of an international nature shared by several States. As long as these waters remain within the territory of a single State, they tend to be treated as that State's sovereign resource. This has given rise to claims by individual States to the exclusive and unfettered control of waters that pass through their territories. On the other hand, the shareability of waters, reinforced by their hydrological unity, has pushed States to seek co-operation first in the use of common bodies of water and then in the use of entire drainage basins. This need for co-operation and accommodation becomes more pressing in areas and instances in which water use begins to approach or to exceed available capacity and in such instances it may even extend beyond the confines of a single drainage basin.

Because of this double character of water as a permanently shareable and temporarily sovereign resource, and because of the hydrological and, in some instances, political, economic and geographical distinctiveness of the drainage basin, the evolution of universally applicable rules for co-operation has been slow and confined to principles such as good neighbourliness, abuse of right, and *neminem laedere*, which however, lacked sufficient precision to be applied in particular situations. The effort to supply rules of general application was undertaken by international conferences and international associations. The International Law Institute and later the International Law Association, in its espousal of equitable utilization, attempted to establish flexible guidelines for what is an equitable share of each co-basin State in the use of the basin waters. The development and general adoption of these or similar guidelines is one way of putting co-operation between States on a firmer basis. If it appears that universal guidelines are premature or impracticable, they may be more easily applied by a regional organization on a regional basis. This is already done by the Council for Mutual Economic Assistance, the European Economic Community and the Organization for Economic Co-operation and Development in the field of transboundary pollution, where common standards and the rules of State responsibility for damage are of prime importance.

Along with the effort to evolve regional or general rules of co-operation between States, there has been a parallel effort to define such co-operation through bilateral and multilateral agreements, beginning with boundary water treaties of limited scope and evolving into treaties of basin-wide application. The latter may generally be divided into agreements which apportion the basin waters between concerned States, as does the Indus Treaty, and those, such as the Columbia River and the Senegal Basin Treaties, which establish a basis for joint development. Treaties not only can be a means of implementing regional or general principles and guidelines, but also may and do substitute for these principles.

One of the most important requirements, if not the most important, for putting co-operation between States in the water resources field on a firm and durable basis is the establishment of an institutional framework for such co-operation. Many bilateral and multilateral treaties establish river or basin commissions or committees. The scope of their functions varies from the purely technical and supervisory to the judicial, in some (still rare) instances. Not only do these entities generally not have a decision-making role, they also lack power to make proposals. The power to initiate proposals (especially, but not exclusively, in the development of standards), along with data-collection, and the role of information clearing-house, is the most promising line of evolution of these institutions in all those situations in which it is not feasible to entrust to them a decision-making capacity. A joint hydrological data collection system and establishment of joint technical organizations for this purpose seems to provide a most flexible and progressive tool to solve at least the most acute problems of international sharing of water resources. Discrepancy in data on quantity and quality of water across State boundaries gives rise to conflicts which can be avoided by the above action.

There are as yet few general principles of universal acceptance in international water law. Two which have been put forward by scholarly bodies are: (1) the right to an equitable share for each co-basin State in the use of drainage-basin waters; and (2) the responsibility of States for water-related activities within their borders which may cause injury in areas outside their jurisdiction. In view of the slow development of general principles, the most promising avenues for the development of international water law are the basin or regional organizations. Common pollution standards and the elaboration of responsibility for damage to individuals outside a State's territory are already in an advanced stage of readiness in some regional organizations of industrialized countries. The appropriate international water administration is of prime importance for the effective and equitable use of international waters. Whenever possible, international water commissions should have the role of information clearing-houses and the power to propose and approve rules, standards and the construction of waterworks. The establishment and support of basin and regional water agencies should be encouraged. In this connexion, it is worth mentioning that the International Law Association has, at its fifty-seventh Conference, approved a report on "Administration of international water resources", with annexed guidelines, and this report has been presented as a contribution to the United Nations Water Conference.

Consideration could be given to the role that the United Nations system should

have in reviewing, collecting, disseminating and facilitating the exchange of
information and experiences on the various questions discussed in this document
through the preparation of studies or the preparation of expert meetings, working groups, as well as in supporting or arranging research, study and technical
advisory programmes.

IV. SECTORAL OPTIONS

While planning should initially be viewed in a comprehensive national or regional context governed by specific government objectives, water management can
help to achieve social and economic goals only through sectoral activities.
The range of alternatives and choice of options which are presented in this
context will now be reviewed briefly.

A. *Rural and Urban Water Supply*

Community water supply is an integral part of the socio-economic infrastructure
of settlements which, apart from water supply and sewage disposal, includes
such broad and diverse components as health and sanitary services, housing,
supply of energy, public transportation, schooling, police services and many
others. Although the immediate objectives of community water supply and sewerage are quite specific (to provide or improve the quality, quantity, availability and reliability of water supply and sewage disposal services) these
are also inseparable ingredients of a number of broader infrastructural objectives, such as reducing the incidence of water-borne and water-related diseases,
creating opportunities for learning and providing employment, and promoting
greater self-reliance and better social organization for the community (particularly for the poor, the aged, women and children). Above a certain minimum
level determined by health considerations, the "appropriate" level of water
supply and sewerage services can only be judged for any given locality in the
light of the development resources (social, economic and physical) available
for establishing and maintaining such services, together with the other components of rural and urban infrastructure.

At present, in a world-wide perspective, the options are quite clear: on the
one hand, the large cities of industrialized countries are provided with water
and sewerage services for the majority of the population through large-scale
networks and in-house connexions, built and maintained with a high level of
technology, adequate financing and the necessary service personnel. At the other
extreme are the isolated dwellings in the rural habitat of developing countries,
where in many instances there is virtually no service of any kind for water
supply and excreta disposal. Between these two extremes, in the majority of
cases, there has been a tendency to transfer virtually unchanged the contemporary concepts, technologies, and social organizations for public water supply
and sewerage from the highly industrialized to the developing countries. Following these efforts, there has grown a recognition over the last few years that
in fact there exists between the two extremes a very wide range of alternatives
with regard to both technology and social organization, and that the selection
of appropriate solutions needs detailed analysis and careful experimentation
based on and geared to the specific social, economic and physical conditions
and objectives of the given location. Although the number of alternatives is

almost infinite as regards specific technological and organizational detail, the various alternatives are rather closely conditioned by one factor, namely, the scale of the system expressed through the number of inhabitants served by a particular public water supply and sewerage network.

In industrialized countries, the resources needed for the establishment of public water supply and sewerage as well as other components of urban and rural infrastructure, did not represent limiting constraints in developing these services. In fact, they have in most instances been able to meet in full the rising and changing levels of demand of the last 50 years. As for other fields of technological development and social organization, the general tendency has been to establish larger and larger systems in line with requirements and the tenets of economy of scale and favouring automation and centralized organization.

Although water supply and sewerage services are usually not among the primary causes and symptoms of the general breakdown of infrastructure experienced by many metropolitan areas in the industrialized countries, at least three major tendencies of increasing concern have been observed over the last few years and even decades. First, the rapidly growing pollution of rivers, lakes and ground water within and around such areas tends to impair the quality characteristics of community water supply. The fact that this quality degradation frequently goes unnoticed or that it may, at times, be accepted as inevitable can only be viewed as a reflection of a basic shift in the patterns of urban water use in these countries. By far the largest quantity of this water is now used for dishwashers, washing machines, lawn sprinkling, car washing, and municipal use. Drinking and washing, the principal original purposes of providing a potable water supply, have now been relegated to a secondary role in relative terms. A second alarming trend in urban water use is the extremely high level of losses in the distribution systems and the low level of efficiency in various domestic and public uses, even in regions which have experienced a general scarcity of water or which are facing this problem in the foreseeable future. This situation may largely be ascribed to cost and price structures, which attribute an incorrect value to water *per se* and tend to increase its demand and use rather than promote efficiency in the use of water. Thirdly, a by-product of attempts to cope with the consequences of pollution and wasteful usage by increasing the treatment of water and sewage is that the cost of providing water supply and sewerage services is beginning to reach alarming proportions in a number of highly industrialized metropolitan areas. This may necessitate a basic revision of existing policies, including the introduction of new cost and price mechanisms, which more nearly reflect the true cost of the health hazards and the environmental degradation involved, and which are likely to encourage a more efficient and rational conservation of water.

In most developing countries the present situation and outlook for public water supply and sewerage is typified by an increasing gap between the demand for capital and skilled manpower to provide the modern technologies and administrative structures required, and the actual scarcity of such resources in the developing countries. Estimates summarized in the report entitled "Resources and needs: assessment of the world water situation" (see pp. 49-50 of this volume) indicate that some $36 billion at least will be needed during the next four or five years, in order to achieve the revised 1980 targets set by WHO for the improvement of urban and rural water supply and excreta disposal in the developing countries. It is also noted in the above report that, even if funds of such magnitude were available, the small pool of trained personnel and limited organizational resources would impose serious limitations on the efficient use of the required capital. It should, furthermore, be borne in mind that the improvement of public water supply and sewerage services are likely to reach desirable social and economic objectives only if other related components of the rural and urban infrastructure (housing, health and sanitary services, schooling, etc.) are improved, in step with water supplies and in a closely interlinked fashion. To the capital and trained manpower needed for the establishment of these services, annual requirements for maintenance, repair, and safe operation have to be added; frequently, these are also of great magnitude. Some modification in the current approach to technical assistance programmes and a significant broadening of the range of technological and organizational alternatives considered — with greater emphasis on small and medium scale systems — appear to be among the crucial elements in finding a solution to this seemingly insoluble dilemma.

Apart from and in addition to greater reliance on small-scale and medium-scale technologies, special attention should be devoted to using, as far as possible, of locally available labour and materials if economical and socially desirable. The fact that technologies of this type are not readily or easily available should not detract from the opportunities offered. An increasing number of encouraging examples illustrate the great potential for local adaptations if a careful analysis is made from both ends: the tasks to be performed on the one hand and the materials and skills available locally on the other. Indicative examples include the manufacture by local potters of aqua-privy fittings in Nigeria; rainwater catchment tanks in Swaziland with linings and internal structures which combine polythene sheeting with mud, sand and a little cement; coagulant aid for water treatment in India using local vegetation; and the use of discarded containers as the basis for chlorine dosers in Sudan. In other countries, development plans in the sector of water supply and sewerage are made in accordance with those of the national construction industry as a whole; they take into account the country's capacity to absorb additional demand for labour and construction materials, and to foster the development of all construction related sectors within the national economy. In Turkey, for instance, comprehensive urban and rural water supply programmes have resulted in the phased development of national pipe manufacturing industry. In Brazil, the national programme for the improvement of urban water supply is almost entirely based on the development of national resources to meet the demand created by this programme. Such comprehensive policies necessitate long-term planning, in order to avoid the creation of a temporary market, which would result in regression after the main works are built, and which would on the whole be detrimental to the economy. Also, it must be ascertained whether locally produced construction materials are reasonably competitive on the international market. Governments and donor organizations could help to promote the dissemination and exchange of local experience and initiate and support research and experimentation in tasks which are beyond local capabilities (e.g. the development of cheap pumps with local repair facilities or the small-scale local manufacture of plastic pipelines). The small and easily movable sanitation unit developed by Oxfam for emergency situations in Bangladesh is a good illustration of this concept.

B. *Protection from Floods and Droughts*

How to use lands exposed to natural hazards (floods, droughts, typhoons, earthquakes, volcanic eruptions, tsunamis, forest fires, locusts, etc.) and how to prevent or reduce the losses caused by such disasters are among the important policy issues at the local, regional and national levels, and are relevant to almost every sector of the economy. Among the numerous problems faced by developing countries, an adequate adjustment to flood and drought hazards is particularly critical. Thousands of people drown annually and floods destroy more than 10 million acres of crops each year in South-East Asia alone, while in the Sahel region the recent drought took a toll of castastrophic proportions in human lives and suffering. Not only are the losses caused by floods and droughts large, but they have been getting larger every decade owing to the continuing movement of population and economic activities onto flood plains and drought-prone areas. The success or failure of strategies relating to natural disasters in general, and protection from floods and droughts in particular, is closely linked to the safety afforded by other infrastructural services, such as land-use planning and regulation, transportation systems, energy supplies, public information and education, and so on.

The basic challenge in meeting problem floods and droughts is to find a set of land-use regulations and management strategies which will permit a more intensive use of the endangered areas but minimize the associated losses. While there is ready agreement on the advisability of abandoning certain lands that are frequently and regularly struck by floods or droughts, there is in many instances complete indifference to infrequent but more serious risks. Thus, while rural inhabitants, particularly in developing countries, live in daily contact with nature and are ready to adapt their lives to its vagaries, town dwellers, particularly in the industrialized countries, live in an increasingly artificial psychological atmosphere and frequently refuse not only to take precautions against collective natural hazards, but also to face the consequences of their refusal. Partial protection from floods or droughts has, more than once, led to an increase of hazards and losses because it has encouraged unjustified encroachment onto the risk areas by housing developments and other economic activities.

In principle there are always four major ways of adjusting to flood or drought hazards: (a) by modifying the flood or drought event (e.g. by weather modification or, in the case of floods, by dykes, reservoirs or watershed management); (b) by modifying the susceptibility to damage (e.g. through land-use regulations, zoning ordinances, government purchase of land or property, flood-proofing, introduction of drought resistant plants, etc.); (c) by modifying loss burden through evacuation, disaster relief, tax write-offs, emergency operations during disaster periods, etc.); and (d) by bearing the loss. Two basic questions are relevant in selecting the actual measures for adjustments: What level of adjustment is appropriate and what is the most satisfactory combination of measures? Fundamentally these are economic questions, although several other considerations may affect the final decision. In some countries the intensive use of hazard-prone areas is the only possibility for economic growth because the whole area is exposed to risk, or alternatively all the available risk-free areas are already densely populated and fully utilized (as in several countries of South-East Asia). Developing countries with high levels of risk but low levels of economic growth should concentrate on those adjustments that can be accomplished with low capital investment, but which are highly effective in saving lives and minimizing property losses (emergency operations, land use regulations, flood warning and evacuation, etc.).

Frequently there is a large gap between what a country can technically attain by effective prevention and management measures with the resources already available to it, and what is actually achieved. Such discrepancies are generally the result of institutional inertia, tending to concentrate on measures that were perhaps appropriate at an earlier phase of development but are no longer satisfactory. Innovation in administrative structures or other types of institutional innovation might, therefore, be one of the most effective ways of improving the efficiency of adjustments to flood and drought hazards. Lack of comprehensive information on the regions and areas exposed to various degrees of flood and drought hazard is also one of the most frequent and most significant obstacles in the formulation and implementation of long-term programmes and policies.

C. *Water for Food and Agriculture*

Community water supply, as well as protection from floods and droughts, are interlinked with other components of the social and economic infrastructure, mainly at the end-product level, i.e. although they are part of a broader infrastructural package, specific water management criteria and services can be established and rendered with a certain degree of independence. In the case of agricultural water development the interrelation with the broader socio-economic framework and with the over-all social and technological structures for food production and agricultural development, is a much closer one. In fact there is not a single detail or phase of agricultural water management and administration which can be planned, built or operated without close co-ordination with other input factors of the agricultural system. On the other hand, there is not a single change or decision within the agricultural and food production system that will not have water-related implications.

For the purposes of a brief overview, the internal relationships between water and agriculture might be grouped at three major levels: (a) the end-product level, within which the local, regional and global demand/supply situation for food and other agricultural products motivates and controls the over-all and long-term trends of agricultural water development through long-term planning, and/or general tendencies affecting the cost and price structures of these products; (b) the input factor level, within which the relative significance and specific water management approaches are determined and conditioned by the given climatic and soil conditions and the general patterns and levels of a region's agriculture; (c) the water supply and management level, within which the specific technological and organizational aspects of irrigation, drainage, fishery development, rural water supply and other components of agricultural water management are designed, constructed and operated on the basis primarily of the general availability of water and the over-all level of efficiency in its use and management within a given location. Needless to say, the above three levels are closely interrelated. Under conditions of general water scarcity, factors at the third level may influence decisions or developments at the second level and, in cases of irrigation of desert or semi-arid lands, the issues of water supply and management may become of major concern even with respect to considerations on the end-product level.

Since agricultural water development relates to man's most vital need for food, it is not surprising that the first clear examples of highly skilled and widely organized water management systems, the fluvial civilizations of antiquity, emerged essentially within this sector. Most of the remaining records and the systematically assessed historical heritage of ancient water management practices and organizations relate to irrigation, drainage and flood control in the valleys of the Nile, Tigris-Euphrates, Indus, Lower Mekong, Yellow and Yangtze rivers; it also seems very likely that fluvial civilizations of a similar type and scale must have developed and flourished for long periods in other arid areas of Africa,

Eurasia, Central and South America and the Pacific region. The history of agricultural water management, like that of other human endeavours, abounds in both successes and failures. About half of the world's total agricultural crop comes from irrigated lands, providing on an average several times the specific yields of dry farming. In many instances, however, irrigation has also brought undesired and unexpected consequences, such as the spread of water-related diseases or the deterioration of valuable croplands by water-logging, salination and alkalification. Social and institutional components or irrigation programmes have frequently been neglected, and the efficiency of water use and management is generally very low.

The rapidly rising levels of demand for food and the food shortages experienced during the last few years leave little doubt that food production must be increased considerably during the years to come, and that irrigated agriculture can and should contribute heavily to this objective. Most of the policy issues relating to the intensification and expansion of food production are, however, tied very closely to the immense intraregional and interregional variability of the physical, social, economic and technological conditions for agricultural production. It is an extremely long and difficult process to bring the end-product level pressures for more food and better nutrition in a global context (expressed clearly by the rapidly rising food prices in almost every country) to the input-factor and water management levels of the various regions and countries. This needs a set of well co-ordinated and highly differentiated efforts at all levels of national and international action. Agricultural production is almost everywhere at a relatively low level with respect to its full potential, and the quasi-industrial type of agriculture which emerged or is emerging in the industrialized countries raises a number of difficult questions regarding its long-term social and ecological impacts, including the high pollution risks for the neighbouring rivers, lakes and ground waters.

Proposals and requests for improved agricultural water supply and management relate mostly and necessarily to lands under less favourable climatic and/or soil conditions than other farmlands of the given country or region. This means that the investments needed for the improvement or extension of such services must be supported by other regions or population groups, through a carefully designed system of governmental policies (economic incentives and regulatory measures). On the other hand, a new irrigation project in one region of a country may adversely affect the welfare of producers in another part of the country. For these reasons, relatively large agricultural water management projects, which will have a significant impact on the market for a product, should be undertaken only after all effects have been taken into account.

In many countries irrigation water is used inefficiently because of inadequate water storage and delivery systems, improperly levelled land and poor choice of crops. In spite of low productivity per unit of land, there is frequently greater pressure to extend irrigable acreage than to improve the cultivation of land already irrigated. Although there might be valid reasons for both tendencies, efforts devoted to the cultivation of land already under irrigation usually deserve priority. In this context, medium-scale and small-scale projects have definite advantages over large-scale ones. They provide more flexibility for local involvement and more potential for experimentation and improvement in the implementation phase. If it is decided to expand the acreage of irrigated agriculture, a number of options usually emerge in relation to the degree of concentration of available development resources. For example, these can be routed to areas exposed to severe droughts (where larger investments are required but where greater crop production levels may be expected), or be dispersed over greater acreage in regions where supplementary irrigation only is needed. A reasonable selection among the emerging options and their satisfactory combination require a comprehensive assessment of development potentials in various regions with regard to both agriculture and integrated water management. In countries of humid or highly variable climate, e.g. in the tropical lowlands of Latin America and Africa, drainage and flood control are indispensable prerequisites for the intensification or expansion of agriculture and demand or opportunities for supplementary irrigation should be looked upon only as a subsequent aspect of agricultural water management. Drainage is, of course, indispensable to, and an integral part of, any irrigation scheme. Its neglect is one of the most frequent and most damaging causes of deterioration in soil fertility in many irrigated areas.

Since irrigated agriculture consumes a large portion of the water withdrawn from a source for that purpose, the selection of irrigated areas in the sequence of natural flow with respect to other uses which rely on the same resource is a question of great importance. If an irrigated area is situated downstream of a large town, it can utilize the return flow of municipal water supply (and eventually save part of the cost of the waste disposal and recycling system too). If, however, it is located upstream of the town it may pre-empt or decrease possibilities for municipal water supply. Such sequential allocation options are particularly relevant in planning for the development of virtually uninhabited areas.

Finally, and most important, it should be emphasized that agricultural water management has a vital role to play in cases where the land's natural water régime is not radically changed by drainage and irrigation; it remains one of the most important input factors under conditions of rain-fed crop production, which represents the backbone of food supply in many parts of the world. In fact, rain-fed agriculture is an overwhelmingly important on-site water use and related technological and managerial practices have far-reaching impacts on, and interrelations with, the availability and quality of water in the surrounding areas. Soil cultivation tools and practices are most significant factors in shaping the flux and storage of water within the soil and farmland areas, and they should be designed and used with a full awareness and recognition of this interrelationship. Similarly, research and experimentation for less water-consuming and more drought-enduring crops is a most important facet of agricultural water management; this might result in a replacement of costly irrigation systems and become by far the most cost-effective solution for increased food production, under dry-land farming conditions in many instances. In some cases where quasi-industrialized agriculture is practised, a reduction of chemical inputs or their replacement by organic alternatives could represent the most cost-effective or the only viable way to prevent or reduce pollution of the nearby aquifers.

It is in this broad context that the interrelations of agricultural water management with other input factors and managerial practices for crop production suggested in the opening paragraph of this brief review, should be viewed, as the corner-stone for the integrated development and management of land and water.

D. Inland Navigation

The establishment and maintenance of a transport system is a major component of regional and national infrastructure, which should develop hand in hand with, or preferably in anticipation of, the growth in agriculture, industry, commerce, tourism and other sectoral activities. Throughout human history inland navigation has been in many regions the most important and in some areas and periods the only mode of transport. During the last few decades its significance has been greatly overshadowed in industrialized countries by the explosive development of railways and of road traffic by lorry and car. There are signs that during the decades to come inland navigation will regain a significant part of its historic role, most particularly in the developing countries and possibly also in Europe and other highly industrialized regions.

The historic usefulness of river systems as waterways and their potential for many developing countries cannot be judged in terms of their navigability for fairly deep-draught vessels only. From ancient Mesopotamia to the Mississippi of the eighteenth century, rivers were navigated much further upstream by exceedingly light, even flimsy craft. The most ubiquitous form of river transportation was the raft, which could be made of any handy material (timber or reed), could be floated downstream from the uppermost tributaries, and could be abandoned, sold, or used to build a house. In areas of dense virgin forest a navigable river was, and in many regions still is, the easiest if not the only means of entry. If the river is long and has navigable tributaries, the extent of penetration may be considerable and may result in a string of settlements and trading ports. An important factor in this connexion is the length and ease of transit between the headwaters of adjacent river systems. When compared with the construction of roads and railways, the major advantage of inland navigation by locally made small and medium-sized vessels, consists in its low investment cost adaptability to local skills and flexibility with repect to gradual expansion.

The continuing significance of inland navigation, which periodically reached outstandingly high levels of technical and social organization in subsequent periods, was motivated by two major factors: (a) the building of navigation canals and (b) the remarkable respect for freedom of navigation and the functional and commercial integrity of waterways within politically divided river systems. The outstanding examples of canal building of antiquity, particularly in Mesopotamia and China, were enthusiastically pursued in Europe and North America, reaching a culminating point in the eighteenth and nineteenth centuries. Ancient examples of basin-wide commercial and functional unity were emulated repeatedly in Europe during the Middle Ages (for example in the basins of the Rhine, the Elbe and the Oder) and the principle of freedom of inland navigation had already reached broad international recognition in 1815 at the Congress of Vienna.

Since transportation costs by inland navigation decrease considerably with the increase of distance traversed without unloading, the great potentials of large-scale interregional waterway systems for highly industrialized and mass-production-oriented societies were also recognized and took shape in the 1920s. This took the form of a proposal for a trans-European east-west waterway through the interconnexion of three river systems, the Danube, the Main and the Rhine. This giant undertaking, the realization of which is well under way and which will probably be completed by the mid 1980s, will permit the short-cut passage of large-tonnage ships (up to 1500 tons) between the North Sea and the Black Sea and it will directly interconnect 13 riparian countries.

The historic significance of inland navigation in general and its functional integrity in politically divided river systems in particular, may be attributed primarily to the fact that the establishment and maintenance of navigable waterways is in most cases of common interest and advantage to all parties concerned. In the case of rivers navigable under natural conditions, the investment and maintenance costs (needed for the survey and marking of the navigation route within the channel, the construction of vessels and harbours, etc.) usually clearly lead to financial benefits and there are generally no serious obstacles to agreement among the parties or countries concerned regarding the sharing of costs and other issues of common interest (such as the standardization of signs and safety rules, custom agreements, unified information on water levels and ice conditions and prediction services, and others). This favourable situation is gradually changing with the increasing use of rivers for purposes other than navigation. Due to diversion for irrigation, for instance, the maintenance of the depth of the navigation channels may require continuing and costly dredging, and the construction of river barrages necessitates the construction of navigation locks (with extra costs charged mostly to navigation). All this slows down river traffic. Further development of stream-flow regulation and of river barrages turns the balance in favour of navigation once again, however, as soon as a situation of more or less complete "canalization" of the river is reached. Under such conditions the flow required for navigation drops to a negligibly small portion of that required under the natural régime, and water depths equal to or considerably greater than heretofore can be maintained by the barrages, even during low flow periods. National or federal Governments, to whom the jurisdiction over navigable rivers in most countries pertains, have an important role to play in harmonizing interests and sharing costs relating to river development under this type of multipurpose setting.

E. *Hydropower and Industrial Water Uses*

Water is one of the essential input factors for industry. The manifold functions of water within industry may be grouped into three major categories: (a) water provides energy for industry through hydropower development; (b) it helps industrial production as a process medium in a great number of functions (cooling, washing, boiling and transportation being the most frequent ones); (c) river systems and the hydrosphere are used to dispose of industrial wastes. In earlier periods, the major role of water for industry was to provide a cheap and easily manageable source of energy for a great variety of manufacturing and mining activities. Very recently (during the last 50 years or so) water power has been largely replaced by the use of coal, oil and nuclear power facilities in most highly industrialized countries, and the disposal of wastes has become the major use or function of water for industry in those regions.

Water-wheels were already in rather wide use in antiquity and water-power, together with wind-power, soon became the major substitute for human and animal power as the demands for flour milling and for manufacturing cloth, paper, iron, beer and other products increased. More than 5000 grist mills were in use during the eleventh century in southern and eastern England alone, and the Bisenzio river in Italy was made to flow through the city of Prato (near Florence) in a network of small canals, so numerous were the mills using this source of power. During the eighteenth and nineteenth centuries the large-scale application of power for mass production in spinning, weaving, pottery and other large factories came primarily not from steam-engines but from an increased use of water-mills and from the invention of the water turbine in 1825 from hydropower plants.

It was only during the first decades of this century that the "economy of scale" principle, and the assumption that the earth's resources for power production from natural resources were virtually inexhaustible, overrode all other considerations, leading to the neglect and abandonment of small and medium-size waterpower plants; on the other hand, the development of thermopower plants and systems with sizes and capacity greatly surpassing hydropower potentials took place in the most highly industrialized regions. It seems likely that, owing to the rising costs of energy production and the related waste-disposal problems, the interest for water-power, including its small and medium size applications, will increase again during the decades to come, even in the industrialized countries. For most developing countries, where capital and skilled manpower are scarce and energy development is to be looked upon in the context of achieving self-reliance, hydropower in general and its small and medium-size potential in particular, are among the possibilities that offer the greatest promise. This is the lesson learnt from the history of industrialization in Europe and North America, also supported by recent achievements in the People's Republic of China, where rural development is being promoted through the use of about 50,000 small-scale hydroelectric plants.

Regarding the use of water as a medium for industrial processing and waste disposal, the great diversity among various branches of industry is a first striking feature. In view of the multitude of specific industries using water in one form or another, one is tempted to focus attention and effort on a few principal uses. This is a reasonable and practical solution as far as the quantitative side of industrial water uses is concerned. Unfortunately, it is very difficult to adopt such a selective approach on issues concerning the chemical, biological and radiological qualities of water, because the presence of negligibly small amounts of some trace elements, toxic substances and viruses in sewage can lead to disastrous large-scale consequences for the aquatic life of the recipient waters. The difficulty in keeping a reliable account of the risks involved is further increased by the fact that, in many cases. the impacts are not directly attributable to one single pollutant but to a combination of several physical, chemical and biological factors, originating from various natural or man-induced sources and relating to various parts of the water system.

Another set of policy issues concerns the striking difference between the gross amounts of water needed for various industrial processes and the amounts that are actually "consumed" (incorporated into the product, or lost through evaporation or seepage) in those processes. This means that through in-plant recirculation and intermediate treatment the net amount of water to be withdrawn from and disposed into the aquifers can be reduced to a very small fraction of the amounts needed for simple "through-flow" technologies. As indicated in the report on resources and needs, the tendency towards more extensive and intensive recirculation of water can already be observed in several industries, particularly in regions where competition for water of acceptable quality is rapidly increasing, but actual achievements still have a long way to go in this regard (see pp. 52-53 of this volume). This slow progress towards a more efficient use and rational conservation of water in industry is especially regrettable in the light of the relatively low level of water-related costs for investment and operation in industry, which rarely surpass 1 per cent of the total costs involved (in striking contrast to agriculture, where water-related costs frequently reach significant proportions). With the technological options available and given the favourable conditions, local, economic, regional and national governments have an efficient, and largely unexploited, tool for influencing industrial development according to broader social interests.

Although complaints and conflicts raised by water pollution of industrial origin date back to mediaeval times, such occurrences were until recently sporadic and localized. It was only during the last three or four decades that industrial pollution has reached such proportions that aquatic life has become extinct in whole rivers and lakes, and large segments of fresh water resources have been made unfit for any human use in several highly industrialized regions. There are at least three major aspects in which industrial pollution differs from all other sources of water pollution and they are largely responsible for recent deterioration in water quality at scales never before experienced: (a) industrial wastes contain a number of new chemical components which are not formed under natural conditions, and consequently there are no natural organisms and processes for their decomposition; (b) whereas an increase in domestic and agricultural wastes for any given location is conditioned rather closely by the number of people in the area and other ecological constraints, there is virtually no such limitation in the amount and the growth of industrial wastes; (in this context quasi-industrial agriculture based on high levels of chemical utilization is closer to industry than to organic agriculture); (c) industry introduces new chemicals and new technologies in such vast numbers and differing so much from year to year that it is virtually impossible to assess and analyse in a reliable fashion their potential impact on water pollution. Success or failure in rationally managing and conserving water resources in the industrialized countries will greatly depend on how far local, regional and national governments will succeed in curbing and remedying industrial pollution.

V. GENERAL CONCLUSIONS

As in the case of other aspects of socio-economic development, there are increasing differences between the highly industrialized and the developing countries in their current approaches to water management. Although there exists a common conceptual framework, and national policies may be expected to tend towards interlinked global strategies, the present and the immediate future are typified by various issues requiring different approaches in these two groups of countries.

In the industrialized countries, water planners and managers are primarily concerned with problems and uncertainties created by pollution and other undesirable environmental impacts. On the other hand, in the developing countries current issues of water management are related to some extent to the benefits and limitations of a somewhat mechanistic transfer or acceptance of concepts, technologies and institutions from the industrialized countries. Within and beyond these polarized patterns, each country and each river basin is, of course, a unique entity, not only in its physical characteristics and hydrologic régimes but even more so with respect to the social evolution and economic activities taking place within and around its boundaries.

In the 6000 years of recorded human history, river basin development and water management have been important catalysts in the emergence of major periods of social and economic development, such as those characterized by (i) production within the great fluvial civilizations of antiquity; (ii) long-distance interregional commerce by inland navigation (which flourished in ancient Mesopotamia and continued until the eighteenth century in Mississippi); and (iii) the evolution of mass-production-oriented industries fuelled by water-power from the early mediaeval periods until the late nineteenth century. Water management is a good indicative example of how far the basic concepts and tendencies of earlier times with regard to technical and socio-economic development have evolved in Europe and North America over the last 60 years. Earlier technological developments had aimed at a better use of natural resources, whereas modern technologies tend to replace these by man-made ones: natural soil fertility by chemical fertilizers, inland navigation by trucks and railways, hydropower by coal, oil and nuclear-fired generation. Although, in essence, all these new technologies rely on natural resources, they induce two most significant alterations: (a) they tend to replace renewable natural resources by non-renewable ones; (b) they require more energy and produce more wastes. The rapidly rising concern about water pollution and the growing scarcity of good quality water in many industrialized countries are clear indications that technical and economic efficiency are an acceptable motivation for development only if supplemented and controlled by ecological considerations and constraints. The recent renewal of interest in the conservation and better utilization of natural soil fertility, and in the application of less energy-consuming and less polluting industrial and transportation technologies, constitutes an important point of departure for achieving social goals based on a common set of interests and policies both for the developing and the industrialized countries.

The "economy of scale" principle, the strongest motivation and argument for the acceptance of large-scale technologies, has its place and role in water management. There are, however, at least four major considerations which suggest the desirability of a cautious attitude with respect to the general and limitless acceptance of this principle: (a) beyond a certain range of size the stability and safety of large structures (dams, reservoirs, pipelines, etc.) could become questionable — even with the most careful technical design — as has been tragically documented by a number of catastrophic failures of large structures during the past few years; (b) large-scale structures and projects provide less opportunity for gradual implementation and feedback from on-site experimentation than smaller ones; this is an aspect of particular significance in water development, where uncertainties with regard to physical design, economic justification and social response to new initiatives are usually both inevitable and of considerable magnitude; (c) centralized decision-making and management give rise to specific difficulties and inherent conflicts in many water-related development programmes; this occurs because both the socio-economic and the physical components of such projects vary considerably at the local level and the continuing involvement and support of the local population throughout all phases of planning and implementation are key factors for success; (d) associated and partially unforeseeable social implications and consequences of large-scale structures and projects (e.g. in terms of relocation of population or the spread of water-related diseases) often become significant and make the justification of projects based on directly accountable benefits questionable.

Thus, the replacement of technologies where "economy of scale" dominates by more broadly based and locally diversified intermediate technologies is one further common factor upon which there can be a convergence of interests for both developing and industrialized countries.

Owing to geographical and climatic conditions, the technological, economic and institutional differences between the industrialized and the developing countries are accentuated by the fact that concepts, technologies and institutional structures for water management were evolved in the industrialized countries during the last hundred years or so under conditions of relative abundance of water. Moreover, resources needed for water development were made available as

needed without undue stress. On the other hand, most developing countries face the
same issues of social and economic development under far greater pressures of
scarcity, either with respect to water as a physical resource, or with respect
to the financial and institutional resources needed for water development, or
both. This is one of the major reasons why many of the concepts and solutions
successfully applied in the industrialized countries over the past decades have
resulted in some failures and disappointment when transferred to developing
countries. There has in fact been a recent recognition in many industrialized
countries of the need to introduce new technologies and new institutional frameworks favouring more efficient use and rational conservation of water resources
both in the industrialized and the developing countries.

In the light of the preceding paragraphs, it might be concluded that, apart
from a decreasing number of areas exceptionally well endowed with water resources and experiencing relatively low levels of demand for water and water-related
services, both the developing and the industrialized countries are facing or
rapidly approaching the stage of water demand management. In contrast to the
supply-oriented or resource-oriented stages, this stage is characterized by high
marginal costs for water supply and other water-related development projects.
Of course, depending on local conditions, supply and demand management stages
of development may coexist at any one moment in different areas of a same country. In the industrialized countries, situated mostly in the temperate and humid
zones with a favourable water régime, this development has resulted primarily
from industrial and agricultural technologies applied during the last few decades, leading to large-scale pollution and wasteful use of water resources. In
most developing countries, which occupy the largest parts of the arid and semi-
arid zones with inherent scarcity of water supplies, the stage of water demand
management is not new. The urgent need to seek rational solutions has been further increased following the rapidly rising levels of demand for agricultural
and community water supply.

There are many specific ways in which various countries and regions may reach
the stage of water demand management. Historical precedent and present issues
are as diverse and site-specific as the general socio-economic and physical
environment within which further evolution will take place. There are, nevertheless, a few characteristic features which in one way or another will become
constituent ingredients of water demand management in most cases:

(a) *Broadening of available options*. Under conditions of relative abundance of
water (in the supply-oriented and the early period of resource-oriented stages
of water management) an increase in supply is virtually the only choice for
development. With an increasing scarcity of water and the ensuing rapid rise
in the marginal cost of water supply, two further groups of development options
emerge and gradually override the previous one: increase of efficiency in using
the water and water-related services already provided, and adjustments in the
development programmes and technologies of water-related economic factors.

(b) *Exploratory planning*. Where and as long as water is abundant and the marginal cost of water development is relatively low, definitive and normative types
of water planning are usually reasonable and practical. Under conditions of increasing scarcity of water, however, the number of structural and non-structural
development options increase greatly and normative planning must gradually give
way to exploratory projections and plans. These are geared to the identification of the constraints and consequences of foreseeable (or assumed) **trends** of
socio-economic development in general, and those relating to various water pol-

icy options in particular.

(c) *Emphasis on non-structural measures.* While major structural measures available within a country or region to cope with the supply of water and water-related services are provided within the supply and the resource oriented stages of water management, non-structural measures (legislation, licensing, pricing, setting of standards, forecasting and warning services, etc.) which aim at a more efficient operation of the water resource system and a socially and economically desirable conservation and continuing reallocation of water are of primary concern during the stage of water demand management.

(d) *Multidimensional organization and policies.* The objectives and functions described in the previous subparagraphs cannot be realized without an appropriate reorganization of structures and procedures for administration and policy formulation. The interrelation between the water management system and the socio-economic system is rather limited in scope and technical in nature when supply is abundant. It gradually becomes broader and more heavily economic in nature during the stage of resource management, and becomes most complex and diversified in the stage of demand management, when a policy orientation prevails. This process involves not only changes in governmental organization, but also requires a large degree of expansion and diversification in educational background and administrative skills for water planning and management.

(e) *Emphasis on research.* All the major features of demand-oriented water management can essentially be summed up by emphasizing the need for a very close and intense linkage between policy formulation and applied research. Under conditions where innovations in technology and social organization become of overriding concern to water management, projection, planning and policy formulation themselves frequently extend into the realms of experimentation and applied research, and cannot be carried out successfully without the continuing support of an interdisciplinary research team.

To sum up, there is no single policy option best suited for all times and all places, and choices will increasingly have to include a judicious blend of structural and non-structural measures. These will, in turn, have to be closely interlinked with a country's or region's planning process. In particular the following considerations will have to be borne in mind:

(1) A complete inventory of waters furthers effective planning and the establishment of priorities.

(2) The same can be said of a complete inventory of water rights.

(3) Water planning should be adequately co-ordinated with planning for the land use that water resources development is expected to serve. Moreover, wherever and whenever any water project is contemplated, an impact statement should be prepared, indicating the potentially adverse as well as the potentially beneficial effects on the hydrological régime, on the ecology, on other water uses and users on local populations in the project area, on related land use, and on the economy in general.

(4) One of the guiding criteria for effective water planning is to determine water demand by successive approximations for the various sectors of the economy, on a basin or regional basis. This activity will have to be co-ordinated with and guided by general economic objectives, and will condition allocation

of the water resource itself and of the required financial resources. Machinery to collect and store the needed information for projection methodology should be established as a priority item.

(5) Physical forecasting and warning services are also an indispensable adjunct of the management process, particularly in situations where extreme conditions (droughts and floods) occur with some regularity.

(6) Consolidation and co-ordination are means of modernizing water administration. One way to achieve this is when the execution of projects is consolidated in regional agencies and the co-ordination and decision-making functions are entrusted to and centralized in one water agency of national scope. The participation of the public is of great importance. It should be provided with avenues of expression at the planning stage so as to obviate an adverse reaction to new legal constraints, and subsequently so as to provide safeguards against an arbitrary exercise of administrative power. The administration should have the power to exert control over all types of water within the hydrological cycle, as well as over waters contained in man-made structures. Ground water and groundwater reservoirs should be fully integrated into the legal régime in view of the hazards of pollution and the possibility of excessively rapid depletion. This control should be as flexible as is necessary to assure effective use of water and to minimize waste. Therefore, latitude should be given to the administration with respect to duration and quantity of the water right, priority of right, and transfer of water and water rights from one place to another and from one use to another. The limitation of use to a definite period of time allows for the correction of past mistakes and enables individual water uses to be fitted more easily into the general scheme and made to correspond to changing technological interpretations of efficiency. Constraints on the transfer of water may be relaxed by eliminating the requirement of appurtenance to a particular piece of land or to a particular use. Quantification of water rights appears essential to the rational and equitable allocation of the resource. Possible abuses of power might be eliminated or minimized by providing administrative or judicial recourse from the decisions of the water administration.

(7) The enactment of comprehensive water legislation to replace or complement the sectoral legislation dispersed in many separate enactments should make the working of the law more efficient. Generally, it should provide for the assimilation of pre-existing water rights into the new legal régime within the shortest period of time consonant with the users' ability to make the transition from the old to the new pattern of use without undue hardship. In an intersectoral context, such legislation should make it possible to view water supply and water requirements as two aspects of a single problem. Thus, it should minimize conflicts between uses, integrate the water demands of all sectors of the economy, facilitate the transfer of water between sectors when this is beneficial to the economy, and encourage the search for appropriate uses for the suitably treated effluent of one sector as part of the supply of other sectors whenever this is technically and economically feasible and advantageous.

(8) Water should not be supplied free of charge. In fact, water charges for water supply and effluent systems can become a most powerful mechanism for allocating water to various sectors of the economy and managing quality, thus influencing demand. When this happens, however, Governments should be aware of the resulting implication with respect to the economy of the basin, region or country concerned. However, the charges need not necessarily reflect the market value of water, but may be geared to social and economic objectives.

(9) In agriculture, the water law should assure a well co-ordinated distribution of water supply, whether from a central government agency, a river basin authority, a district or project organization, a users' association, or a combination of all or any of them. But the construction and maintenance of works down to the field level should be the responsibility of the entity in charge of water distribution. There should be a minimum of return flow; in practice there is bound to be some, and the law should regulate its ultimate disposition.

(10) For domestic and municipal water use a good law should help to solve the problems of securing and protecting an adequate water supply, regulate consumption and regulate disposal of the effluent at the most reasonable cost. The assurance of safe drinking water to rural populations should be as much a responsibility of government as is that of water supply to municipalities, even if no piped water supply exists. This requires, in particular, the establishment of protective zones around wells and springs and along watercourses, and regulation of activities (including effluent disposal) within such zones and, where necessary, on watersheds and across ground-water aquifers. Furthermore, priority of domestic use needs to be reinforced by quantitative as well as qualitative control of industrial consumption which might endanger potable water supplies.

(11) In the industrial sector, in addition to the distribution of water, adequate pollution control is of particular importance. Here effluent charges or effluent limitations geared to the desired level of technology or to water quality standards can be included in the legislation. Power development, especially in the context of its nuclear aspects, which may impose a heavy environmental burden on future generations, may require the inclusion in the legislation of provisions concerning environmental impact statements, consolidation of licensing in one agency, and the establishment of strict safety standards for the operation of power plants and their monitoring for the discharge of effluent. The use of dry cooling towers may be considered wherever feasible in order to minimize adverse impacts on the environment.

Overview of Thematic Papers

INTRODUCTION

In an aide-mémoire dated 15 August 1975, the Secretary-General invited Governments to submit thematic papers, for presentation to the United Nations Water Conference, in addition to the national reports prepared for the regional prepatory meetings. Paragraph 11 of the aide-mémoire stated that:

> "Governments are invited to propose thematic papers for presentation to the Conference at Mar del Plata. It is suggested that these papers should concentrate on specific issues relevant to the main themes to be considered at the Conference. Such papers will deal in detail with national experiences in water management likely to be of world interest or with the results of the research undertaken by national institutions or scientists relevant to world water management."

By the end of November 1976, 215 thematic papers had been received in response to the aide-mémoire and the survey that follows is intended to facilitate their consideration by the Water Conference.

A. *Geographic Coverage*

The table below shows the region of origin of the 215 papers received, the regions being those of the United Nations regional commissions; for the sake of convenience, the papers from the United States of America, the Union of Soviet Socialist Republics and Canada are included in the total for Europe.

Europe including the USSR, the United States of America and Canada	136
Asia and Pacific	31
Africa	25
Latin America	21
West Asia	2
Total	215

---

*The present document was prepared by the secretariat of the United Nations Water Conference and subsequently reviewed, revised and endorsed by an intergovernmental working group convened at United Nations Headquarters from 6 to 10 December 1976 by the Secretary-General of the Conference. The names of the members of the working group are given in annex I.

**The numbers within brackets in the text of the present document refer to the serial numbers of the thematic papers and corresponding abstracts. In most cases, quotations are taken from the abstracts. For further information, see *Water Development and Management*, edited by Asit K. Biswas, Pergamon Press, Oxford, 1978.

Thus, 136 of the papers, or about two thirds of the total number of those received, are from the developed countries and this geographic coverage has a bearing on the subjects dealt with.

B. *Subject Coverage*

The wide spectrum of water resources development includes water policy, planning and management, the assessment and appraisal of water sources and uses, and supportive technology, research, education and training etc. From this spectrum, based on the topics covered by papers presented to the Conference, the following picture emerges.

	Number of papers
Water policy and planning objectives, including institutional and legislative problems	81
Assessment of water availability, including surface and ground waters	42
Water quality	6
Improvement in the management of water demand	3
Community water supplies	19
Use of water in agriculture	17
Use of water in energy and industry	11
Problems in the development of technology and research	9
Environment and health considerations	20
Flood loss and drought management	6
Utilization of shared water resources	11
Education and training	5

From the geographic and subject coverage of the papers, it will be seen that:

(a) The great majority of the papers deal with questions relating to policy formulation and planning objectives, including institutional and legal problems;

(b) Various aspects of the assessment of water availability, including surface and ground waters, have received more attention than problems of water use and development; here again, the assessment of ground-water availability and the monitoring of water quality are given more attention than questions pertaining to surface waters and non-conventional sources such as the sea or brackish waters;

(c) A good number of papers deal with the environmental impact of water development, both in the developing and the developed countries;

(d) A preponderant number of papers deal with the problems associated with the provision of community water supplies to both urban and rural communities;

(e) After community water supplies, problems associated with the use of water in agriculture come next in priority;

(f) Although a large number of papers deal with community water supplies, problems associated with excreta disposal have not received commensurate attention;

Overview of Thematic Papers   113

(g) On the whole, there has been relatively little coverage of important subjects like rural water supplies (only five papers), the development of appropriate or intermediate technology and other related aspects such as the transfer of technology, inland navigation (only one paper) and recreation and fisheries (a few papers refer to these questions); neither has much attention been paid to strategies for combating water-related diseases (one paper only); floods, droughts and earthquakes (six papers), problems of education, training and specialization (five papers), and salination and salinity problems (only two papers);

(h) There have been no papers as such on pricing mechanisms, financial problems or capital needs.

The desirability of focusing on new ideas, concepts and techniques and on aspects of national experiences that are likely to be of much wider and more general interest or validity to many other similarly placed countries or regional groupings have been important criteria in preparing the following broad overview of the principal points covered in the thematic papers.

I. PROBLEMS OF PLANNING AND POLICY FORMULATION

A. *Policy and Planning*

1. *Policy*

Increasing attention is being paid in many countries to formulating and strengthening water policy and planning objectives. The definition of objectives and the setting of goals and targets to be achieved over specified time-spans is the essence of the planning process. It would be pertinent to take into account objectives for different sectoral uses of water, such as the provision of community water supplies, rural as well as urban, the provision of water for the production of food and other agricultural products, water for industries and for the generation of hydropower, strategies for mitigating losses arising out of extreme conditions like floods or droughts or, in the most general sense, the use of water for the benefit of man. In the formulation of water policies and short-term and long-term plans, this basic human dimension should be considered as the key element and the main motivation for water resources development. Such an over-all human perspective has been counselled by the Holy See (61).* In considering any aspect relating to the planning and development of water resources, France (181) has also drawn attention to the fact that it is necessary to have this broad approach to the role of water as the basis for the sustenance of life and as the foundation for the civilizations that have grown up on the banks of rivers throughout the history of man.

Some notable examples of comprehensive water resource planning on a national scale are provided in the thematic papers by Denmark (207), the United States of America (92), Iraq (204), Japan (76), the Ukrainian SSR (140), Iran (27), Mexico (100, 102 and 103), Canada (157), Yugoslavia (58), the United Republic of Tanzania (153), Italy (98), Romania (45), the Byelorussian SSR (47) and the USSR (128, 130, 131, 132, 133, 166).

The abstraction of water in Denmark is presently estimated at 770 million cubic metres a year — 290 million cubic metres for industry, 10 million cubic metres

---
*The number in brackets indicates the number given to the paper referred to at the Water Conference. For the papers, see *Water Development and Management*, edited by Asit K. Biswas, Pergamon Press, Oxford, 1978.

for thermal power plants, 140 million cubic metres for agriculture and 330 million cubic metres for the population. In the year 2000, these figures are expected to increase to 1150 million cubic metres for the country as a whole, 380 million cubic metres for industry, 50 million cubic metres for thermal power plants, 170 cubic metres for agriculture and about 550 cubic metres for the population. In contrast, similar national data developed by the United States of America's New Water Assessment and Appraisal Programme indicates that between 1975 and 2000, total water withdrawals will decline by about 14 per cent, while total consumptive uses will increase by about 20 per cent.

This illustrates the sound basis for undertaking long-range planning on the basis of demand projections.

Iraq (204) has also created a scientific basis for the development of water resources by estimating the projected requirements by 1995, totalling to 67.6 billion cubic metres per year, of which irrigation alone accounts for 52.1 billion cubic metres. Estimates have also been made of the total water resources of the country (106 billion cubic metres) and the hydropower potential (56.1 billion kilowatt hours). Similar estimates for the Ukrainian SSR (140) show that the total stream discharge is 80 billion cubic metres (49 billion in a dry year) and the demands of the people and the economy are estimated at 32 billion cubic metres.

Considerable importance is attached to the creation of adequate storage capacity to help use this available resource for national needs. Since 1948, 13 large dams and reservoirs have been constructed in Iran (37), regulating more than 22 billion cubic metres of water, annually irrigating 4 million hectares and ensuring an installed capacity of 1800 megawatts, and six additional large dams are under construction, regulating an additional 1 billion cubic metres annually and generating 134 megawatts of power. The fourth plan started in 1968 and is scheduled to continue through to the eighth plan, which will be completed in 1993.

Estimates of national resources are not in themselves adequate indicators of sufficiency of supply. Mexico (100) points out that "although the supply is sufficient to meet future requirements, this will require new action involving more efficient use of water for the prevention of pollution and control of water quality". Based on this concept, Mexico (102) viewed the planning process as a process for determining targets, in respect of quantity as well as quality, both at the regional and central levels, in the short, medium and long terms. The design of an information system to support the planning process on a continuous basis is an important feature of the planning mechanism. It is therefore pointed out that "Mexico's National Water Plan is a pioneering effort in the world". Canada (157) also offers an interesting experience in comprehensive river basin planning initiated over the past five years for the Canadian river basins under the provisions of the Canada Water Act of 1970. The USSR reports on its long experience in the comprehensive and integrated planning of water resources development, the preparation of "water economy budgets" for river basins (128, 133, 166) hydrological forecasting for operational planning (131) and economic and organizational principles that are adopted (132). Yugoslavia (58) reports on its experience in the preparation of comprehensive water management plans for individual river basins in the country and their planned integration into a national plan, taking into account the regional imbalances and priorities in the national, economic and social plans. The United Republic of Tanzania (153) adopts a similar approach for the preparation of a long-term national plan as the synthesis of several subplans for different regions of the country. The planning process, which started in 1971, is expected to be concluded in 1978, culminating in the formulation of a national plan.

The importance attached to the formulation of a national water policy in Italy (98) is evidenced by the legislation adopted by the Senate on the problems of water supply, conservation, regulation and pollution control and the decision to convene a National Water Conference to discuss and adopt appropriate policies to achieve national objectives. The long-term national programme adopted in 1976 by Romania (45) is estimated to span 30 years, by which time the multipurpose development of the river basins in the country is expected to be completed. The goals for a 15-year period have already been established. On the other hand, a number of countries, such as the Byelorussian SSR (47), formulate development plans on the basis of both one-year and five-year periods.

Thus, it will be seen that long-term planning practices vary from country to country. In some countries, the formulation of perspective plans indicates the ultimate potential in different river basins, while in others the periods of planning are taken as 30 years, 15 years and five years, in addition to which there are annual plans. Evidently, the plans for shorter periods (e.g. five years) are more closely integrated into the over-all economic and social development plans than are the plans for longer periods.

2. *Regional planning*

The regional concept discussed below includes both intranational and transnational regions and comprises three types of zones, namely (i) river basins; (ii) distinct homogeneous geographic zones like the karst, coastal or arid zones; and (iii) administrative units, such as states, in countries with a federal structure.

In the context of regional planning, the comprehensive development and use of the Volga basin reported by the USSR (133), the Dnieper river basin, reported by Ukrainian SSR (139), the Vistula and Odra river basins in Poland (10), and the Tone and Ara river systems in Japan (76) are examples of the comprehensive planning of individual river basins. In the same context, Zaire (184) emphasizes the importance of the multipurpose development of the potential of the Zaire river basin not only for the benefit of the country itself but for the basin as a whole, such development comprising drinking water supply, navigation, fisheries, agriculture and energy development (the dam at Inga on the Zaire has one of the most powerful hydropower potentials in the world). Finland (51) has valuable experience in regional planning for the development of water resources. On the other hand, there are examples of regional plans evolved in a comprehensive manner for regions with common geographic or other features. The Dinaric karst region in Yugoslavia (54) is a good example of planning for the development of multipurpose water resources in a distinct geographic region, to be used for industry, power generation, etc. Remarkable results are reported to have been achieved in the construction of various projects, notably reservoirs and tunnels, under difficult and complex karst conditions. South Australia (114) and New South Wales (115) have reported on their integrated approach to preparing outline plans for the ultimate development of water resources. These are examples of planning at the state level in the context of a federal structure.

Another example of regional planning occurs in the coastal zones in the United States of America (190) and Canada (154). The geographic coverage of the management programme for coastal zones in the United States includes not only coastal waters, but the shore-lands whose uses have a direct and significant impact upon the coastal waters. Planning also takes into account "local concerns for the on-shore socio-economic impacts of off-shore oil and gas exploration and production". The Province of Prince Edward Island in Canada is cited (154) as an illustration of the importance of co-ordinating development based on multidisciplinary research.

Arid zones constitute another distinct category in regional planning. Israel (105) concentrated on the satisfaction of demands in the 1950s, management of demand in the 1960s and pollution control in the 1970s. In the case of the minor river basin of Gaja Creek (600-square kilometre catchment) in Hungary (6), the objective was to balance demand and supply, storage being a factor of fundamental importance in striking such a balance.

The above examples illustrate the variety and complexity of regional plans for the development of water resources and the need to consider certain specific regions, such as coastal or arid zones, apart from national and river basin planning.

3. *The integration of water planning into over-all planning*

In the formulation of long-term plans and regional plans, new innovative methods and techniques are being constantly developed. Planning is no longer unidirectional, neither is it limited to a single objective and there is an increasing recognition of the need to integrate water planning and management into national, social, economic and environmental goals; (USSR, 132, 166), Denmark (208, 209); the United States (92) also points out that such management should take into account both quantity and quality. Discussing the methodological aspects of water planning, Argentina (89) points out that the use of water "is clearly a question not of ordinary supply and demand, but rather of a derived demand". Quantification of demand and allocation of water, both quantitatively and qualitatively, become important components of water planning.

4. *New methods and techniques of planning*

This limitation of the river basin as a unit for planning logically leads to increasing efforts to effect interbasin transfers. The efforts by the USSR (165 and 166) to achieve a territorial distribution of water resources by redirecting northern and Siberian rivers towards the southern incline and establishing a unified water management system for the country are of interest in this context. The demonstrable feasibility, both technical and economic, of such interbasin transfers encourages reversals of the natural direction of river flows and would radically alter the basis and traditional concepts of planning and policy making.

The dynamic concept of the relativity of the water resources potential reported by Yugoslavia (55), which deals not only with conventional parameters of quantity and quality but also the parameter of potential energy (head) is an interesting analytical tool; the methodology indicated for eliminating waste in usage is also of interest. The use of pumped storage, increased reservoir construction on natural streams and the interbasin transfer of water are some of the planning and management techniques reported from Spain (63). Techniques to estimate the useful volumes of water for different purposes are also described by Spain (65). The conjunctive use of surface and ground water for integrated planning is emphasized by Iran (15) and the Sudan (27).

The use of mathematical models for the integrated development of surface water and ground water is reported by Iran (15), and the computerized optimization of power production from a reservoir system by the use of a mathematical model is cited by Austria (13). These are examples of the increasing use of the technique of mathematical modelling and computerization in the solution of a variety of problems involved in the process of planning.

B. Institutional Arrangements

In several countries a number of interesting patterns are evolving in the building of an appropriate institutional framework for the organization of multiple-purpose water resource development.

The establishment of 16,200 water authorities in the Federal Republic of Germany (142), 10,500 of which are "organized according to the legal provisions on water and soil authorities", are instances of this trend. The other interesting feature of this type of organization is the principle of "self-administration". It is also significant that the authorities are organized in "one of the most densely populated industrial areas of the world, the German Ruhr district". A somewhat similar principle seems to govern the organization of water resources development in Yugoslavia (56) within the context of its "self-management system". Representatives of citizens, water users and water-management enterprises govern the water-basin authorities.

Under a common agreement between the federal Government and the provinces, Argentina (85) has established seven river-basin committees which are inter-jurisdictional bodies. As there are 99 river basins in Argentina, this fruitful work will be continued. *Waterschappen* (water control boards) in the Netherlands (189) deal chiefly with dams and dikes and with problems of water control and water pollution in their districts. The interrelationship between the economic and organizational principles of water management is emphasized by the Union of Soviet Socialist Republics (132). The new water authorities set up in the United Kingdom for river basin management have facilitated an integrated approach to the problem of water development in that country. The authorities integrate all functions and are vested with powers to license all development and seek information about resources and demands. Romania (44) reports on the establishment of a water-management information and decision-making system, while Poland (12) follows system-oriented regional management patterns, as in the case of the urbanized and industrialized region of Upper Silesia and the agricultural region of the upper Notec river.

The problems of assuring national co-ordination and the development of a national approach to water assessment, research and management in a federal structure where the constitutional responsibility devolves on the states is reported by Australia (110). An important mechanism for achieving this national approach was the formation of the Australian Water Resources Council in 1963. More recently, a statement of water policy acceptable to all members of the Council was formulated. The collaborative intergovernmental basis evolved in Australia is of interest to countries with a federal structure, where an active role in the field of water development is assigned to individual states.

C. Legislation

The closely related question of providing a suitable legal and legislative framework for the development of water resources is becoming increasingly important not only in European countries like Poland (9) and Spain (67) but also in countries of the African region such as Botswana (73).

Poland (9) enacted a new Water Law in 1974 which is much more comprehensive than either the Water Law of 1962 or the Water Decree of 1922, and covers such questions as irrigation and drainage, as well as the water supply for cities and rural settlements.

Spanish water law (67) contains certain interesting premises, for example, while all running waters are public, "ground water brought to light by an individual on a property and rain water that falls on that property are private".

In arid countries such as Botswana (73), individuals who control ground-water rights and water boreholes acquire the ability to control vast communal grazing areas. The issues of water rights and land control are now closely interwoven and this has resulted in profound changes in the socio-economic fabric of societies traditionally based on the collective ownership of land, but where new features of individual ownership are becoming apparent.

Thailand (31) has prepared a Ground-Water Act providing "for the control of engagement in ground-water activities, which include drilling for ground water, the use of ground water and the disposal of water or liquids into the aquifer through a well". Under the Act, private ownership of ground water is permitted only outside the area proclaimed by the ministry as a "ground-water area". Moreover, the ownership of ground water is confined to "only depths not exceeding those stipulated in the ministerial regulations". A system of permits is contemplated. Excessive pumping of ground water in Japan (171) is known to lead to land subsidence, which is of the order of 10 centimetres per year in an area such as Osaka and legislation is therefore needed to control ground-water pumping.

Apart from legislation on such individual aspects of water use and development, the present trend is to promulgate a complete and comprehensive legislation in the form of a water code or water law. Australia (114) reports the recent enactment of a new Water Resources Act providing for the first time in Australia a complete water resources code in one piece of legislation, covering surface and underground water management and water quality control, and providing formal mechanisms for the co-ordination of planning and for the involvement of the public in the water resources management process.

Legislation, its form and content, is an integral part of the socio-economic structure and policies adopted by Governments. This intrinsic inter-relation between economic, organizational and legislative principles and regulations is emphasized by the Union of Soviet Socialist Republics (132).

II. ASSESSMENT OF RESOURCES AND NEEDS

The assessment of resources and the assessment of needs are dealt with jointly, since they are interrelated.

A. Assessment of Resources

The following aspects of the question are dealt with below: surface water, ground water, collection of data (an aspect which is common to both surface and ground water), non-conventional sources and matters related to water quality assessment.

1. Surface water

In recent times, there has been an increasing interest in the assessment not only of water resources at the national, subregional and regional levels but also of the resources of the earth and of the components of the water budget for the world as a whole. In this connexion, mention must be made of the outstanding contribution of the USSR (127) to the International Hydrological Decade, in the shape of a monograph which evaluates and calculates "the components of the water budget for Europe, Asia, Africa, North America, South America, Australia and Oceania, the Arctic and the Antarctic. At the same time, it evaluates the water budget of dry land, [57] lakes ... and [25] reservoirs ... the fresh-water budget of the Pacific Ocean and the water budget of the entire globe". The monograph also includes a forecast of changes in the earth's water resources under the impact of human economic activities in 1985 and 2000.

The techniques for forecasting changes include the establishment of indicators of the current use of water resources and long-term water requirements, the two components that go into the preparation of what in the USSR are termed "long-term water economy budgets for river basins" (128).

The USSR (125) also reports on the results of interesting research on the use of aerological observation data for 35 South American stations between 1966 and 1970 for the computation of the atmospheric water budget over the South American continent as a whole and, based on this, the computation of monthly values of precipitation minus evaporation, not only for the continent but for its various physical and geographic zones. Similarly, the monthly amounts of evaporation from the La Plata basin were estimated from a study of the atmospheric budget over the basin. This aerological approach offers interesting possibilities for an assessment of the water resources of other continents and water basins, particularly those where few records have been taken in the past.

Global evaluations of this nature contribute to an understanding of deficiencies and surpluses of different geographical regions and continents and, at the same time bring into focus methodological deficiencies in the techniques of resource estimations.

The estimation of available surface water resources involves not only an assessment of the total surface resources, but also a determination of their distribution in time and space. The requirements of assessment vary with the nature of the projects. The difference in the requirements for irrigation projects, hydroelectric projects and water supply projects is pointed out by Spain (65), which underlines the importance of such parameters as the percentage of inflow, the distribution of flow and precipitation and the physical geography of the basin. A lower rate of guaranteed success in the earlier stage is permissible in irrigation projects. In hydroelectric projects greater economic efficiency is assured only when a percentage of the mean flow is guaranteed, which in turn requires a greater rate of guarantee in studies on the exploitation of resources. A higher guaranteed flow is warranted in studies on water supply.

But whatever the nature of the project and the guarantee of success in the
exploitation of resources, the basic requirement for planning is the collection
of hydrological data. In view of this, a number of countries have been attach-
ing considerable importance to making an inventory of the surface-water
resources by strengthening hydrometric networks. This activity has received
an enormous impetus in the International Hydrological Decade, which ended
recently, and it is to be hoped that this aspect will continue to receive the
attention it merits in the International Hydrological Programme, which has
succeeded the Decade. In addition to traditional hydrometric networks, the
successful utilization of complexes of representative basins has been reported
by France (174), particularly in the calculations of flood levels and annual
run-offs in the Sahel region of Africa. The concept of representative basins
is recommended as a useful tool in the assessment and inventory of surface-
water resources in developing countries (174).

In several countries, in addition to rainfall, snow-fall acts as an important
source of river waters and a number of countries have therefore been actively
engaged on snow surveys and forecasting the total annual discharge of the
streams, based on the measurement of snow accumulation and the computation of
snow melt run-off. Argentina (82) reports on its experience of 25 years of
snow surveys conducted by the Argentine Water and Electric Power Agency, which
uses the forecasts of stream-flow based on snow surveys in the operation of
projects for the generation of power and for irrigation. Similar is the case
with USSR (131) where the main source of water for most of the country's rivers
is snow melt, which accounts for between 60 per cent and 90 per cent of the
annual run-off of the rivers. Seasonal forecasts of stream-flow from snowmelt made at the beginning of March have a "lead time" ranging from three to
seven months. Statistics show that the probability of maintaining a marginal
error of no more than 20 per cent ranges from 75 per cent to 90 per cent.
The Ukrainian SSR (138) also reports on its experience of hydrological forecasts and their use in day-to-day water-management planning. Not only is
forecasting a useful tool in the operation of reservoirs and, in the more
general sense, in system operation, but long-term forecasts are issued giving
the volume and maximum or minimum flow of regulated and unregulated rivers.
This aspect of long-term forecasting is particularly useful in predicting
impending droughts or floods.

Successful water planning and management require not only adequate and well-
distributed hydrometric networks in the field, but also sound, scientific and
systematic arrangements for the collection and processing of the hydrological
data that are collected from such networks. In this respect, methods of
electronic data-processing using computer facilities are becoming more and more
popular in many developing countries. For instance, Kenya (168) and the
United Republic of Tanzania (152) report on their initiation of computer
systems for data storage and retrieval, including the preparation of magnetic
tapes. Argentina (83) reports on the setting up of a multidisciplinary working
group to analyse hydrological data, with powers to establish commissions composed of specialists in different subjects. As a result of the efforts made
by the working group, a number of studies have been made and 83 working papers
covering a variety of subjects have been prepared.

The experience of the United States (161) points to the desirability of having
a principal fact-finding agency for data collection "that is independent of
the missions of water-management agencies", at the same time ensuring communication between the data collector and the data user. Further, there is a
reciprocal influence between the data base and water policy.

The ever-increasing demand on available surface-water resources and the growing need to explore ways and means of augmenting traditionally available supplies is illustrated by the Jonglei Canal project in the southern part of the Sudan. An enormous quantity of water is lost in the extensive swampy areas of the Sudd. It is estimated that 42 billion cubic metres of water are lost annually, half of the quantity of water at Aswan, on the Nile, which is 84 billion cubic metres. Considerable importance is attached by Egypt (16) and the Sudan (30) to the projects for increasing the Nile yield. The first phase of the Jonglei Canal project is expected to save 4 billion cubic metres of water.

2. Ground water

There is increasing interest, in almost all parts of the world, in a systematic extensive and comprehensive investigation of ground-water prospection, use and development. Examples of such interest are afforded by a number of countries in Europe, Africa, Asia and Latin America. The following aspects of ground-water development have to be considered:

(a) Use;

(b) Planning and prospection;

(c) Problems associated with the artificial recharge of aquifers;

(d) Advanced methods for prospection and development;

(e) Some special categories of ground water, such as mineral and thermal waters.

(a) Use. At the present time, ground-water consumption in the Soviet Union (129) amounts to approximately 700 cubic metres per second, i.e. only about 7 per cent of the estimated recoverable resources of 10,000 cubic metres per second. Of the present use, approximately 320 cubic metres per second are for urban water supply, about 190 cubic metres per second for agricultural water supply and pasture watering and 160-170 cubic metres per second for the irrigation of cultivated land. Ground water is used to supply approximately 60 per cent of the Soviet Union's total urban water supply needs and 80 per cent of its agricultural water supply needs (129). Similarly, at present "about 90 per cent of the stable water resources which are formed on the territory of the German Democratic Republic are already used in an average year. ... Twenty-five to 30 per cent of the water demand is covered by ground water" (60).

Finland (48) made a detailed survey of all aquifers with a daily yield of more than 250 cubic metres to help communities within reasonable distances which might possibly resort to this source for their water supply needs. It is anticipated that all the available ground-water areas would be put to use by the year 2000; the amount of ground water obtained would be 1.6 million cubic metres per day — making use of about 40 per cent of the known ground-water resources for the whole country in place of the present 22 per cent.

The USSR (120) reports on the various methods being taken for protecting ground waters against pollution, including the proper location of industrial enterprises, the establishment of sanitary protection zones, pumping tests, the injection of water into strata in order to extract the polluted water, the burial of highly toxic waste in deep strata, comprehensive monitoring, etc.

(b) Planning and prospection. In order to facilitate rapid increases in the use of ground water, extensive planning and prospection is undertaken in almost

all countries in the different continents. The use of ground water is particularly important in the arid zones of the world. The Federal Republic of Germany (145) points out that "in humid zones, for example, a discharge rate of 1000 cubic metres per day demands a catchment area of 1 square kilometre in a sandy aquifer with a recharge rate of *circa* 50 per cent of 730 millimetres per annum precipitation. In an arid zone with an annual precipitation of only 73 millimetres and a maximum recharge rate of 5 per cent of the same discharge of 1000 cubic metres per day demands under the same hydrogeological conditions a catchment area of 100 square kilometres." This points to the comparability of 100 square kilometres in an arid area to 1 square kilometre in a humid area, which underlines the importance of ground water in arid zones.

Ground-water prospection is carried out in almost all African countries. Extensive drilling is reported from the Ivory Coast (46); 150 bore holes totalling 8500 metres of drilling were done in one year, ending 1 April 1976.

Mapping is in various stages of progress in the African countries; for instance, 1:1,000,000 maps covering 15 hydrological units were prepared in Somalia (38). Prospection has been in progress in the sedimentary basins of the southern and north-eastern parts of Benin (99). A systematic regional assessment has been taken up in individual river basins in the Sudan like the Gash at Kassala (26) and also for the country as a whole (27). In the Sudan, the total rural water demand is estimated at 275 million cubic metres, ground-water resources at present providing 23.2 per cent of this amount. The total annual recharge is estimated at 1381 million cubic metres, of which 143 million cubic metres represents use. There is considerable interest in ground-water development in Egypt (18) including the Nile valley, the delta, the coastal areas and the desert. The construction of the Aswan Dam is known to have introduced profound changes in the ground-water régime of the country. France (176) carried out a comprehensive hydrological study in the Sahel which resulted in the production of three types of maps on the scale of 1:500,000, showing: (i) initial flow-rates of ground water; (ii) the average cost of ground-water exploitation; and (iii) the suitability of water for irrigation. A comparison of these three maps would make it possible to choose the most suitable regions for agricultural development.

In Latin America, Argentina (79) reports that, although general hydrological exploration is fairly well advanced in the country, extensive areas remain to be appraised. Also in Argentina, the ground-water potential in parts of the pampa plains was evaluated by the Federal Republic of Germany (146), using modern methods of exploration, including interpretation of air-borne photography, remote sensing and geophysics, to prepare maps on the scales of 1:50,000, 1:100,000 and 1:500,000.

In Sweden, hard rock aquifers play an important role. Techniques, based on geological, tectonic and geophysical methods, are used to find areas in hard rocks with a proper fractual pattern with enough free space to store infiltrated water. The methods and experience of Sweden (71) would be of interest to areas in Africa, the Arabian shield, the Indian subcontinent, Australia, Brazil and other similar parts of the world.

Some of the problems encountered in planning the development of ground-water resources are the reconciliation of possible conflicts in their potential use and prevention of the pollution of natural resources. Australia (113) points out potential conflicts between urban and industrial use, irrigation, wild life and recreation interests in the case of the Swan coastal plain. Although these have not yet developed into major problems, it is obvious that careful management will be required as development takes place in the future.

(c) Artificial recharge of aquifers. Considerable interest has been shown in problems relating to the artificial recharge of aquifers. The USSR (134) reports on two main trends, regional and local. The main types of research reported from the USSR are experimental infiltration in basins, the injection of water into absorption boreholes and experimental work on filtration columns. The Ukrainian SSR (136) also reports on the use of open infiltration works (basins, channels), in addition to water injection boreholes to assist in artificial replenishment. In the case of the Burdekin delta in Australia (118) surplus water from the river was pumped to recharge the ground-water supplies and the scheme involved the construction of pumping stations, distribution channels and excavated recharge pits.

Sweden (71), when reporting on its 80-year experience in artificial recharge, points out that the most suitable geological formations in arid and semi-arid areas are coarse alluvial deposits and sedimentary rocks. The infiltration process is simple and can be operated by unskilled labour under limited supervision.

(d) Advanced methods for prospection and development. An interesting new approach has been evolved by Hungary (2), which postulates that the water balance "is a socio-economic-hydrogeological estimate of the hydrogeological consequences of withdrawal rather than a comparison of water demand with some resources figure regarded as constant". Mathematical modelling techniques are being developed in Hungary for the determination of safe yields according to this dynamic concept. Modelling as an aid in the problems of ground-water exploration and development is also reported from the German Democratic Republic (59). The use of natural and artificial tracers and salt injections in the investigations of karst waters is reported from Austria (43). Airborne photography, remote sensing, geophysics and nuclear techniques are among the advanced techniques that have to be used, particularly in the developing countries, to a greater extent than hitherto for ground-water exploration and development.

(e) Mineral and thermal waters. The USSR (124) reports interesting research on the use of mineral, thermal and industrial water resources "for heat-power engineering and as a source of useful substances". Carbonaceous mineral waters have been exploited in the south of the country and nitric thermal waters in the neighbouring areas. Known supplies of thermal waters amounting to 3.5 cubic metres per second are reported to have been used to produce electrical energy and to supply heat. Mineral and thermal waters are also reported to have been used in the industrial production of iodine and bromine. There are a number of countries that have such mineral and thermal springs and the work reported by the USSR would be of value to those interested in using such water resources not only for spas but for other economic purposes, such as those cited by the USSR in its paper.

3. *Collection of data*

The USSR (130) reports on an integrated national recording system for water and water use consisting of three subsystems, one for recording surface water, one for recording ground water and a third for recording water use. An integrated system of this kind, comprising not only data on available resources of surface water and ground water but also including the details of its utilization for development purposes, will be of interest to many countries that are in the process of building up data collection systems to help in their national planning.

4. *Non-conventional sources*

In addition to the conventional sources of surface and ground waters, non-conventional sources such as sea water and brackish water, induced precipitation and geothermal waters, are increasingly being used for a variety of purposes, for example, for community supplies or for industry.

Sea water and brackish water. Reporting on its use of desalting technology to meet its fresh-water needs, Kuwait (25) mentions the results of the experiments on the various desalting processes, leading to the conclusion that "the multistage flash is the most reliable method for large-scale plants, both technically and economically". The plants in Kuwait serve the dual purpose of satisfying demands for both power and water. There does not seem to be any irrefutable evidence to warrant the conclusion that the multistage flash is indeed technically and economically the most reliable method. For instance, research is now being undertaken in experimental plants in Japan (173) employing the reverse osmosis technique, with a view to providing pure water while using a more practical sea-water desalination method at lower cost and with less energy consumption. Another interesting example of the use of desalinated water comes from the Colorado river basin in the United States of America (191). A desalting plant with a capacity of 104 million gallons per day (4.6 cubic metres per second) is to be constructed in Arizona for the purpose of improving the quality of the Colorado river water delivered to Mexico.

Induced precipitation. Considerable interest has been evinced in research and experimentation on weather modification, including precipitation management technology and anti-hailstorm plans. Studies in the United States (191) show that precipitation management technology could increase the annual run-off in the upper Colorado river basin by 15 per cent, at a cost ranging from $1.50 to $3 per acre-foot. Argentina (90) draws attention to the need for a careful cost-benefit assessment in the attempts at artificial weather modification.

Geothermal water. In the United States (191) studies are under way in southeastern California on the desalting of geothermal brine and the generation of electricity from geothermal energy. The water developed under this programme could be used to augment existing supplies.

The intensive research and experimentation being carried out with a view to augmenting traditional water supplies from non-conventional sources such as those described above are indications of the acuteness of the water scarcity in certain parts of the world.

5. *Water quality assessment*

Apart from the measurement of quantity, observations on the quality of both surface and ground water constitute an important part of the assessment of available resources. Thus, water quality measurements are introduced as integral parts of observational networks in many countries. The monitoring of quality is also considered to be one aspect of the fight against pollution.

France (175) has underlined the close interrelationship between quality management and quantity management, "which is achieved in identical fashion:

regulation and economic incentives". A similar plea is made by the United States of America (108) for a closer integration between water quality and water quantity planning both by State and local agencies. Under the terms of the Danish Environment Protection Act of 1973, Danish regional authorities submit water quality plans for streams, lakes and coastal waters (210), the primary purpose of which is to indicate for what uses the different water areas are suited.

The automatic monitoring of water quality forms part of the water management information and decision-making system in Romania (44). The case of the pump-storage project in Austria (41) is somewhat unique in the sense that the monitoring of quality of waters in the reservoirs of manifold origin has for its aim the determination of stratification and flow superposition of waters of different quality in the reservoir.

As in the case of surface waters, great care is necessary in the determination and preservation of the quality of ground waters. For instance, in Finland (48), there are varying amounts of iron and manganese in the ground-water resources and various methods are developed for their removal.

Australia (109) points out the need to establish some mechanism for continually updating any set of water quality criteria, since even for the relatively well studied agents there are still many unknowns, such as the effect of critical receptors. Although in Norway (185), "most of the land area and most water basins are still at the stage of no industrial activity going on", the Government is preparing three new laws — a planning law, a comprehensive pollution law and a product control law — as new instruments for the water quality management of unpolluted and slightly polluted water resources. As the situation in many developing countries is comparable in the sense that many of the streams are still unpolluted or slightly polluted, the experience of Norway will be of interest to such countries.

B. *Assessment of Needs*

An essential element in the process of planning, besides the assessment of resources, is an assessment of needs. Estimates of needs have to take into account not only present requirements for various sectoral uses but also projected requirements for the future, so that reasonable demand projections for the foreseeable future may provide the necessary perspective for planning. A number of countries have been making estimates of present and future demands for water for different purposes. There appears, however, to be a need to rationalize the basis for such estimates and also to introduce an element of uniformity in order to make them as far as possible comparable, at least in the same international river basin.

At the same time, the keen competition for water has made it necessary, at least in countries where future prospects are extremely competitive, to foster the concept of management of demand as distinct from management of supply. Management of demand proceeds from the premise that "no supply system can be dimensioned economically for covering completely the peak demands, but certain restrictions in supply must be anticipated". Proceeding from this, concepts have been evolved in Hungary (5) of "supply restriction indices", "shortage tolerances", and the "determination of risk indices", etc.

III. COMMUNITY WATER SUPPLY

This question may be considered under three broad headings, namely, urban water supply, rural water supply and sewage disposal and treatment.

A. *Urban Water Supply*

The increasing trend of urbanization in all the regions of the world is causing strain on metropolitan and urban water supply systems already in existence, as much in the developed world as in the developing world.

There are interesting papers on the problems caused by expanding water needs in large metropolitan areas like Madrid in Spain (66), Helsinki in Finland (50), Tokyo and Osaka in Japan (74 and 75) and Bangkok in Thailand (70).

The Madrid water-supply system (66) is extraordinarily complex, consisting of water resources drawn from eight rivers (two more rivers will be added to the system later), 12 reservoirs with a capacity of about 900 million cubic metres with plans to build four new reservoirs by the year 2000, with a capacity of 1500 cubic metres. In addition, there are 441 kilometres of major canals, six water treatment plants and a distribution network about 4000 kilometres long.

The Helsinki (50) metropolitan area is served by the Päijänne Tunnel, 120 kilometres long, which, when completed, will probably be the longest tunnel in the world constructed through rock. The cross-section of the tunnel is 15 square metres and its discharge capacity will be 13 cubic metres per second. About 4 million cubic metres of crushed rock are involved in the construction work.

In Austria (77), "usually, centres of consumption can be supplied with ground water or spring water from the vicinity". The use of surface water is practically limited to industrial purposes. The problems of water supply in Austria are being met by encouraging the establishment of a water supply network through the construction of large-scale plants and the granting of public subsidies in this respect.

In large metropolitan areas in Japan (75), like Tokyo and Osaka, "water has willy-nilly become a factor restricting social and economic development". The principal water sources for Tokyo and Osaka are the Tone and Yodo rivers. It will be difficult to envisage further development after 1985, when the water resources development projects now under way will have been completed. A large-scale reorganization of water undertakings "was recently examined and promoted" in Japan (74). The purposes of the reorganization are to strengthen the financial and management basis of the undertakings, utilizing water effectively, equalizing water prices in wide areas and lowering water costs. Some new concepts are also being developed, such as the adoption of advanced water-treatment techniques, for example carbon absorption and ozonation, the use of low-quality water sources and the reuse of waste water for purposes such as toilet flushing.

In the metropolitan areas of Bangkok in Thailand (70), one third of the water supply is at present extracted from ground-water sources and two thirds from surface run-off diverted from the Chao Phraya river. The pumping of ground water has now exceeded the safe yield and consequently is lowering the groundwater level by 3 to 4 metres per year. Therefore, the policy is to use surface water as much as possible and this, in its turn, is making the preparation of a basin plan for the river necessary to facilitate a rational allocation of available river water for different purposes.

The enormity of the problem of a potable fresh water supply, even in the developed countries, is indicated by the feasibility studies reported by Norway (186), concerning the possibility of low-cost tow transportation of unpolluted, potable fresh water in large quantities from Norway to the Netherlands in very large (1 million cubic metres capacity) light-weight flexible containers. The economics of small containers are also included in the scope of the study. Tanker transportation of potable water could at best be a temporary solution to meet occasional periods of water shortage.

B. *Rural Water Supply*

The United Republic of Tanzania (151) has evolved a comprehensive policy for rural water supply in terms of which targets have been set to provide clean, potable water within easy reach to every individual in the rural area by 1991 and a crash programme is being implemented to provide every village with a permanent source of potable water within the next five years. The United Republic of Tanzania estimates that efforts must be made to provide water to 20 million people in the rural areas between 1973 and 1991. A concerted effort is being made to deal with the principal constraints arising out of shortages of trained manpower equipment, transport facilities and finance. Similarly, Guyana (183) plans to provide improved water supply to the entire country by 1985. A phased long-range water supply improvement programme has been undertaken to facilitate the achievements of this target. These are two examples of efforts being made by countries to implement the recommendations of Habitat: United Nations Conference on Human Settlements.

Thailand (35) is evolving a comprehensive policy and programme for the extension of water supply facilities for domestic use in rural areas, including pipe-distributed water systems, surface waters, ground water from deep-drilled wells, etc.

Argentina (88) points to the need for an efficient functioning of the financing machinery to assure the allocation of sufficient resources for this vital purpose.

C. *Sewage Disposal*

Although problems of sewage disposal and treatment have not received, on a global scale, the same attention as problems of water supply, some countries have been developing various methods for the treatment of urban and industrial sewage. For instance, the USSR (122) has been adopting a variety of methods which can be classified as (a) chemical and physico-chemical; (b) biological; and (c) mechanical.

Another interesting approach has been the co-ordinated treatment of both urban sewage and urban storm-water drainage as in the case of Chicago in the United

States of America (162). The Flood Water Management Plan and the Tunnel and Reservoir Plan (TARP) interphase closely with the Waste Water Management Program. The Federal Republic of Germany (149) points out that the construction of about 1000 facultative anaerobic/aerobic lagoons in Bavaria represents a very efficient stage in a sewage treatment plan. Facultative aerobic lagoons combined with biological stages are inexpensive and do not need skilled maintenance, and hence are of interest to many other countries.

The above review of the problems of water supply and sewage disposal shows the enormous complexity of the problem and the wide variety of conditions in different countries of the world. The establishment by the Netherlands (169) of an International Reference Centre for Community Water Supply, which "operates as the nexus of a network of regional and national collaborating institutions in 30 developing and industrialized countries" is therefore opportune.

Over the last two decades, in a number of countries, bilateral, multilateral, governmental and intergovernmental organizations have done or are doing considerable work in the field of community water supplies, including waste disposal. The United States of America (94) calls attention to the adaptation and transfer of existing technology as well as the development of new technology and focuses upon the relationships of technology to the requisite human and financial resources and institutions in this most important sector of water use.

IV. THE USE OF WATER IN AGRICULTURE

A. *Irrigation Development*

One of the most important uses of water is in agriculture. Water is one of the most important inputs in current efforts to increase food production in many countries and parts of the world and, in general, to raise agricultural productivity and production, along with a variety of other related inputs. Moreover, the agricultural use of water is the most predominant; more than 90 per cent of the water used is in irrigation. In almost all the countries of the world, considerable importance is therefore attached to the development of irrigation.

The USSR (167) has cited the examples of the Kakhovka and Saratov projects for the production of grain, the Golodnaya and Karshinskaya projects for cotton and the Kuban and Kazyal-Orda projects for rice. Some major multipurpose storage reservoir projects were formulated and constructed in Thailand (34) but agriculture in about three quarters of the land is still rain-fed. Apart from major projects, a number of small projects are being undertaken in many countries to increase the irrigated area. Since 1968 Thailand (33) has initiated 11 electrical pumping projects on the right bank of the Mekong, the project areas being of a reasonable size, between 500 and 1,000 hectares. A programme of development of new irrigation networks has been taken up in Indonesia (24), covering the development of simple irrigation/reclamation systems of about 550,000 hectares. The individual areas range in size from several hundred hectares to 2000 hectares, which can be developed easily.

These examples point to the desirability of combining major, medium, and minor irrigation projects in the strategy for the development of irrigation.

An agricultural programme is reported by Guyana (182) involving gravity drainage into the ocean together with pumping into the Canje river to benefit an area of 50,000 hectares. The importance of irrigation in the economies of the Sudan (30) and Egypt (21) is illustrated by the giant Jonglei Canal, which is one of the projects undertaken in order to increase the yield from the Nile and promote the use of drainage water for irrigation in Egypt. In Egypt 50 per cent of the irrigation water becomes drainage water and is again reused in combination with canal water. At present, 4.8 billion cubic metres of drainage water are thus reused out of an estimated potential of 12.2 billion cubic metres.

B. *Management of Water for Higher Efficiency*

Apart from the extension of irrigation, one of the most important problems in agriculture is to improve the management of irrigation water and use it more economically and efficiently within the existing systems. In Egypt (19), intensive work is being undertaken on water requirements for crops, irrigation rotation, water losses, improvement of irrigation efficiency, integrated land and water conservation and management. Egypt (20) is also attempting to evolve remedial measures to combat the growth of weeds and hyacinth in the river and canal systems with manual and mechanical methods and through the use of chemical herbicides and biological controls. The same is true of the Sudan, which is currently engaged in intensive research on evaporation (28) and crop-water uses in irrigated and rain-fed agriculture (29), with a view to maximizing agricultural production.

Bangladesh (40) has reported the results of its experiments in adjusting the time of seeding in order to exploit the full potential of HYV rice in the irrigated areas. Seeding IR-8 in mid-January and transplanting it in mid-February was found to yield the best results.

In the Federal Republic of Germany (143) agricultural drainage is considered far more important than irrigation. Agricultural irrigation is basically supplemental irrigation, especially in dry years and concerted efforts are being made to cut down on water consumption in irrigated agriculture. The change-over to a sprinkler irrigation system is reported to have resulted in savings of more than 500 million cubic metres of water per year. The withdrawal of surface water has decreased considerably — to less than half the previous amount — whereas the use of ground water for irrigation has shown a marked increase.

Modern irrigation practices assure a highly efficient irrigation system in Israel (150). The agricultural output of irrigated crops per cubic metre in real terms increased in Israel from $US 8 in 1962 to $US 15 in 1973.

C. *Salinity Control and Drainage*

Irrigation projects have to cope with problems of salinity and waterlogging, thus making it necessary to incorporate measures for salinity control and drainage in an integral manner in the planning, design and operation of irrigation systems.

Irrigation development in Australia (111) over the past 90 years has raised naturally saline water tables in large areas and a $A 40 million (1975) programme is proposed to mitigate waterlogging and salination in areas in Victoria. Extensive economic and political factors are taken into account in the "multi-objective" planning procedures.

Another type of salinity problem is the one caused by salinity intrusion in estuaries. The Gambia has presented a case study (216) of the Gambia river, where the tidal influence is felt up to 520 kilometres inland because of low gradients; a mathematical model was formulated, based on field measurements, "to serve primarily as a prediction model and to determine from it a salinity control system within an integrated development plan".

D. *Soil Erosion and Conservation*

Another important factor in maintaining and increasing agricultural productivity is the undertaking of measures to combat soil erosion and conserve soil and water.

Kenya (23) underlines the need to conserve land and water resources by analysing the situation with regard to rates of erosion and sedimentation within some of the catchment areas in the country. River sedimentation is also a serious problem in Argentina (80), which is therefore undertaking not only a quantitative assessment of the transport of sediments but also an analysis of river dynamics and their effects on the various uses of the resources. The problem is so serious in the mountain regions of the Federal Republic of Germany (141) that the Government for the first time submitted the problem for discussion at an international seminar in 1974, and subsequently undertook remedial measures. The Federal Republic of Germany also implemented a project in Brazil (148) involving investigations in the Parnaíba basin.

E. *Integrated Land and Water Management*

The above examples emphasize the necessity for developing and conserving land and water in an integrated manner in the interest of agricultural production. The United States of America (96) also emphasizes the concept of integrated land management to achieve multi-objective goals.

In relation to the use of water in agriculture, the greatest imperative in the present situation is the formulation of a comprehensive and integrated policy involving the extension of irrigation and of rain-fed cultivation, improved agricultural efficiency, better management practices and other related measures. Also, as the United States (93) points out, "those institutions and land operators responsible for implementing and operating agricultural water resources projects must have a role in planning and decision-making, if full returns from the projects are to be realised". Water must receive prime consideration as an essential input in a well thought out over-all agricultural strategy to be implemented in accordance with the political and socio-economic conditions in different countries.

V. THE USE OF WATER FOR HYDROPOWER GENERATION

One of the significant uses of water is hydropower generation. Notwithstanding the many major hydropower projects being undertaken in countries and regions throughout the world, there exists a tremendous potential still to be developed and efforts are therefore being made in many countries to make a systematic study of regional and national hydropower potential. In Yugoslavia (54) considerable funds have been devoted to the development of the water power potential in the Dinaric karst region. Remarkable results have been achieved in the construction of various projects, notably reservoirs and supply tunnels, under difficult and complex karst conditions.

Even in the case of hydroelectric projects already constructed and in operation, studies are being conducted to facilitate optimization of power generation, and in this connexion a number of different and sophisticated techniques, such as mathematical simulation models are currently in use. In Austria (13), a mathematical model was developed to study the potential for optimization, using methods of non-linear programming. Although in this case the method was developed for a study of the problems in hydroelectric power production, it is applicable to any kind of reservoir operation in the field of water management. Simulation models in water management with special reference to hydroelectric production are the subject of detailed studies by France (178). In relation to hydropower production, the paper points out that analytical methodology has to take into account whether power generation is a high priority objective or of low or no priority in the case of the reservoir under consideration.

Discussing the problems it has encountered in the development of hydroelectric power, Thailand (32) points out that the demand for hydropower generation has been increasing very steeply during the last two decades. For instance, energy generation in Thailand increased at an average rate of 32 per cent from 1964 to 1970 and 15 per cent from 1971 to 1975. Rates of load growth will still be high for several years to come. This is true not only of Thailand, but of several other countries and regions of the world, notwithstanding the efforts to use other sources such as lignite, natural gas and oil, as well as non-conventional sources. The development of hydropower assumes particular importance in the context of the current energy crisis. In the United States of America (158) a number of different energy technologies are emerging to place new and significant demands on water and related land resources. Of particular relevance are coal conversion, shale oil, geothermal power and nuclear energy. Although, as a result of these new trends, the traditional "energy-development/water-demand relationships" are undergoing a change, in many of the developing countries with a still considerable unused hydropower potential, emphasis will continue to be placed on hydropower generation for a long time to come.

VI. THE USE OF WATER IN INDUSTRY

The high priority accorded to industrialization in the developing countries involves additional demands for water, which sometimes enters directly into the production process for consumptive use (in breweries, for instance) and in other cases has auxiliary uses. In the developed countries, where the rate of industrialization remains high even today, the demand for water is also great. Thus the use of water for industry is becoming increasingly important in every country of the world.

It is becoming more and more necessary to reuse and recycle water for industrial purposes. The Byelorussian SSR (47) reports that one of the main trends in the use of water for industry is the effort to introduce recycling for supply purposes and to achieve the maximum reuse of waste water. Austria also reports an increase in the use of water.

Japan (170) has a system of industrial water supply utilities that is unparalleled elsewhere. In 1962, 8.2 per cent of the total industrial water (fresh water) was supplied by this system and the ratio increased remarkably to 26.4 per cent in 1973. At present more than 30 per cent of the industrial water in Japan is supplied by industrial water supply utilities. The industrial water supply systems making use of treated sewage that are now under construction in Japan are indicators of the difficulties encountered in securing adequate water sources. Japan (172) is naturally devoting thought and effort to stimulating the efficiency of industrial water use by increasing the extent to which recycling is practised. In 1958 19.6 per cent of the water used by industry was recycled and the proportion increased to 62 per cent in 1973. The capacity of waste-water recycling differs according to the scale and type of the industry concerned. For example, the recycling capacity of the iron and steel industry and the chemical industry in 1973 was 83.1 per cent; for the textile industry it was only 6.7 per cent. Thus, measures for new water sources are constantly under investigation in Japan, for example additional potential for recycling, the utilization of treated sewage, desalinated sea water, etc.

Different combinations of internal water re-use and waste recovery are being tried in the pulp and paper industry in Finland (49). Industrial production per unit of water in real terms increased in Israel (150) from $US 0.90 in 1962 to $US 1.8 in 1973. This has been mainly due to the enforcement of closed-cycle cooling systems. A great deal of interest has been evinced in conducting research on problems related to the use of water in industry, and water research in the United Kingdom (1) is partly financed by industry and partly by the Government.

The growth in the production of thermal and atomic energy has been accompanied by an increased demand for water in the USSR (121 and 126) and it is reported that in the case of ordinary thermal and atomic power stations, the total water requirements for cooling are comparable to those for irrigation. This fact brings out the importance of water even in the case of thermal and nuclear power stations.

VII. WATER FOR TRANSPORT, RECREATION, TOURISM AND CONSERVATION

A. *Transport*

The only paper on the theme of water for transport is the one presented by the United States of America (159). This underlines the need to pay greater attention in times to come to problems of water transport in the many rivers and lakes throughout the world. Water transport is of crucial importance to the economies of the land-locked countries in particular.

The many rivers, the Great Lakes and the protected coastal waters of the United States provide one of the largest and most efficient shallow-draught navigation systems in the world and it is expected that the barge operators will maintain, if not increase, their present share of traffic. A study needs to be made of the operation and maintenance of the shallow-draught system and the operation of the barge industry throughout the world and action should be taken to improve the situation in both developed and developing countries, but particularly in the latter. This is especially important in the present context of oil and energy crises, in which other modes of transportation would entail prohibitive costs.

B. Recreation, Tourism and Conservation

Here again, as in the case of water transport, the only paper is the one presented by the United States (164). This underlines the necessity for greater consideration to be given to these matters in future in the multiobjective planning of the development of water resources. The United States points out that "allocation of water to recreation, tourism and conservation of living resources should be a full partner in the planning process, along with kilowatts of hydropower, acre-feet of irrigation water, cubic feet per second of water supply or sewage dilution and minimum flow for navigation".

VIII. ENVIRONMENTAL CONSIDERATIONS

These may be considered under the following five headings:

(a) Environmental policy for water management;

(b) Industrial pollution;

(c) Regional environmental planning;

(d) Some special cases;

(e) Health considerations.

A. Environmental Policy

Environmental policy in the USSR (119) takes into consideration the impact of reservoirs on the hydrological régime, changes in the water and ground ecosystems and in the populations' social and economic living conditions. Every effort is made to ensure that the construction of reservoirs does not have undesirable consequences; increasing sums are being spent on such measures and their range is constantly being expanded. The main trends in the protection of reservoirs from surface run-off in urban areas of the Ukrainian SSR (135) are various systems of dealing with urban run-off and industrial effluents, including separate, partially separate, combined and multiple systems for the aforementioned two sources of river-water pollution.

A number of measures to this effect are being undertaken in the Ukrainian SSR (137), including legislative (regulatory) measures, state inspection, technological measures and measures for the planning of water-quality control.

Similar measures constitute the key elements of Swedish policy in the management of water quality (72); as a result, the pollution load of the waters, which are vulnerable because of the Swedish climate, has been considerably reduced. The policy is based on a system of permits, controls and State subsidies. The technological measures are far-reaching and include chemical purification as a standard requirement for municipal waste water and predominantly internal measures with respect to industrial processes.

Denmark (208 and 209) follows an integrated approach to the planning of water supply and waste-water discharge, as well as to physical planning (urban construction, industries, farm land, recreation areas, etc.). Environmental considerations in Australia (117) include such factors as eutrophication, the control of aquatic weeds, heavy materials, limological environment, collection of base-line data, etc. In the formulation of medium-term and long-term water and environmental policy, France (188) uses methods based on game-plan techniques.

The experience of Australia (109) in establishing quality criteria is of interest to many countries. In the first place the criteria serve two major purposes. They provide the basis for assessments of both the short-term and long-term consequences of any agent (pollutant) at any concentration in the aquatic environment. A second and more recent use is in the area of natural resource usage and environmental planning. At this point, it will be of interest to note that, while the establishment of criteria is considered useful in Australia, its absence is considered to have a beneficial impact in Sweden (72). This brings up the point that the principle of the establishment of criteria and the actual criteria fixed would naturally have to take into account the specific national characteristics and conditions in different countries.

B. *Industrial Pollution*

An interesting approach in the fight against pollution is reported by Finland (49), citing the typical case of the control of water pollution caused by the pulp and paper industry. There is a theoretical optimal resultant that can be regulated, involving different combinations of internal water reuse, waste recovery and the external treatment of effluents. A general model for the optimization of results is presented in the paper, along with a plea for a careful analysis of the cost-effectiveness ratio of the different measures proposed for pollution control, with priority being accorded to the method with the least cost.

Romania (44) has instituted a system that automatically monitors water quality and issues a warning in the event of accidental pollution.

Hungary (3) uses simulation models for pollution control and for the evaluation of pollution control alternatives. Pollution control is of great importance in Austria (77) in view of that country's importance as a recreational and tourist centre and its geographical situation as an up-stream country, in other words as a source of flow of surface water discharging into the Danube, the Rhine basin to the west and the Moldau to the north. Elaborate arrangements are made for the collection and treatment of waste water both from the public sewerage system and the industrial effluents.

The USSR (121, 126) reports on problems of water discharge from thermal and atomic power stations and their effect on the hydrobiology of water bodies.

Systems for cooling steam by means of combined aeration condensation equipment, methods for the purification and reuse of discharged water, "prospects for devising thermal power stations in which there is no discharge of water", using low potential thermal effluent for agricultural purposes, fish breeding and shipping and, in general, the design of hydrotechnical equipment with minimal environmental repercussions are among the trends to be seen in the efforts to protect water resources in the USSR.

The United States (97) deals with the problem of pollution from toxic substances and, in this, traces the evolution from the initial difficult attempts to list the toxics as a first step toward controlling them to the subsequent development of criteria for their identification. It is pointed out that the current concept of control is primarily built on an industry-by-industry basis rather than on a pollutant-by-pollutant basis. The fight against pollution is to be waged not only on a technological plane but also on the organizational and economic plane. The close interrelationship between the organizational, economic and technological approaches is emphasized by the USSR (123).

In the Byelorussian SSR (47) "biological purification installations are used to ensure the desired quality in waste water discharged into reservoirs in conformity with the regulations governing the protection of surface water from pollution by waste water".

In the field of technology, sophisticated techniques such as parametric modelling, as described by France (179), are being used to represent the growth of river pollution.

C. Regional Environmental Planning

A number of instances are reported of environmental planning of specific geographic regions, for example, of the Tejo estuary in Portugal (211), of the Danube river in Hungary (3) and of the Laguna de Bay basin in the Philippines (214). Both in the case of the Tejo estuary and the Laguna de Bay basin, environmental studies include protective measures including biological and ecological aspects along with the physical. Water quality studies in the Danube use simulation models.

D. Some Special Cases

Norway and Sweden (106) report an important case of long-distance transportation of air-borne pollutants, especially polluted acid precipitation. The acidity of the precipitation affects the chemical and biological conditions in fresh-water systems in southernmost Norway and in southern and western Sweden. The chemistry of the lakes and streams in the areas mentioned is influenced by the acid. There are also adverse effects on forest growth and fish production. Control of the emission of the relevant pollutants at the international and national levels is being considered as a measure to remedy the situation.

Elsewhere, the decision by Egypt (17 and 18) to construct the Aswan High Dam "was the result of thorough investigations and comprehensive studies (of the environmental impacts of the dam) conducted for several years by Egyptian engineers and experts, together with the world's most prominent dam experts and consultants".

An interesting aspect of the environmental effects of water control projects is reported from Austria (42). Extensive work on flood control, avalanches and torrent control is being undertaken there and is combined with the interests of town and country planning and environmental control. "Within the framework of area planning, alpine valleys endangered by avalanches have been divided into danger zones, where building is prohibited, zones endangered to a certain extent and safe zones." This is a good example of co-ordination between projects for planning water control and those for town and country planning.

Excessive pumping of ground water causes land subsidence in Japan (171 and 205), exceeding more than 10 centimetres per year in a place like Osaka. Controls on ground-water pumping rates are viewed as a part of the environmental protection of the regions involved.

E. Health Considerations

Although the importance of the implications of water development projects to considerations of public health are indirectly alluded to in a number of papers, a full discussion of the epidemiological considerations of drinking water and sewage disinfection is dealt with in a contribution from the Federal Republic of Germany (144). Not only has chlorination been one of the most widely used practices for the disinfection of microbiologically contaminated surface water for drinking purposes, but it is sometimes being resorted to in the treatment of sewage effluent, which is then used for recreational purposes. Recent experience is quoted to show that this cycle of chlorination (i.e. sewage effluent chlorination — river water — drinking water production with chlorination during treatment) "may give rise to epidemiological consequences, as the chlorinated organic substances may be carcinogenic. Therefore, there does exist a conflict situation, as on the one hand, chlorination of drinking water is usual and necessary to cut down the ... risk (of infection) and on the other hand may include the possibility of non-infectious epidemiological complications with regard to cancerogenity."

The rapid economic growth of Japan led to a deterioration in water quality as a result of the untreated discharge of harmful or organic substances. Such industrial effluents as mercury, cadmium, etc., were detrimental to human health and led to cases of minamata and other diseases. As a result, Japan (206) established strict standards for harmful substances such as mercury and PCB, in terms of biological accumulation rate, release from bottom deposit, diffusion in given waters and so on. As a result of these stringent over-all countermeasures against harmful substances, water quality has recovered remarkably.

IX. NATURAL HAZARDS: FLOODS, DROUGHT AND EARTHQUAKES

Ethiopia (62) divides disaster situations into two categories: instantaneous and cumulative. Both floods and drought situations can be caused either by instantaneous or cumulative factors. Earthquake situations are perhaps more instantaneous than cumulative, although their ultimate occurrence is also the final outcome of invisibly accumulative factors operative over a long period prior to their visible eruption.

A. *Floods*

Five papers deal with the flood situations. The newly-approved Unified National Programme of Flood Plain Management in the United States (107) advocates mixing flood plain occupancy and flood control strategies, treating flood control, flood insurance, flood plain regulations, flood zoning and like measures within a common management framework. Canada (156) is undertaking to prepare flood-risk maps as a basis for joint agreement on designated flood-risk areas. Zoning and other restrictions on land use are also contemplated. Stressing the economic significance of the development of flood control, Hungary (7), where 30 per cent of the population lives in flood plains, points out the importance of cost-benefit analysis based on flood damage surveys, the calculation of risk and the economic significance of flood control development.

Austria (42) is threatened by avalanches, mud flows and floods and problems of control are looked upon as components of physical planning, as mentioned in paragraph 135 above. Argentina (80) discusses its approach to the problem of controlling floods within the context of its experience in river-basin management, erosion and sedimentation.

B. *Drought*

There are two papers dealing with the problems of drought. Ethiopia (62), in this connexion, draws particular attention to the cumulative disaster that occurred in the country in 1973 and 1974. In this specific context, the technology for improving the water supply is reviewed, with a discussion of the merits of capital-intensive and labour-intensive techniques, the use of modern synthetic materials and the need for proper co-ordinated surveys and investigations of different disaster situations.

The second paper, from Australia (116), discusses the response of ground-water systems to drought. One of the advantages generally claimed for ground water is that it is more reliable in situations of drought when surface-water resources become scarce as a result of failure of rainfall. Experience in Australia is quoted to show that in some areas, aquifers react markedly to drought — for instance, by a decline in water level and yield, an increase in salinity, a reduction in base flow of streams and increased time lag in response to recharge events. In order to evaluate this response, an approach is put forward involving the concept of storage/flow ratio to determine the likely degree of effect of a drought on an aquifer. "This is the ratio of the volume of ground-water storage up-gradient of any chosen section to the flow through the section and it thus has the dimension of time. Since the relationship between storage and flow is not linear, the ratio is not constant for a given system but it is particularly useful in characterizing the ground-water flow régime." This approach is of interest to many countries which are dependent on ground-water sources, particularly to meet drought situations.

C. *Earthquakes*

An Argentinian paper (91) describes the advances made in the study and application of earthquake-resistant arrangements in Argentine dams and also refers to the use of mathematical models to study dam dynamics, the assessment of the risk of damage and the extent of seismicity brought about by the filling of reservoirs.

X. THE USE OF SHARED WATER RESOURCES

Many of the major rivers in the world are international. It is, therefore, natural that their management and development presupposes close co-operation among the countries sharing a basin. A wide variety in the form and content of international treaties and agreements for the utilization of shared water resources is reported from a number of countries in Europe, America, Asia and Africa.

Finland (53) has a treaty with Sweden dealing with the Tornio river, providing for a system of joint administration covering all the different possible kinds of use of that watercourse and dealing with the whole of the drainage area of the river. A treaty with the Soviet Union deals with utilization of the watercourses bordering the two countries and provides for a joint commission to meet regularly but infrequently to deal with questions, as they arise, relating to all the rivers and lakes of common interest. Finland also has treaties with Norway in the case of one border watercourse.

Switzerland (69) informs and consults its neighbours before entering into negotiations with them on common matters pertaining to water use, flood control and pollution control. Treaties often provide for the establishment of joint commissions, whose recommendations are adopted unanimously and are generally followed. Switzerland distinguishes between "contiguous watercourses" (that is, where a river follows an international boundary) and "successive watercourses" (that is, where a river traverses two or more countries) and points to an interesting feature which is gaining in importance in international relations, namely the principle of interstate solidarity consistent with absolute territorial sovereignty.

Citing the example of bilateral and multilateral co-operation in which it is involved, Hungary (8) draws attention to the principles of absolute territorial sovereignty, the theory of rights acquired, absolute territorial integrity, easement laws, the principle of common property/common interest and good neighbourliness and points out that co-operation in the management and development of international river basins does not conflict with the concept of absolute national sovereignty.

Yugoslavia (57) urges international co-operation in research in such fields as pollution control, nuclear contamination, disposal of thermal wastes and water management, and advocates the development of an international legal framework for international co-operation.

From the North American continent, the United States and Canada (215) report on their experiences regarding the 1909 Boundary Waters Treaty between them, in terms of which a binational body, the International Joint Commission, was set up to deal with problems that arose along the boundary, and certain rules or principles were specified to govern the Commission in the exercise of its jurisdiction. Although the examples described are unique to Canada and the United States, many of the basic principles perhaps have potential for broader application to other countries facing similar situations along their common borders.

From Asia, Bangladesh (39) presents its experience regarding the development of its water resources in the basins of the Ganges and the Brahmaputra, both of which are international. Bangladesh urges that "the United Nations and the international agencies initiate a programme of assistance and collaboration in the realization of the great potential that exists in the development and use of the waters of international rivers".

Australia (112) reports on the problems it has encountered in the use of shared water resources. These are internal problems and are not international in the usual sense. Under the federal constitution of Australia, agreements have to be drawn up among the states for the administration of interstate rivers. For instance, the Murray-Darling system rises in the states of New South Wales and Victoria, forms the boundary between them and flows into South Australia. The Australian tradition is one of "solving potential disputes by political agreements between governments, which are then followed by parallel legislation in identical terms". The River Murray Waters Agreement of 1914 is one such agreement. The powers of the Commission are examined as a case study from the standpoint of their adequacy to meet current needs. The Australian experience is of interest to other countries with federal constitutions that encounter similar internal interstate problems.

To facilitate the use of shared water resources, joint intergovernmental institutions have been set up for data collection, planning and development in a number of countries. The plans and problems reported by Liberia (14) and the establishment of the Mano River Union are examples of this effort.

Egypt (22) cites the example of the hydrometeorological survey of the catchments of Lakes Victoria, Kyoga and Mobutu-Sese-Seko, which is jointly undertaken by all the countries sharing the Nile basin (Egypt, the Sudan, Uganda, the United Republic of Tanzania, Kenya, Rwanda and Burundi, with Ethiopia as an observer and Zaire likely to join the project) as a good example of international co-operation in the utilization of the shared water resources of the Nile system. The project, in which the technical personnel of all the countries pool their efforts in the field of data collection, is a good example of the way in which regional basin-wide projects of this nature facilitate the pooling of the scarce resources of all the basin countries for their common benefit, to help them to overcome critical constraints in respect of men, material and money.

XI. EDUCATION, TRAINING AND RESEARCH

Major emphasis has been placed in the United States of America (95) on utilizing the research and educational capabilities of the nation's universities. While, in general, this coupling of programme needs with the universities' abilities has been effective, certain difficulties are reported as having been encountered, particularly concerning the level of university activities in water-related programmes. Any generalization in attempting to answer this problem seems to be hazardous and the extent of involvement of the universities should naturally be dependent on specific national situations in the different countries, but, in general, at least in the case of many developing countries, there appears to be great need for a much higher level of involvement in water development activities on the part of the universities.

The traditional activities of hydrology, namely water measurements and the obtaining of data, are no longer enough to meet today's needs. As pointed out by Spain (64), many new specialized disciplines have entered into the domain of hydrology, automatically changing the face of the "future", for instance automation, mathematical modelling, systems engineering, environmental concerns, forecasting and prediction, pollution control, internal and international water law, and exploration of the possibilities of obtaining additional supplies from non-conventional sources such as desalination, weather modification, geothermal water, etc.

Another important development is in the establishment of international institutions for training and research especially related to water management and development. For instance, France (187) is planning to establish an International Water Management Training and Research Centre to train water management officials, both French and foreign. The Centre is to be situated "on the Mediterranean coast, where a complex of high-level public and private organizations for study, teaching and research is now being developed". Argentina (78) has played a leading role in joint Latin American efforts for nearly 30 years, starting with the establishment of the first Chair of Water Law at the University of Mendoza and, recently, through the establishment in 1970 of the Institute for Water Economics, Legislation and Administration (INELA), the only institution in the region that provides instruction and training in these subjects. In-service training and applied research are valuable tools for preparing staff to work efficiently at various administrative levels.

In addition to the research content of relevant programmes, the aspect of research management has recently been coming to the fore. The organization of water research in the United Kingdom (1) represents a machine in which the Government, the independent multipurpose water authorities and other interested parties work together to conduct research in accordance with the priorities of both water users and government expenditure. The Water Research Centre in the United Kingdom is controlled by the users and financed partly by industry and partly by the Government.

XII. PROBLEMS OF TECHNOLOGY

While there is considerable scope for the application of traditional and conventional technology to the solution of the problems of water management and development in many countries of the world, there is a great need for a systematic and concerted effort to apply and develop new technologies to help in finding solutions to the problems encountered in the water-related fields. Satellite and computer technologies are examples of the application of new methods and approaches to the solution of some intractable problems.

The United States and Argentina are pressing for the application of remote sensing methods and techniques in the field of hydrology and water resources management. In the United States (163), the NIMBUS, TIROS, NOAA and GOES satellite systems and related rapid data-processing systems have made it possible to develop an improved system of weather forecasting. Remote sensing can also supply information on problems such as the degradation of the environment, resources development, the planning and monitoring of river basins, weather modification and the development of hazard warning systems. Experiments have been conducted in an area of the Pampas in Argentina (87), using LANDSAT multispectral imagery. Infra-red colour imagery from SKYLAB was used for the same region and for a region in north-west Argentina. It was observed that the differences in ground colour were closely related to the depth and salinity of ground water. Computer technology is being widely used and developed to solve the problems of data storage and retrieval in many countries. The techniques of mathematical modelling are being extensively used to solve a variety of problems, both in the assessment of surface-water and ground-water resources and in the study of pollution problems. The use of numerical models is described by France (180) for the generation of long time-series of the natural temperature of river waters. Various aspects of seismic studies have been emphasized by Argentina (84 and 91), such as the determination of a "potential maximum earthquake"; studies on dam dynamics and the extent of seismicity brought about by the filling of reservoirs.

There is an imperative need to intensify scientific and technological research relating to water and to promote regional and international co-operation in hydraulic research, as urged by Argentina (81 and 86).

Mexico (101) discusses technological progress in the water resources field and calls attention to the need for new technology to be applied to ensure more efficient water management and for appropriate technologies to be designed to maximize the extent of water exploitation, as well as the need to determine the concept and content of appropriate technologies in the field of water resources. Mexico (104) also draws attention to the need to establish stronger ties amongst the countries of the third world to assist them in their efforts to combat underdevelopment. It therefore proposes the establishment of a committee on the transfer of technology among nations, especially to the countries of the third world. This points to the need to promote adequate institutional mechanisms to facilitate an effective transfer of technology not only between the developed and the developing countries but also among the developing countries themselves, within the framework of the arrangements being considered for economic and technical co-operation among the developing countries.

XIII. POINTS FOR CONSIDERATION BY THE CONFERENCE

From the body of abstracts and those papers available at the time this document was prepared, it has been possible to identify some policy suggestions for the consideration of the Conference. In some instances what amounted to essentially the same suggestions appeared in a number of different papers, while other papers made no policy suggestions and dealt only with technical matters. In order to avoid duplication, the suggestions listed below incorporate similar ideas and, for this reason, there is no reference to specific papers.

Problems of planning. (1) Efficient national water policy and planning should be based on the objective estimation of available water resources with a view to obtaining the maximum improvement of community water supply, agricultural and industrial requirements with regard to future needs and environmental protection. A number of countries have reported the methodology and techniques they use in formulating long-term plans for river basins and continents. The laying down of some basic guidelines, principles and procedures would help in the adoption of compatible methodology.

(2) Apart from river basin planning, efforts to undertake planning for geographically homogeneous regions like coastal zones or arid regions need to be encouraged.

(3) The main guidelines of water resources development must be in agreement with prospective economic and social growth. Long-term forecasting and planning methods facilitate a comprehensive solution of water problems and the co-ordination of the development of various sectors of the economy on different levels and make it possible to take full advantage of scientific and technological achievements.

(4) In planning studies the use of mathematical models and computerized methods to take full advantage of benefits from existing development need to be encouraged, particularly in relation to the conjunctive use of surface and ground waters.

(5) Apart from legislation on individual aspects of water use and development, the present trend towards promulgating complete and comprehensive legislation in the form of a water code or water law needs to be encouraged.

Assessment of resources. (6) Methods for the estimation of available water resources using aerological observations for the computation of the atmospheric water budget need to be developed for use in connexion with large river basins, regions and continents.

(7) Available hydrological data on surface and ground waters, which is continuously being collected at the national level, should be studied and analysed by multidisciplinary teams to provide adequate information for planning purposes and should be updated on a routine and continuous basis.

(8) In the case of surface and ground waters, an assessment is needed of present and potential use for different purposes, in addition to an assessment of economically exploitable resources.

(9) The assessment of resources should be improved by using modern means such as remote sensing, nuclear and geophysical methods, etc.

(10) In the case of ground waters, intensive work needs to be carried out on economical methods of artificial replenishment and of locating ground waters in fractured zones in hard rocks.

(11) Mineral and thermal waters need to be inventoried in the different countries which possess such resources and their industrial potential, in addition to their potential for use as spas, needs to be studied and developed.

(12) Work needs to be intensified on less costly methods of drawing on non-conventional sources of water, such as desalinated sea water or brackish water, and induced precipitation.

(13) The development of forecasting methods is of particular importance for developing countries and should be included as part of quantitative and qualitative assessment of water resources.

(14) Effective decision-making methods in the management of water quality should be based on techniques of natural water quality regulation that have been proved in practice and should be based on uniform methods and standard equipment for measuring characteristics of water quality and quantity.

(15) The establishment of quality criteria should take into account the specific national characteristics and conditions in different countries.

Assessment of needs. (16) There is a need to rationalize the basis of estimates of needs with a view to facilitating a greater measure of compatibility.

(17) A methodology for the management of demand needs to be evolved, refined and adopted, using such concepts as "supply restriction indices", "shortage tolerances", "risk indices", etc.

Community water supply. (18) Some countries have reorganized their water supply arrangements so as to strengthen the financial and management basis of metropolitan and urban water supplies, use water effectively, reduce losses, equalize water prices over wide areas and reduce water costs. New concepts are being developed, such as the use of advanced water treatment techniques, for example carbon absorption and ozonation, the utilization of low quality sources and the reuse of waste water for purposes such as toilet flushing. These trends (reorganization and the use of new concepts) need to be encouraged, where they are found to be necessary and desirable.

(19) Rural water supply projects and programmes for implementing them on a priority basis are being undertaken in some countries and should be encouraged in others to achieve the targets in the field of community water supplies set by Habitat: United Nations Conference on Human Settlements.

(20) The planning of community water supplies should envisage sanitary norms and drinking water standards fixed by the respective countries, protective measures against diseases, the organization of medical control, and skilled service for water supply and treatment works.

The use of water in agriculture. (21) In the strategy for the development of new irrigation facilities, a judicious combination of major, medium and minor schemes appears desirable.

(22) A more efficient use of water per unit of agricultural product is desirable.

(23) In the execution of schemes to combat salinity and waterlogging, economic and policy issues need to be taken into account in the planning procedures and the affected farmers need to be involved in the planning and implementation of schemes.

(24) Soil and water conservation measures are to be undertaken within the framework of integrated land and water management for increasing agricultural production.

The use of water for hydropower generation. (25) In addition to the undertaking of new hydropower projects, efforts are needed to optimize power generation from existing hydro projects by improved reservoir regulation.

The use of water in industry. (26) The recycling and reuse of water for industrial purposes should be practised to the fullest extent possible taking into account the scale and type of the industry; this is true even for industrial units where some degree of recycling is already practised.

(27) Water-saving technologies are to be encouraged in order to minimize the use of water in industry.

Water for transport. (28) A study needs to be made of the operation and maintenance of the shallow-draught system and the operation of the barge industry and action should be taken to improve the situation.

Water for recreation, tourism and conservation. (29) In the planning of water projects, greater consideration needs to be given to the interests of recreation, tourism and the conservation of living resources.

Environmental considerations. (30) The range of environmental considerations at present receiving attention in relation to water projects needs to be expanded in order to become more comprehensive and include not only physical, chemical or biological changes, but also the resulting social and economic changes.

(31) In combating industrial pollution, a careful analysis needs to be made of the cost-effectiveness ratio of the different measures proposed for pollution control and priority accorded to the method entailing the least cost.

(32) To mitigate adverse environmental repercussions of water discharge from thermal and atomic power stations, cooling systems and hydrotechnical design practices and procedures need to be improved to reduce potential hazards.

(33) Studies need to be undertaken to evaluate the best possible approach to controlling pollution on an industry-by-industry or pollutant-by-pollutant basis, in accordance with national requirements in the light of the nature and level of industrial development.

(34) Techniques like simulation, parametric modelling and computerized analysis need to be developed to facilitate solutions to problems in the field of pollution control.

(35) Environmental planning is being undertaken not only at the national or river-basin level but also at the level of specific geographic regions such as estuaries, coastal zones, etc., wherever such an approach is warranted by the nature of the problems inherent in such regional development. This should be done not only in relation to water projects in isolation, but in close liaison with other related activities like town and country planning or regional development.

(36) In dealing with problems of public health, a careful evaluation is needed of potential conflict situations such as the chlorination of sewage effluents and the chlorination of drinking water production so that epidemiological consequences are avoided.

(37) With relation to the long-distance transportation of air-borne pollution, especially acid precipitation, the different approaches to the control of the emission of relevant pollutants should be considered, bearing in mind the available range of technical solutions.

Natural hazards. (38) In the mitigation of flood loss, balanced consideration must be given to structural measures such as dikes and levees and also to non-structural measures like flood plain regulations, flood zoning, the preparation of flood-risk maps, flood insurance, etc. and measures for upstream watershed management should be integrated into the over-all flood control plans.

(39) In the assessment of the response of ground-water systems to drought, the effect of drought on aquifers needs to be determined, based on concepts like the storage/flow ratio, in order to characterize the ground-water flow régime in periods of drought.

(40) In seismic areas, earthquake-resistant arrangements for dams and other hydraulic structures must be duly provided in order to minimize the risk of damage. An assessment should also be made of the extent of potential seismicity brought about by the filling of reservoirs.

Education, training, research and technology. (41) National universities need to be more heavily involved in water development, but the actual level of involvement in each country should depend upon the specific features, characteristics and needs of the national situation.

(42) It is important that greater use be made of existing international institutions specifically dealing with water management and administration to impart education and training to water management officials from different countries throughout the world.

(43) Maximum use should be made of new technologies like remote sensing, computer technology, etc., to help countries to survey, explore and develop their water resources.

(44) There is an imperative need to promote greater co-ordination in the field of water resources research, including the design of appropriate technology, the adaptation of technology and an effective transfer of technology both between the developed and developing countries and among the developing countries themselves.

ANNEX I

MEMBERS OF THE INTERGOVERNMENTAL WORKING GROUP CONVENED BY THE SECRETARY-GENERAL OF THE UNITED NATIONS WATER CONFERENCE

Argentina	Juan Eduardo Fleming, First Secretary, Permanent Mission of Argentina to the United Nations
India	E. C. Saldanha, Member (Planning and Progress), Central Water Commission, New Delhi
Japan	Takashi Kuramata, Associate Director, Senior Researcher, Nomura Research Institute, Social and Economic Systems Department, Kamakura
Sweden	Malin Falkenmark, Ministry of Agriculture
Union of Soviet Socialist Republics	Boris V. Smirnov, First Secretary, Permanent Mission of the Union of Soviet Socialist Republics to the United Nations
United States of America	Frank Thomas, Professor of Geography, Georgia State University, Atlanta
Venezuela	José Luis Mendez-Arocha, Executive Secretary, Water Commission, National Development Plan

Mar del Plata Action Plan:

RECOMMENDATIONS

A. *Assessment of Water Resources*

In most countries there are serious inadequacies in the availability of data on water resources, particularly in relation to ground water and water quality. Hitherto, relatively little importance has been attached to its systematic measurement. The processing and compilation of data have also been seriously neglected.

> **To improve the management of water resources, greater knowledge about their quantity and quality is needed. Regular and systematic collection of hydrometeorological, hydrological and hydrogeological data needs to be promoted and be accompanied by a system for processing quantitative and qualitative information for various types of water bodies. The data should be used to estimate available precipitation, surface-water and ground-water resources and the potentials for augmenting these resources. Countries should review, strengthen and co-ordinate arrangements for the collection of basic data. Network densities should be improved; mechanisms for data collection, processing and publication and arrangement for monitoring water quality should be reinforced.**

To this end, it is recommended that countries should:

(a) Establish a national body with comprehensive responsibilities for water-resources data, or allocate existing functions in a more co-ordinated way, and establish data banks for the systematic collection, processing, storage and dissemination of data in agreed formats and at specified intervals of time;

(b) Expand and extend the network of hydrological and meteorological stations, taking a long-term view of future needs, following as far as possible the recommendations of the United Nations specialized agencies on standardization of instruments and techniques and comparability of data, and use existing meteorological and hydrological data series for the study of seasonal and annual fluctuations in climate and water resources. Such analysis could also be used in the planning and design of networks;

(c) Establish observation networks and strengthen existing systems and facilities for measurements and recording fluctuations in ground-water quality and level; organize the collection of all existing data on ground water (borehole logs, geological structure, and hydrogeological characteristics, etc.) systematically index such data, and attempt a quantitative assessment so as to

---

General note. Many recommendations for action contain references to national or country action, organization, policies and legislation. A number of countries with federal systems of government interpret such recommendations in the light of their constitutional division of responsibilities. Actions, organization, policies and legislation in these countries accordingly will be taken at the appropriate level of government.

determine the present status of and gaps in knowledge; increase the search for, and determination of, the variables of aquifers, with an evaluation of their potential and the possibilities of recharge;

(d) Standardize and organize as far as possible the processing and publication of data so as to keep the statistics up to date and take advantage of the observations made in stations operated by different institutions;

(e) Include consideration of diseases associated with water as an integral part of water assessments and the consideration of the interrelationships of water quality, quantity and related land use;

(f) Make periodic assessments of surface- and ground-water resources, including rainfall, evaporation and run-off, lakes, lagoons, glaciers and snowfields, both for individual basins and at the national level, in order to determine a programme of investigation for the future in relation to development needs; intensify programmes already under way and formulate new programmes wherever needed;

(g) Provide the means for national mechanisms so established to use, as appropriate, modern technologies (remote sensing, nuclear methods, geophysical techniques, analogue and mathematical models) in collecting, retrieving and processing data on the quantity or quality of water resources; manual data-processing methods may still satisfy the simple requirements of small collections, although it may be necessary to introduce various degrees of automation, ranging from small punch-card machines to large electronic computing systems;

(h) Standardize measurement techniques and instruments, and automate stations as appropriate; reference should be made to international standards and recommendations adopted by Governments through various international organizations;

(i) Support and promote national contributions to regional and international programmes on hydrological studies (e.g. the International Hydrological Programme and Operational Hydrological Programme);

(j) Co-operate in the co-ordination, collection and exchange of relevant data in the case of shared resources;

(k) Appropriate substantially increased financial resources for activities related to water resources assessment and to establish or strengthen related institutions and services as necessary;

(l) Establish or strengthen training programmes and facilities for meteorologists, hydrologists and hydrogeologists at professional and subprofessional levels;

(m) Prepare an inventory of mineral and thermal waters in countries possessing such resources with a view to studying and developing their industrial potential as well as their use as spas;

(n) Develop methods for the estimation of available water resources using aerological observations for the computation of the atmospheric water budget in large river basins, rivers and continents;

(o) Provide for the studying and analysing of hydrological data on surface and ground water by multidisciplinary teams so as to make adequate information available for planning purposes;

(p) Include the development of forecasting methods in quantitative and qualitative assessment, especially in the developing countries;

(q) Include effective decision-making methods in the management of water quality, based on techniques of natural quality regulation that have been proved in practice;

(r) Take specific national characteristics and conditions into account in different countries in assessing water quality and establishing water-quality criteria.

International organizations and other supporting bodies should, as appropriate, and on request, take the following action:

(a) Surface water

(i) Offer technical assistance, at the request of interested Governments, to review the adequacy of existing networks and make available the use of advanced techniques such as remote sensing;

(ii) Offer technical assistance, including personnel, funds, equipment and training, to strengthen the networks and to establish laboratories for comprehensive water analysis;

(iii) Offer assistance and facilities for the establishment of data banks, processing and periodic publication of data by modern methods of electronic data processing, archiving and retrieval;

(iv) Help in making qualitative and quantitative assessments of surface-water resources, both gross and economically usable quantities, for different sectoral uses;

(v) Strengthen, in general, technical assistance programmes for the development of integrated national data systems.

(b) Ground water

(i) Offer assistance for the establishment or strengthening of observational networks for recording quantitative and qualitative characteristics of ground-water resources;

(ii) Offer assistance for the establishment of ground-water data banks and for reviewing the studies, locating gaps and formulating programmes of future investigations and prospection;

(iii) Offer help, including personnel and equipment, to make available the use of advanced techniques, such as geophysical methods, nuclear techniques, mathematical models, etc.

(c) Snow and ice

Advise on international standards and the establishment of observation networks regarding snow and ice in order to permit international exchange of this information, especially concerning international rivers.

B. Water Use and Efficiency

In many areas of the world, water is wasted or used in excess of actual needs. Often water is not used efficiently for agricultural purposes owing to losses in transit, unsuitable irrigation systems or lack of institutional co-ordination. Since irrigation is the principal water user in a great many countries, and since water and land capable of being cultivated are becoming increasingly scarce, there is a special need to achieve greater efficiency in the use of both these resources. At the same time, there is an imperative need in some regions to increase total agricultural production and productivity in order to increase food production. Furthermore, a large portion of the world's population does not have reasonable access to safe water supply and lacks hygienic waste-disposal facilities. In urban and industrial areas, the provision of adequate facilities and services for treatment of wastes generally lags behind the provision of water supplies, with consequent problems in water-quality management. In many parts of the world only a small part of the potential for hydroelectric power generation has been developed, even though the utilization of these resources may, in many cases, be very attractive as a result of the world energy situation. The growth of population also calls for ever larger areas for recreation and fisheries. In many regions, rivers also constitute one of the main means of communication and the potential for inland water transport should be developed. The value of inland water resources for food production should be recognized as important to protein supply.

Instruments to improve the efficiency of water use

Since water is a limited and valuable resource and since its development requires high investment, its use must be efficient and must secure the highest possible level of national welfare.

> **Effective legislation should be framed to promote the efficient and equitable use and protection of water and water-related ecosystems. Pricing and other economic incentives should be used to promote the efficient and equitable use of water.**

To this end it is recommended that national institutions for water resource management should:

(a) Carry out research studies on the actual and potential quantities of water to be used by the various sectors, and encourage effective application of the results of these studies;

(b) Create incentives for increasing the efficiency of water use, such as financial assistance by Governments or credits for the adoption of new technologies, and introduce where appropriate scales of charges that reflect the real economic cost of water or that rationalize subsidies within the framework of a sound water policy;

(c) Evolve appropriate procedures for economic methods of reusing and recycling water, and where relevant introduce dual water systems for drinking and other uses;

(d) Enforce clear punitive arrangements to encourage the reduction or elimination of contaminant discharges which do not conform to standards, and provide adequate powers of applying deterrents and punishments;

(e) Promote, and develop by means of suitable incentives and appropriate policies, the efficiency of waste-water purification systems and the adoption of less polluting technologies;

(f) Take measures to encourage the use in productive activities of technologies which consume little water or which reuse it;

(g) Because water is a valuable and scarce resource deliberate administrative policies should be established, such as measuring supplies, licensing diversions, charging for water and penalizing wasteful and polluting acts;

(h) Encourage the use of associations of water users or other local community organizations to instil a collective responsibility in the decision-making process for the programming, financing and care in the use of water;

(i) Use school programmes and all public media to disseminate information concerning proper water use practices.

Efficiency and efficacy in regulation and distribution of the resources

National mechanisms for the management of water resources should apply the best measures to improve the existing systems and the best available techniques for planning and design of conservation and distribution systems in the most efficient way and should equally attend to proper maintenance, control at the regional, national and farm level and operation of delivery systems to increase efficiency.

To this end, it is recommended that:

(a) Measures be taken to utilize ground-water aquifers in the form of collective and integrated systems, whenever possible and useful, taking into account the regulation and use of surface-water resources. This will provide an opportunity to exploit the ground-water aquifers to their physical limits, to protect spring and ground water from overdraught and salinity, as well as to ensure proper sharing of the resources;

(b) Studies should explore the potential of ground-water basins, the use of aquifers as storage and distribution systems, and the conjunctive use of surface and subsurface resources to maximize efficacy and efficiency;

(c) Systems analysis and modelling techniques should be applied to improve efficiency and efficacy in storage operation and distribution systems;

(d) Studies should explore further the possibility of effecting interbasin transfers of water; special attention should be given to environmental impact studies;

(e) Measures should be taken to ensure systematic planning of the distribution of water among the various users as a prerequisite for full and rational utilization of the volume of water available for exploitation;

(f) Programmes should be strengthened for the dissemination of existing information and experience;

(g) Studies should explore the extent to which new effluents generated from new demands will effectively reduce the scale of projected resource development.

Measurement and projections of water demand

In many countries no systematic measurements are being made for planning purposes concerning the use and consumption of water by sectors. The absence of this information has hampered the use of more sophisticated methods of estimating future requirements. Where projections have been made they have not been based on uniform norms or comparable methodologies.

In order to project future water needs it is desirable to have data on use and consumption and quality by type of user and also the information necessary to estimate the effect of the application of different policy instruments (tariffs, taxes, etc.) in influencing the various areas of demand. The demand for water for different purposes should be estimated at different periods of time in conformity with national development goals to provide the basis and the perspective for the planned development of available water resources.

To this end, it is recommended that national bodies responsible for water resource management should:

(a) Initiate action to estimate the demand for water for different purposes, e.g., community water supply, agriculture, industry hydroelectricity, etc.;

(b) Ensure that statistics on the use and consumption of water should be organized, improved and amplified on the basis of those prepared by the existing services, supplemented by censuses, surveys, etc.; censuses on productive activities should include information on volumes of water used, sources of supply, coefficients of reuse, and quality data;

(c) Identify the targets to be achieved over different periods of time, taking into consideration the anticipated population growths, and the priority to be given in such matters as the number of people to be served with reasonable access to safe water supply; areas to be irrigated under different crops, and specific production per unit of water; and the units of hydropower to be installed to satisfy anticipated demand;

(d) Endeavour, as far as is practicable, to adopt the norms and methodologies recommended by the United Nations in making such demand projections;

(e) Base their approach to long-term demand estimates on the use of methodologies involving models which include the population and population location variable. In this context, countries should also take into account an evaluation of the over-all demand for water-consuming basic goods and services on the part of the population;

(f) Consider conservation as an explicit policy, bearing in mind changes in demand, water-use practices, lifestyles and settlement patterns;

(g) Evolve appropriate methodology for the management of demand, using suitable concepts, such as "risk indices".

International organizations and other supporting bodies should, as appropriate, assist, at the request of countries or subregional intergovernmental organizations, in the drawing up of demand projections for countries as well as for river basins in accordance with the commonly accepted norms and techniques.

Community water supply and waste disposal

In order to implement recommendation C. 12 of Habitat: United Nations Conference on Human Settlements,* the decade 1980-1990 should be designated the international drinking water supply and sanitation decade and should be devoted to implementing the national plans for drinking water supply and sanitation in accordance with the plan of action contained in resolution II below. This implementation will require a concerted effort by countries and the international community to ensure a reliable drinking-water supply and provide basic sanitary facilities to all urban and rural communities on the basis of specific targets to be set up by each country, taking into account its sanitary, social and economic conditions.

To this end it is recommended that countries should:

(a) Set targets for community water supply and waste disposal and formulate specific action programmes to attain them, while evaluating the progress made at regular intervals;

---

*Report of Habitat: *United Nations Conference on Human Settlements* (United Nations publication, Sales No.: E.76.IV.7), chap. II; see also *Habitat in Retrospect*, Margaret R. Biswas, *International Journal of Environmental Studies*, January, 1978.

(b) Establish standards of quality and quantity that are consistent with the public health, economic and social policies of Governments, ensuring by appropriate measures, duly applied, that those standards are observed;

(c) Ensure the co-ordination of community water-supply and waste-disposal planning with over-all water planning and policy as well as with over-all economic development;

(d) Adopt policies for the mobilization of users and local labour in the planning, financing, construction, operation and maintenance of projects for the supply of drinking water and the disposal of waste water;

(e) Consider carefully inequalities in the standard of drinking water and sewerage services among the various sectors of the population. As far as possible, design programmes so as to provide basic requirements for all communities as quickly as possible, generally deferring the provision of improved services to a subsequent stage. Priority should be given to the provision of drinking water and sewerage services in areas where the quality and quantity of water supplied is inadequate, for instance, in rural areas and urban fringe areas populated by low-income groups;

(f) Ensure that the allocation of funds, of other resources and of all forms of economic incentives to community water-supply and sanitation programmes reflects the urgency of the needs and the proportion of the population affected;

(g) Promote the construction of facilities by granting low-interest loans or subsidies to communities and to other entities concerned with water supply and sanitation;

(h) Provide, where needed, additional well-drilling capability or other equipment for the establishment of local drinking-water supply facilities;

(i) Review the organizational infrastructure for community water supply and sanitation and set up, where it is considered appropriate, a separate department for this purpose;

(j) Prepare long-term plans and specific projects with detailed financial implications;

(k) Develop a financing system capable of mobilizing the resources needed for the implementation of the national programme for water supply and sanitation, as well as for the operation and maintenance of these services, for instance, by a system of revolving funds to ensure continued financial support for the execution of long-term programmes. This system should make it possible to bridge the gap between production costs and payment capacities;

(l) Provide mutual assistance in the transfer and application of technologies associated with these programmes;

(m) Carry out special water-supply and waste-treatment programmes as national or regional undertakings or as activities of non-profit organizations, such as users' associations, where local resources do not make it possible to achieve the desired goals;

(n) Adopt pricing policies and other incentives to promote the efficient use of water and the reduction of waste water, while taking due account of social objectives;

(o) Seek to promote in rural areas with low population density, where it seems appropriate, individual water-supply and waste-water disposal systems, taking account of sanitary requirements;

(p) Carry out a programme of health education, parallel with the development of community water supply and sanitation, in order to heighten the people's awareness with respect to health;

(q) Establish, at the national level, training programmes to meet immediate and future needs for supervisory staff;

(r) Provide inventory and protection of water-supply sources;

(s) Provide additional facilities and possibilities for drinking water supply during natural hazards;

(t) Use water effectively, reduce losses, equalize water prices by purposes for which the water is used over wide areas and reduce water costs due to reorganization models of some countries' water-supply arrangements so as to strengthen the financial management basis of supplies in metropolitan, urban and rural areas. Develop new concepts, such as the use of advanced water-treatment techniques, the utilization of low-quality sources and the re-use of waste water. These trends (reorganization and the use of new concepts) need to be encouraged where they are found to be necessary and desirable. Rural water-supply projects and programmes for implementing them on a priority basis are being undertaken in some countries and should be encouraged in others to achieve the targets in the field of community water supplies set by Habitat: United Nations Conference on Human Settlements.

International organizations and other supporting bodies should, as appropriate, and on request, take the following action:

(i) Provide technical assistance to countries in the preparation of long-term plans and specific projects;

(ii) Consider adapting their criteria for financial assistance in accordance with the economic and social conditions prevailing in the recipient countries;

(iii) Promote research, development and demonstration projects for reducing the costs of urban and rural water-supply and waste-disposal facilities;

(iv) Promote public health education;

(v) Support research, development and demonstration in relation to predominant needs, particularly: (a) Low-cost ground-water pumping equipment; (b) Low-cost water and waste-water treatment processes and equipment, with emphasis on the use of materials and skills likely to be available to rural communities for installation, operation and maintenance;

(vi) Strengthen the exchange of information, *inter alia*, by arranging expert meetings, and development of a clearing-house mechanism.

Agricultural water use

The increase of agricultural production and productivity should be aimed at achieving optimum yield in food production by a definite date, and at a significant improvement in total agricultural production as early as possible. Measures to attain these objectives should receive the appropriate high priority. Particular attention should be given to land and water management both under irrigated and rainfed cultivation, with due regard to long-term as well as short-term productivity. National legislation and policies should provide for the properly integrated management of land and water resources. Countries should, when reviewing national policies, institutions and legislation, ensure the co-ordination of activities and services involved in irrigation and drainage

development and management. It is necessary to expand the use of water for agriculture together with an improvement in efficiency of use. This should be achieved through funding, providing the necessary infrastructure and reducing losses in transit, in distribution and on the farm, and avoiding the use of wasteful irrigation practices, to the extent possible. Each country should apply known techniques for the prevention and control of land and water degradation resulting from improper management. Countries should give early attention to the improvement of existing irrigation and drainage projects.

In this context, countries should:

(a) Bear in mind principles of integrated land and water management when reviewing national policies, administrative arrangements and legislation, and pay heed to the need to augment present levels of agricultural production;

(b) Undertake or continue studies on the relationship between land use and the elements of the hydrological cycle at the national and international levels;

(c) Consider appropriate incentives such as safeguarding water rights for farmers and encourage holders of irrigated land to adopt management practices compatible with long-term resource management requirements;

(d) Plan and carry out irrigation programmes in such a way as to ensure that surface and subsurface drainage are treated as integral components and that provision of all requirements is co-ordinated with a view to optimizing the use of water and associated land resources;

(e) Provide financial resources and qualified manpower services for better water-use and management practices, proper maintenance, control and operation of distribution systems, and joint use of surface and ground water and eventually waste water, paying due attention to the needs of small-scale agriculture;

(f) Intensify work on determining crop-water requirements, integrate schemes for swamp reclamation and drainage in schemes for comprehensive river development, bearing in mind their effect on hydrological régime and the environment; give due attention to problems of salinity intrusion, particularly in coastal areas, and integrate measures for salinity control;

(g) Give attention to problems of soil and water conservation through good management of watershed areas which includes a rational crop distribution, improvement of pastures, reforestation, avalanche and torrent control, as well as the introduction of appropriate agricultural soil conservation practices, taking into account the economic and social conditions existing in the respective watershed areas;

(h) Adopt appropriate pricing policies with a view to encouraging efficient water use, and finance operation and maintenance costs with due regard to social objectives;

(i) Adopt appropriate measures for instructing and encouraging water users in efficient animal or farm husbandry and farm management. Particular attention should be paid to groups not reached by formal education;

(j) Take steps to complete irrigation and drainage projects currently under construction as expeditiously as possible, so that benefits on past investment accrue without delay;

(k) Take related health and environmental aspects into account in the planning and management of agricultural water use.

To this end it is recommended that:

(a) The institutional machinery responsible for water management should possess sufficient means and powers for the management of water for agricultural purposes, bearing in mind the physical interdependence of surface and ground water and in accordance with all its uses;

(b) Measures should be adopted for the supervision and control of water distribution and use, taking into account livestock and irrigated crop farming needs in keeping with the type of crop, soil and zone, the level of agricultural technology which can be attained, and the risk of soil erosion and salination of the soil and water, with the adoption, as far as possible, of arrangements to measure the amount of water supplied;

(c) The main cause of waste in the use of water should be identified and corrected, but also the limitations on the adoptions of sophisticated — even if more efficient — irrigation methods should be taken into consideration;

(d) Steps should be taken to increase the efficiency of water use in existing irrigation systems by improving watercourses, land levelling and improving water management on farms and in distributaries;

(e) Irrigation plans should be formulated (preferably by stages) which coordinate the implementation of the infrastructure with rural development and the promotion of suitable technology, *inter alia*, control of water-associated disease; the improved management of soils; the introduction of new species; and provision for the training of personnel and the use of the necessary technical assistance;

(f) Agricultural practices that will regulate the run-off in humid areas should be promoted, particularly where periods of heavy rains alternate with periods of drought, with a view to improving the efficiency of measures against flooding and achieving better organization and regulation of water supplies;

(g) Irrigation projects should be based on detailed soil investigations and consequent land classification;

(h) More attention should be given to procedures for more effective utilization of water at the village level, such as through better irrigation practices, the appropriate use of mulch for kitchen gardens as well as cash crops, and where feasible, the use of companion cropping. These and other measures can extend the responsible use of water, improve agricultural production and nutrition, and ease the onerous conditions of agricultural labour of special importance to the rural women, on whom so many burdens fall;

(i) In the strategy for the development of new irrigation facilities, a judicious combination of major, medium and minor schemes would be desirable;

(j) A more efficient use of water per unit of agricultural product is desirable;

(k) In the execution of schemes to combat salinity and waterlogging, economic and policy issues need to be taken into account in the planning procedures and the affected farmers need to be involved in the planning and implementation of schemes;

(l) High priority should be given to the adoption of urgent measures for soil and water conservation within the framework of integrated land and water management in order to increase agricultural production without destroying those resources.

International organizations and other supporting bodies should, as appropriate, and on request, take the following action:

(i) Assist countries in the preparation of master plans and programmes and definitive project reports on the use of water in agriculture, including land use, irrigation, dry farming techniques, drainage, flood control, salinity intrusion, swamp reclamation and soil and water conservation;

(ii) Strengthen the exchange of information, *inter alia*, through the organization of expert and other meetings.

Fisheries

Plans for the use of water resources and for territorial development should take into account the use of water for fisheries, in order to increase the supply of proteins to the world population.

To this end it is recommended that countries should:

(a) Protect, conserve and exploit rationally their fisheries resources, avoiding the effects of natural or human pollution and co-ordinating the relevant regulations with interested countries sharing water resources;

(b) Develop research and information dissemination programmes concerning fisheries;

(c) Promote intensive fisheries activities including aquaculture by establishing the needed additional infrastructures and facilities, at the same time avoiding the introduction of unsuitable species into the local ecosystem;

(d) Where a reasonable cost-benefit ratio is expected make provision for fish passage facilities and other actions needed to avoid damage to aquatic systems, as initial elements of project design and funding;

(e) Regulate, restrict or prohibit the use of certain polluting substances, especially toxic and organoleptic substances, to prevent their entry into waters. These measures are required to protect human health and the aquatic ecosystems upon which life is dependent.

International organizations and other supporting bodies should, as appropriate, and on request, take the following action:

(i) Assist countries in preparing plans, programmes and facilities for the protection, development and utilization of fishery resources in connexion with water resources development in order to augment world protein supplies;

(ii) Assist countries in research and information dissemination programmes in support of increasing fishery production;

(iii) Assist countries in controlling toxic and other pollutants damaging to aquatic systems and to human health.

Industrial water use

In many countries problems associated with the use of water in industry need to be studied in greater depth and in a more systematic and comprehensive manner than hitherto, in both their quantitative and their qualitative aspects, including questions of input and output quality, level of treatment required, if any, and recycling of water. These matters may be crucial to the attainment of industrialization targets in the developing countries.

To this end it is recommended that countries should:

(a) Initiate studies on the present and potential use of water by specific industries, including such aspects as recycling, substitution for and reduction of water inputs and use of low-quality waters for cooling and waste management;

(b) Make an assessment of factors relating to the quality and quantity of water and industrial wastes as important criteria in decision-making on industrial locations within the framework of land-use planning;

(c) Evolve appropriate procedures for economic methods of re-using and recycling water, including corrective treatment for industries, and explore the possibilities for using waters of qualities commensurate with the purposes for which they are needed;

(d) Take into account the water requirements of industries in the planning and formulation of water-development projects, paying due attention to the necessary safeguards against adverse health and environmental impacts arising from industrial activities and to the needs of small-scale and rural industries;

(e) Include waste treatment or other appropriate measures to eliminate or reduce pollution as an integral part of municipal and industrial water-supply systems;

(f) Provide stimulating investments and other economic incentives and regulations to use water efficiently, to treat wastes at their source and, where advantageous, jointly with domestic waste;

(g) Adopt the necessary measures to ensure that the use and disposal of effluents is consistent with the requirements of health and environmental quality;

(h) Carry out a policy aimed at promoting research and the establishment of industrial technologies that use little water and produce little or no waste and also of technical processes for the recovery of usable substances in waste waters;

(i) Take note of the targets and recommendations of the Lima Declaration and Plan of Action on Industrial Development and Co-operation evolved at the Second General Conference of the United Nations Industrial Development Organization in 1975, which should greatly expand use of water by industry in certain countries.

International organizations and other supporting bodies should, as appropriate, and on request, take the following action:

(i) Assist countries in making an assessment of water requirements for industrial purposes in the different countries, subregions and river basins, and evolve economical methods for the re-use and recycling of water, where necessary;

(ii) Strengthen programmes for the exchange of information, *inter alia*, by arranging expert and other meetings;

(iii) Support or arrange research and study programmes, particularly in relation to pricing policy and also methods of water and waste-water treatment which are conducive to a reduction in cost of treating effluents;

(iv) Evolve a common international statistical data base that will relate water use, particularly the effects of water quality available, to process technologies, and the degree of re-use and recycling.

Hydroelectric power generation

In the formulation of plans for the development of the electricity sector, it is necessary to give attention in all cases to the advantages offered by multi-purpose hydroelectric projects, including pumped storage, that ensure the continued enjoyment of this renewable resource without serious damage to health and the environment.

To this end it is recommended that countries should:

(a) Make national inventories of potential hydroelectric projects to be promoted and supplemented with a view to determining which projects, because of their characteristics, can satisfy electricity and water-flow demands on a long-term basis;

(b) Undertake studies on the multiple and integrated development of the water resources in watersheds with hydroelectric potential;

(c) Integrate plans for the development of hydropower generation with the over-all development plans for both the energy and water sectors, taking into account the potential savings in foreign exchange which can accrue therefrom;

(d) Evaluate the impact of the non-consumptive use of water for power generation on other consumptive uses in order to harmonize the two aspects of water use;

(e) Prepare detailed project reports for specific projects to facilitate their financing;

(f) Collect data on the present and future use of water for power generation, so that this aspect of power development can become an integral component of multipurpose river basin development;

(g) Include in studies on the assessment and feasibility of hydroelectric projects potential tourism, recreational, ecological and psychological benefits, for commercial and social purposes, as well as their multiplier effect on the national economy;

(h) Encourage small-scale hydroelectric installation to meet local energy needs, whenever economically, environmentally and socially acceptable;

(i) Give consideration to pumped storage hydroelectric projects as a source of peaking power;

(j) In addition to the undertaking of new hydropower projects, optimize power generation from existing hydro-projects by improved reservoir regulation.

International organizations and other supporting bodies should, as appropriate, and on request, take the following action:

(i) Assist in preparing long-term plans for utilizing the potential for power development in river basins in the different countries;

(ii) Assist in preparing definite project reports to help Governments in seeking investment finance for specific projects;

(iii) Promote the elaboration of detailed load surveys at the national and subregional levels and in individual river basins.

Inland navigation

Plans for the use of water resources and for territorial development should take account of the use of water for inland navigation consistent with other objectives of multipurpose development and with special regard to the needs of land-locked countries.

To this end it is recommended that countries should:

(a) Carry out studies which include the use of rivers and the modernization of port installation and shipping equipment as an integral part of combined regional land and water transport systems, taking into consideration the needs of the land-locked countries;

(b) Ensure in programmes of comprehensive and integrated multipurpose river basin development, the design and maintenance or improvement of navigation systems which are based upon consideration of the special hydraulic and other technical requirements necessary to efficient inland navigation;

(c) Maintain programmes for the collection of hydrometeorological data in river basins used for navigation in order to provide adequate systems for prediction of water levels;

(d) Adopt regulations which make it compulsory to instal equipment in ships to avoid the discharge of untreated organic and chemical effluents into the water and to construct installations in ports to receive and treat tank and bilge wastes. Furthermore, the dumping of radio-active wastes should be prohibited;

(e) Ensure that all vessels transporting oil or hazardous substances comply with the highest safety standards so that accidental spills may be avoided to the greatest extent possible. Severe penalties for non-compliance are necessary.

International organizations and other supporting bodies should, as appropriate, and on request, take the following action:

(i) Assist countries in preparing plans, programmes and projects for inland water transport, especially taking into consideration the needs of the land-locked countries;

(ii) Assist countries in the construction of basic facilities such as navigation channels and locks and the maintenance of waterways, mapping, navigation charts, etc.;

(iii) Assist countries in building up the requisite technology within the countries.

C. *Environment, Health and Pollution Control*

Large-scale water-development projects have important environmental repercussions of a physical, chemical, biological, social and economic nature, which should be evaluated and taken into consideration in the formulation and implementation of water projects. Furthermore, water-development projects may have unforeseen adverse consequences affecting human health in addition to those associated with the use of water for domestic purposes. Water pollution from sewage and industrial effluents and the use of chemical fertilizers and pesticides in agriculture is on the increase in many countries. It is also recognized that control measures regarding the discharge of urban, industrial and mining effluents are inadequate. Increased emphasis must be given to the question of water pollution, within the over-all context of waste management.

Environment and health

It is necessary to evaluate the consequences which the various uses of water have on the environment, to support measures aimed at controlling water-related diseases, and to protect ecosystems.

To this end it is recommended that countries should:

(a) Review the implementation of the recommendations of the 1972 United Nations Conference on the Human Environment relating to the water sector (recommendations 51-55)* and take such action as is necessary to accelerate the pace of their implementation;

(b) Arrange for scientific, systematic and comprehensive studies of the environmental impact of water projects as an integral part of the process of preparing project reports for water development;

(c) Ensure an interdisciplinary approach to such studies so that the full and all-round impact of the water projects can be assessed in a more comprehensive, effective and co-ordinated manner than would otherwise be possible;

(d) Promote research and systematic measurement of the effects that development projects have had on the environment and on other natural resources;

(e) Develop suitable procedures to evaluate the qualitative and quantitative environmental impacts of water projects;

(f) Investigate the possibility of the spread of diseases related to water as a result of large-scale water projects as the project is formulated and take appropriate action in conjunction with the implementation of the project so that no untoward health hazards result from its implementation;

(g) Ensure that due consideration is given to fisheries, wildlife protection and preservation and water-weed control in the planning and construction of water projects;

(h) Develop and regulate the establishment of facilities for tourism and recreation in conjunction with all natural and man-made reservoirs, taking special precautions in the case of drinking-water supply reservoirs;

(i) Promote rational methods of treatment and management of surface watersheds and their vegetation cover so as to avoid erosion and the consequent sedimentation in reservoirs, watercourses and river banks, and to normalize run-off patterns;

(j) Take into account the need for improvement of catchment areas of the national hydrological basins which generate the water resources to be used, in keeping with their degree of degradation and provide for the costs of such measures;

(k) Improve institutional arrangements for the observation and control of the impact that public and other works may have on water resources and the environment; and promote the participation of all governmental agencies responsible for health and environment from the earliest stages of planning, both

---

*Report of the United Nations Conference on the Human Environment (United Nations publication, Sales No.: E.73.II.A.14), chap. II, sect. B.

during the implementation and the subsequent monitoring of any socio-economic development scheme and in the formulation and application of relevant legislation and regulations;

(l) Identify, protect and preserve superlative examples of unique and scenic lakes, rivers, springs, waterfalls, wildlife and natural areas which embody inspirational national heritage values, and provide opportunities for international tourism;

(m) Recognize that fresh-water and coastal wetlands are among the most vital and productive of ecological systems because of their values for flood-water storage, as breeding grounds for fish and wildlife, and for their recreational and scientific use. Nations are encouraged to develop plans to ensure that important wetland areas are not indiscriminately destroyed;

(n) Recognize that while monetary values are often difficult to assign to the benefits of water as a recreational, cultural, aesthetic and scientific resource, the benefits are none the less real and substantial, and should be taken into consideration in the environmental assessment of development projects;

(o) Recognize that water planning and management should be based on ecological knowledge. Every water project must have as one of its goals to eliminate negative effects on public health and minimize the negative environmental impact; new water-supply projects must be linked with hygienic excreta-disposal practices, in order to provide the community with safe drinking water;

(p) Study and investigate water-related diseases in general and the influence of water as a working environment on those working in it;

(q) Recognize that the range of environmental considerations at present receiving attention in relation to water projects needs to be expanded in order to become more comprehensive and include not only physical, chemical or biological changes, but also the resulting social and economic changes;

(r) Recognize that to mitigate adverse environmental repercussions of water discharge from thermal and atomic power stations, cooling systems and hydro-technical design practices and procedures need to be improved to reduce potential hazards;

(s) Recognize that environmental planning is being undertaken not only at the national or river-basin level but also at the level of specific geographic regions such as estuaries, coastal zones, etc., wherever such an approach is warranted by the nature of the problems inherent in such regional development. This should be done not only in relation to water projects in isolation, but in close liaison with other related activities like town and country planning or regional development;

(t) Recognize that in dealing with problems of public health, a careful evaluation is needed of potential conflict situations such as the chlorination of sewage effluents and the chlorination of drinking-water production so that epidemiological consequences are avoided.

International organizations and other supporting bodies should, as appropriate, and on request, take the following action:

(i) Strengthen the exchange of information;

(ii) Support research and studies on the techniques for carrying out ecological surveys and on conditions affecting the incidence of diseases associated with aquatic environments;

(iii) Implement the recommendations of the 1972 United Nations Conference on the Human Environment relating to the water sector (recommendations 51-55);*

(iv) Make an assessment of the environmental impact of water projects and help to take suitable action to prevent undesirable consequences;

(v) Identify and protect waterscapes of international significance within the framework of the UNESCO Convention for the Protection of the World Cultural and Natural Heritage.†

Pollution control

Concerted and planned action is necessary to avoid and combat the effects of pollution in order to protect and improve where necessary the quality of water resources.

To this end it is recommended that countries should:

(a) Conduct surveys of present levels of pollution in surface-water and ground-water resources, and establish monitoring networks for the detection of pollution;

(b) Establish, where necessary, laboratories for the systematic and routine analysis of water samples, including physical, chemical, bacteriological and biological analysis;

(c) Regulate the discharge of industrial, urban and mining wastes into bodies of water by the establishment of the necessary control measures in the context of an over-all water management policy, taking account of qualitative and quantitative aspects;

(d) Apply such legislation and regulatory measures and such systems of incentive charges as to the discharge of pollutants that certain quality goals will be reached within certain periods of time. The discharge into the aquatic environment of dangerous substances that are toxic, persistent and bio-accumulative should be gradually eliminated;

(e) Devote careful attention to the availability of water and the effects of environmental pollution when deciding on the location and selection of facilities;

(f) Conduct research on and measurement of the pollution of surface and ground water by agricultural fertilizers and biocides with a view to lessening their adverse environmental impact;

(g) Adopt the general principle that, as far as possible, direct or indirect costs attributable to pollution should be borne by the polluter;

(h) Increase the number and improve the operation and establish comprehensive monitoring of facilities and technologies for the treatment of waste water, giving greater attention to alternative (especially low-energy) methods of waste treatment and land application or other economic use of wastes;

(i) Encourage the development and use of substances which minimize hazards to human health and the environment, taking into account in particular toxicity, biodegradability, bio-accumulation and eutrophication;

---

*Ibid., chap. II, sect. B.
†Adopted by the UNESCO General Conference on 16 November 1972.

(j) Increase efforts to monitor and assess the effects of the deposition of airborne pollutants in water from distant sources and reduce the total emission of such pollutants, i.e. by applying the best available technology that is economically feasible;

(k) Harmonize and use, where possible, uniform criteria, methods and standards for assessing and monitoring water quality, compiling data and classifying waters with regard to their use;

(l) Prepare and continuously update a list of water pollutants and a harmonizing terminology in the field of water pollution control, in collaboration with existing international organizations engaged in similar work;

(m) Promote the use of infiltration techniques when the nature of the effluents and the terrain makes it possible to do so without endangering surface and ground-water resources;

(n) Set up adequate institutions, where necessary with appropriate co-ordinating machinery, and strengthen those that already exist, to enable them to be more effective in the fight against pollution;

(o) Apply appropriate land-use planning as a tool for preventing water pollution, especially in the case of ground water;

(p) Establish quality standards for the various beneficial uses of water, whenever possible, taking into account the degree of development and the social and economical conditions of each region;

(q) Ensure fast decontamination of water pollution during natural and man-made hazards;

(r) Counteract with all appropriate measures the introduction into water of toxic substances likely to result in environmental hazards such as DDT, polychlorinated biphenyl (PCB), mercury and cadmium, taking into account the special requirements of developing countries;

(s) Where practical, seriously encourage and conduct biological control research where chemicals are used in the control of water-related organisms;

(t) In combating industrial pollution, undertake a careful analysis of the cost-effectiveness ratio of the different measures proposed for pollution control and priority accorded to the method entailing the least cost;

(u) Recognize that studies need to be undertaken to evaluate the best possible approach to controlling pollution on an industry-by-industry or pollutant-by-pollutant basis, in accordance with national requirements in the light of the nature and level of industrial development;

(v) Recognize that techniques like simulation, parametric modelling and computerized analysis need to be developed to facilitate solutions to problems in the field of pollution control;

(w) With relation to the long-distance transportation of airborne pollution, especially acid precipitation, recognize that the different approaches to the control of the emission of relevant pollutants should be considered, bearing in mind the available range of technical solutions;

International organizations and other supporting bodies should, as appropriate and on request, assist developing countries by providing equipment, funds and personnel to enable them to determine quality levels and to face the problems posed by water pollution.

D. Policy, Planning and Management

Increased attention should be paid to the integrated planning of water management. Integrated policies and legislative and administrative guidelines are needed so as to ensure a good adaptation of resources to needs and reduce, if necessary, the risk of serious supply shortages and ecological damage to ensure public acceptance of planned water schemes and to ensure their financing. Particular consideration should be given not only to the cost-effectiveness of planned water schemes, but also to ensuring optimal social benefits of water resources use, as well as to the protection of human health and the environment as a whole. Attention should also be paid to the shift from single-purpose to multipurpose water resources development as the degree of development of water resources and water use in river basins increases, with a view, *inter alia*, to optimizing the investments for planned water-use schemes. In particular, the construction of new works should be preceded by a detailed study of the agricultural, industrial, municipal and hydropower needs of the area concerned. Water-management plans may be prepared using systems analysis techniques and developed on the basis of already adopted indicators and criteria. This analysis would take into account the economic and social evolution of the basin and be as comprehensive as possible; it would include such elements as time horizon and territorial extent, and take into account interactions between the national economy and regional development, and linkages between different decision-making levels. National policies must provide for the modernization of existing systems to meet the requirements of the present day.

National water policy

In a number of countries, there is a need for the formulation of a national water policy within the framework of and consistent with the over-all economic and social policies of the country concerned, with a view to helping raise the standard of living of the whole population.

> **Each country should formulate and keep under review a general statement of policy in relation to the use, management and conservation of water, as a framework for planning and implementing specific programmes and measures for efficient operation of schemes. National development plans and policies should specify the main objectives of water-use policy, which should in turn be translated into guidelines and strategies, subdivided, as far as possible, into programmes for the integrated management of the resource.**

To this end it is recommended that countries should:

(a) Ensure that national water policy is conceived and carried out within the framework of an interdisciplinary national economic, social and environmental development policy;

(b) Recognize water development as an essential infrastructural facility in the country's development plans;

(c) Ensure that land and water are managed in an integrated manner;

(d) Improve the availability and quality of necessary basic information, e.g. cartographic services, hydrometry, data on water-linked natural resources and ecosystems, inventories of possible works, water demand projections and social cost;

(e) Define goals and targets for different sectors of water use, including provision of safe water-supply and waste-disposal facilities, provision for agriculture, stock-raising, industrial needs and transport by water, and development of hydropower in such a way as to be compatible with the resources and characteristics of the area concerned. In estimating available water resources, account should be taken of water re-use and water transfer across basins;

(f) Develop and apply techniques for identifying, measuring and presenting the economic, environmental and social benefits and costs of development projects and proposals. Decisions can then be based on these factors, appropriate distribution of costs can be determined, and the construction and operation of projects can be carried out in such a way that these matters receive continuous consideration at all stages;

(g) Undertake the systematic evaluation of projects already carried out, with a view to learning lessons for the future, particularly in relation to social benefits and ecological changes, which evolve slowly;

(h) Formulate master plans for countries and river basins to provide a long-term perspective for planning, including resource conservation, using such techniques as systems analysis and mathematical modelling as planning tools, wherever appropriate. Projects arising out of the national plans should be well investigated and appropriate priorities should be assigned to them;

(i) Maintain in the planning and management of national water resources as a fundamental aim and as a high priority the satisfaction of the basic needs of all groups of society with particular attention to the lowest income groups;

(j) Periodically review and adjust targets in order to keep pace with changing conditions. Long-term guidelines for water management might be prepared for periods of 10 to 15 years and should be compatible with master plans. Planning should be considered a continuous activity and long-term plans should be revised and completed periodically — a five-year period seems advisable in this respect;

(k) Undertake the training of personnel specializing in planning principles and methods as well as farmers and other users of water so that they are involved at every stage of the planning process. This should include training to improve the expertise in economic analysis so as to ensure that proper cost-allocation studies are undertaken;

(l) Evaluate water-tariff policies in accordance with general development policies and direct any readjustment and restructuring that may be found necessary, so that they may be effectively used as policy instruments to promote better management of demand while encouraging better use of available resources without causing undue hardship to poorer sections and regions of the community. Water charges should as far as possible cover the costs incurred unless Governments as a policy choose to subsidize them;

(m) Document and share their experience in planning with others.

International organizations and other supporting bodies should, as appropriate, and on request, assist countries to:

(i) Evolve and formulate national water policies;

(ii) Strengthen the existing institutions at the national level and existing intergovernmental organizations at the subregional level, and create new institutions where needed;

(iii) Prepare national master plans and, where necessary, river-basin plans and identify projects;

(iv) Prepare feasibility reports for projects identified in such general planning studies, which have some prior assurance of financing by interested donor countries or agencies;

(v) Prepare definitive project reports where feasibility studies have been established;

(vi) Actively promote planning techniques and procedures by arranging information exchange, convening working groups and roving or country seminars, as appropriate, and by disseminating the results of relevant case studies and research studies;

(vii) Give urgent attention at the national, regional and international level to developing national expertise in the application of planning techniques by all appropriate means;

(viii) Promote various available measures and techniques in public participation and pay particular attention to ways of adapting appropriate techniques to the particular circumstances of countries.

Institutional arrangements

In many countries, water interests have been divided among numerous agencies without adequate co-ordination and without adequate links to other aspects of national planning.

Institutional arrangements adopted by each country should ensure that the development and management of water resources take place in the context of national planning and that there is real co-ordination among all bodies responsible for the investigation, development and management of water resources. The problem of creating an adequate institutional infrastructure should be kept constantly under review and consideration should be given to the establishing of efficient water authorities to provide for proper co-ordination.

To this end, it is recommended that countries should:

(a) Adapt the institutional framework for efficient planning and use of water resources and the use of advanced technologies where appropriate. Institutional organization for water management should be reformed whenever appropriate so as to secure adequate co-ordination of central and local administrative authorities. Co-ordination should include the allocation of resources with complementary programmes;

(b) Promote interest in water management among users of water; users should be given adequate representation and participation in management;

(c) Consider, where necessary, the desirability of establishing suitable organizations to deal with rural water supply, as distinct from urban water supply, in view of the differences between the two in technologies, priorities, etc.;

(d) Consider as a matter of urgency and importance the establishment and strengthening of river basin authorities, with a view to achieving a more efficient, integrated planning and development of the river basins concerned for all water uses when warranted by administrative and financial advantages;

(e) Secure proper linkage between the administrative co-ordinating agency and the decision-makers.

Legislation

Legislation in many countries, though often complex, lags behind modern water management practices and techniques and perpetuates an undesirable framentation of administrative responsibilities. Provisions which regulate water management are often contained in different laws and regulations. This may make it difficult to know and apply them. In some instances there are cases of incompatibility between legal provisions of a national character and regulations emanating from regional or local authorities, or between traditional rights and the State's role in controlling water resources.

> **Each country should examine and keep under review existing legislative and administrative structures concerning water management and, in the light of shared experience should enact, where appropriate, comprehensive legislation, for a co-ordinated approach to water planning. It may be desirable that provisions concerning water resources management, conservation and protection against pollution be combined in a unitary legal instrument, if the constitutional framework of the country permits. Legislation should define the rules of public ownership of water and of large water engineering works, as well as the provisions covering land ownership problems and any litigation that may result therefrom. It should be flexible enough to accommodate future changes in priorities and perspectives.**

To this end, it is recommended that:

(a) An inventory and a critical examination of rules (whether written or unwritten), regulations, decrees, ordinances and legal and legislative measures in the area of water resources and development should systematically be carried out;

(b) A review of existing legislation be prepared in order to improve and streamline its scope to cover all aspects pertaining to water resources management; protection of quality, prevention of pollution, penalties for undesirable effluent discharge, licensing, abstraction, ownership, etc.;

(c) Although legislation should generally be comprehensive, it ought to be framed in the simplest way possible, and be consistent with the need to spell out the respective responsibilities and powers of governmental agencies and the means for conferring rights to use water on individuals;

(d) Legislation should allow for the easy implementation of policy decisions which should be made in the public interest, while protecting the reasonable interests of individuals;

(e) Legislation should define the rules of public ownership of water projects as well as the rights, obligations and responsibilities and emphasize the role of public bodies at the proper administrative level in controlling both the quantity and quality of water. It should appoint and empower appropriate administrative agencies to carry out this controlling function and to plan and implement water-development programmes. It should also spell out, either in primary or subordinate legislation, administrative procedures necessary for the co-ordinated, equitable and efficient control and administration of all aspects of water resources, and land-use problems as well as the conflicts which may arise from them;

(f) Legislation should take into account the administrative capacity to implement it;

(g) Countries should document and share their experience so as to have a basis for possible improvement of their legislation;

(h) Priority should be accorded to the effective enforcement of the provisions of existing legislation, and where necessary, administrative and other arrangements should be strengthened and rendered more effective to achieve this objective.

International organizations and other supporting bodies should, as appropriate, and on request, assist countries to:

(i) Improve and streamline existing legislation and prepare new draft legislation; *inter alia* to establish professorships and institutes in water law;

(ii) Arrange the exchange of information and disseminate the results and experience of selected countries for the benefit of others.

Public participation

It is commonly acknowledged that decisions should be made in the light of the expressed views of those likely to be affected by the decision.

> **Countries should make necessary efforts to adopt measures for obtaining effective participation in the planning and decision-making process involving users and public authorities. Such participation can constructively influence the choice between alternative plans and policies. If necessary, legislation should provide for such participation as an integral part of the planning, programming, implementation and evaluation process.**

To this end, it is recommended that:

(a) Countries should develop adequate legislative provisions, educational programmes and participatory activities that will increase public awareness and encourage public participation, as well as emphasize the value of water and the danger of its relative scarcity or abuse;

(b) Countries employing such measures and techniques should document and share their experience;

(c) Every effort should be made to convince the public that participation is an integral component in the decision-making process, and there should be a continuous two-way flow of information;

(d) In the field of community water supply and sanitation special emphasis should be given to the situation and the role of women.

Development of appropriate technology

In many developing countries efforts are being made to hasten and develop local and appropriate technologies using local experience and raw materials; to hasten economic development these efforts require encouragement, expansion, and financial and institutional support.

> **The concept and content of appropriate technology related to water-resource development and management should be perceived in the context of each particular socio-economic situation and its available resources. Developing countries need to build up technological capability at the national and regional levels. Priority should be given to technologies of low capital cost, and the**

use of local raw materials and resources taking environmental factors into account. Developed countries should accelerate the process of transfer of experience and know-how, technical assistance and training to developing countries. The developed countries should encourage and improve the conditions for the transfer of information and know-how. There is also a need for transfer of technology among the developing countries themselves.

In this context, the following considerations are pertinent:

(a) Results of research programmes may not be readily and immediately transformed into applicable technologies; a transitional phase of experiment and adaptation is often needed to evolve the required technologies;

(b) Imported technologies for the management of water resources may require — as an intermediate phase in the transfer of technology — further study and experiment concerning the suitability of their adaptation to available resources and prevalent socio-cultural, economic and environmental conditions.

(c) Water scarcity will often have a decisive influence on the development of appropriate technology. It may require in some cases a shift from traditional to relatively complex technologies;

(d) Self-reliance has become an objective in many developing countries. Efforts should be made to promote indigenous abilities and to develop appropriate technologies that use to the full local experience and resources. These efforts require institutional and financial support.

To this end it is recommended that countries should:

(a) Review the adequacy of existing institutional arrangements for the development of appropriate technologies in water resources management, and provide support for their development;

(b) Provide every possible encouragement and support to national institutions concerned with the development of appropriate technologies in water resources development;

(c) Provide the resources to enable professionals to observe what has been achieved in their field of expertise in other countries and to acquaint themselves with possible improvements in the technologies they are using at present;

(d) Encourage the widest possible diffusion of acquired knowledge on the development of appropriate technology; establish and expand enterprises and productively apply the appropriate technologies that have been developed;

(e) Review the extent of public participation in the planning, construction, operation and maintenance of water projects and take steps to ensure a greater level of participation, through consultations and the transfer of knowledge starting at the village level;

(f) Make the fullest use of labour in water projects, keeping in view the need to strike a suitable balance between labour-intensive and capital-intensive technologies, emphasizing the need to reduce unemployment and underemployment particularly for unskilled labour;

(g) Promote attempts to manufacture such items as pumps, engines, steel, polyvinyl chloride (PVC), asbestos cement and pre-stressed concrete pipes and water treatment reagents, from locally available resources. In the promoting of this idea the use of local materials with advanced technology should be encouraged. Appropriate precautions should be taken in the manufacture and use of potentially dangerous materials such as PVC and asbestos;

(h) Develop facilities for the servicing and maintenance of installed hydraulic equipment, including the manufacture of spare parts;

(i) Promote the standardization of equipment to help solve operational problems resulting from shortages of spare parts;

(j) Promote the standardization of specifications, design and plans of equipment and hydraulic work;

(k) Promote subregional and regional arrangements for the planning, design and construction of water projects and the exchange of information with other regions where similar conditions prevail;

(l) Promote intraregional technical co-operation to even out the prevalent disparities in technological development among countries while encouraging technological innovation in planning, instrumentation and equipment and the exchange of information with other regions;

(m) Ensure that water facilities to be manufactured from local resources do not create health hazards;

(n) Develop emergency programmes to supply water to areas affected by drinking-water shortage;

(o) Make all efforts to improve the cost-benefit ratio while taking into regard the requirements of environment and health protection and local and socio-economic aspects involved.

International organizations and other supporting bodies should, as appropriate, and on request, take the following action:

(i) Make a review of the adequacy of existing constitutional arrangements for the development of appropriate technology in the water resources field;

(ii) Support national efforts to manufacture construction materials, to service imported equipment, to manufacture spare parts and to manufacture the equipment itself;

(iii) Evolve standard designs and plans, wherever possible;

(iv) Strengthen subregional, regional and interregional arrangements for the planning, design and construction of water projects, through the provision of personnel and other such facilities;

(v) Provide funds to enhance the transfer of technologies and to adapt these technologies to local needs;

(vi) Support and strengthen institutions for the promotion of appropriate technology, at the village level, *inter alia*, by organizing workshops, seminars, and appropriate consultations.

It is further recommended to the Economic and Social Council that the relevant recommendations and resolutions of the United Nations Water Conference be transmitted to the Preparatory Committee for the United Nations Conference on Science and Technology for Development at its second session in order to ensure that water-management problems and the problems of appropriate water technologies be given priority attention in the preliminary national and regional analysis undertaken in the preparatory process for the Conference as well as by the Conference itself.

E. *Natural Hazards*

There are extensive areas of the world where severe hydrometeorological phenomena frequently occur and cause great damage, leading to loss of life and setbacks in development. Experience shows that, with appropriate combinations of engineering works and non-structural measures, damages can be substantially reduced. It is necessary to plan ahead and co-ordinate the measures that need to be taken to avoid and reduce the damage produced by severe hydrometeorological phenomena. These should be studied and the losses in the most affected areas should be evaluated, taking into account their physical, economic and social characteristics, in order to forecast the likely nature and frequency of damage.

Flood loss management

Floods are major hazards for many countries because flood plains of large rivers are invariably densely populated and properties of considerable value are located on them. The flood losses can be decreased by comprehensive structural and non-structural precautions and by the organization of emergency services, including expanding the hydrological services to aid in forecasting floods and related events.

There is a need in many countries to strengthen programmes to reduce the losses associated with floods within the framework of programmes for land and water management and for disaster prevention and preparedness generally.

To this end it is recommended that countries should:

(a) As part of general land and water management programmes:

(i) Provide the maximum feasible scope for flood mitigation in reservoir design and operation, having regard, however, to the main function of the particular reservoir;

(ii) Take into consideration the effect of catchment use on the amount and timing of run-off;

(iii) Make provision for the zoning and management of flood-prone lands with due regard to the economic and social consequences of the different uses;

(iv) Plan well in advance and provide effective flood protection by structural and non-structural measures proportionate to the magnitude of the risk;

(v) Provide adequate financial resources to improve catchment areas for the retention of flood waters and soil erosion control and encourage local participation in the implementation of such measures;

(vi) Provide adequate funds for satisfactory maintenance of flood protection works;

(b) Develop flood forecasting and warning systems as well as flood-fighting and evacuation measures to minimize loss of lives and property in case of flooding. Disaster assistance which includes preventive health services should be included in developmental processes;

(c) Improve the collection of data on damage caused by floods so as to provide a better basis for the planning, design and management of measures for the mitigation of flood loss, and to evaluate the performance of measures taken;

(d) Develop flood-risk maps as a basis for public information programmes and action by Governments to regulate development in flood-prone areas;

(e) Give appropriate consideration to structural measures such as dikes and levees and also to non-structural measures like flood-plain regulations, flood zoning, the preparation of flood-risk maps, flood insurance, etc. and integrate measures for up-stream watershed management into over-all flood control plans.

Drought loss management

In the recent past droughts of exceptional severity have caused major hardships in many areas of the world. Such disasters can arise again at any time. In consequence, steps to mitigate the effects of drought in such areas is a top priority. In order to remedy the situation, structural and non-structural and emergency measures should be adopted and for this purpose the development and management of water resources as well as drought forecasting on a long-term basis should be viewed as a key element.

> **There is a need to develop improved bases for planning land and water management in order to make optimum use of land and water resources in areas subject to severe drought. Comprehensive programmes should be formulated for the progressive implementation of the development of water resources for the benefit of drought-affected areas: specific short-term and long-term objectives, as well as targets, should be outlined. There is also a need to study basic meteorological processes with a view to formulating long-term forecasts in weather behaviour in any given area.**

To this end, it is recommended that countries should:

(a) Undertake studies on climate, hydrometeorology and agronomy and on local management techniques in order to define the best means of extending and intensifying rain-fed cultivation while incurring a minimum of risk from scarcity of rain;

(b) Make an inventory of all available water resources, and formulate long-term plans for their development as an integral part of the development of other natural resources, and within this framework prepare medium-term and long-term plans for the development of these water resources. These activities may require co-ordination with similar activities in neighbouring countries;

(c) Consider the transfer of water from areas where surplus in water resources is available to areas subjected to droughts;

(d) Intensify the exploration of ground water through geophysical and hydrogeological investigations and undertake on a regional scale large-scale programmes for the development of wells and boreholes, to be explored in groups where appropriate for water for human and livestock consumption, taking into account the needs of pastures while preventing overgrazing and avoiding over-exploitation of underground aquifers;

(e) Determine the effect of drought on aquifers and in the assessment of the response of ground-water systems to drought, basing such assessment on concepts such as storage/flow ratio in order to characterize ground-water flow regions in periods of drought;

(f) Arrange to complete as expeditiously as possible feasibility reports for well-defined surface water projects and for the implementation of projects deemed to be feasible;

(g) Make arrangements for the proper maintenance of existing wells and the development of new ones, using the resources and energies of the affected population in rural areas on the basis of self-help, supplemented by State assistance and external resources;

(h) Undertake studies on technologies geared to the improvement of water pumps, efficiency of uses and the reduction of losses from evaporation, seepage, transpiration, etc;

(i) Develop drought-resistant plant species;

(j) Set up systems for the observation and control of the processes of desertification and carry out research on the basic causes of drought;

(k) Strengthen institutional arrangements, including co-operation among various agencies, for the preparation and dissemination of hydrological, hydrometeorological and agricultural forecasts and for the use of this information in the management of water resources and disaster relief;

(l) Wherever possible, institute a deliberate policy for the transfer of population from drought-prone areas to other suitable regions with the view of reducing harmful effects on the ecosystem and promoting long-term rehabilitation programmes;

(m) Evolve contingency plans to deal with emergency situations in drought-affected areas;

(n) Study the potential role of integration of surface and underground phases of water basins utilizing the stocks of water stored in ground-water formations in order to maintain a minimum supply under drought conditions.

Management of flood and drought loss

International organizations and other supporting bodies should, as appropriate, and on request:

(i) Further the development of hydrologic models as a basis for flood forecasting and river system management generally;

(ii) Study risk evaluation and other aspects of flood-plain zoning and management and disaster prevention;

(iii) Provide technical and other assistance in implementing flood control and flood protection works as well as the management of the catchment areas;

(iv) Arrange an initial programme of information exchange on drought loss management and long-term weather forecasting through expert meetings and subsequently take appropriate follow-up action.

F. *Public Information, Education, Training and Research*

Public information and extension service

In order to ensure maximum attention to the proper utilization, protection and conservation of water, it is of decisive importance that all citizens be made aware of fundamental matters relating to water. For that reason education and research have to be efficiently supplemented by the provision of broad information to the public. Effective public information aims at the creating of a general as well as personal responsibility for the crucial water issues. It is considered an essential task for Governments to motivate the citizens to adopt a sound view on matters concerning their daily handling of water. Given a general feeling of responsibility for the local resources, people will be aware of the importance of the protection and conservation of water.

Countries should accord priority to conducting programmes for national information campaigns directed to all people concerning the proper utilization, protection and conservation of water.

In this context it is recommended that countries should:

(a) Direct information to all citizens, first of all through the normal channels offered by primary and adult education and in connexion with regular health programmes and information schemes for parents;

(b) Initiate special information campaigns conducted by the use of brochures, newspapers, radio and television, and other forms of popularization;

(c) Prepare people for the consequences of changed life patterns which could be the effect of improved water availability in areas where water shortage formerly restricted various activities;

(d) Provide information in a simple manner and adapted to local conditions concerning land-use, social traditions, climate, geology and infrastructure;

(e) Inform people of the negative ecological, hydrological and sanitary consequences of misuse of water;

(f) Emphasize the risk for the spreading of water-borne diseases in connexion with pollution of water;

(g) Carry out programmes for broad public information repeatedly and make a continuous review of the results.

Education and training

Many countries share problems in educating, training and retaining properly qualified and experienced personnel at all professional and subprofessional levels. There is uncertainty as to the precise extent of these problems and an urgent need to isolate and remedy them. A number of national and subregional training establishments have been doing useful work in the training of middle-level subprofessionals, particularly in the subjects of hydrology, hydrogeology, water desalination and hydrometeorology. A number of fellowships offered by the United Nations system and other bilateral and multilateral agencies have been used for the training of professionals. Nevertheless, the total impact of all this effort has not been such as to remove the element of the shortage of trained manpower as a critical constraint.

> **Countries should accord priority to conducting surveys to determine national needs for administrative, scientific and technical manpower in the water resources area. Law-makers and the public in general should be informed about and sensitized to this problem.**

> **Training programmes should be implemented to give water management planners an understanding and appreciation of the various disciplines involved in water resources development and utilization; to provide professional, technical and skilled manpower in hydrology, hydrogeology, hydraulics, social, biological and health sciences and water desalination; and to provide managers for water resources systems, operators for water distribution and for treatment plants and monitors for water quality installations. Extension services at the farm level should also be organized.**

In this context, the following considerations are pertinent:

(a) Education and training are necessary for all levels of personnel dealing with water resources development, such as professionals, subprofessionals, water users, village level workers, etc.;

(b) Programmes should provide for refresher and in-service training for existing staff to disseminate new developments in methods and techniques;

(c) Incentives must be developed to induce staff to remain in work areas where the training they have received is relevant;

(d) Management training should be provided for senior staff on a variety of matters, including techniques of project negotiation and administration;

(e) Available training at both the professional and subprofessional levels often requires substantial qualitative rather than quantitative improvement as a first priority;

(f) Countries, in particular those offering fellowships of training for overseas students or acting as hosts to regional training centres, should be sensitive to the "brain drain" from developing countries and should co-operate in reducing its incidence;

(g) Regional educational and training centres for administrative and subprofessional staff should be encouraged, but attention is drawn to the fact that suitable persons for subprofessional posts will often not possess a common regional language; smaller countries cannot afford to develop individual programmes and some economical means must be devised of sharing such programmes;

(h) A balance must be struck between the employment of international expertise and developing indigenous experience in planning and executing water development projects.

In this context it is recommended that countries should:

(a) Ensure that the contemplated manpower surveys cover all aspects of water resources management, including the appraisal of water resources, various water uses, water associated diseases and related methods such as computer technology, application of instruments, modelling and management techniques.

(b) Make a comprehensive assessment of the requirements of manpower in the professional and subprofessional, senior, junior and middle-level categories of personnel;

(c) Conceive manpower surveys for water development as integral components of over-all surveys of the need for trained manpower in all sectors of economic development in the nation, so as to provide really effective instruments for policy planning and project implementation;

(d) Improve the working and living conditions for national professional experts to facilitate and encourage them to teach and to develop research in their own countries;

(e) Make an inventory of cadres who emigrate abroad and create conditions that would encourage their return to their own countries.

Further, in connexion with training programmes, countries should:

(a) Take steps to strengthen and expand the facilities and existing institutions, universities, colleges, polytechnics and training centres by providing more teachers, teaching materials, etc., so that the quantity and quality of their output can be increased;

(b) Review the curricula of the existing institutions and training centres and expand them to include subjects pertaining to water resources development, the conservation of land and water resources, the teaching of basic anti-pollution measures for lessening pollution and other waterborne diseases in rural communities, the training of farmers in the practice of irrigated agriculture, and the training of technicians in community and industrial water supply and sanitation;

(c) Take steps to establish training programmes, on-site training and training centres for water and sewage-treatment plant operators and water distribution operators as well as training in other areas where a special need exists;

(d) Consider the establishment of special training schools attached to colleges and schools or to national water-development agencies on a permanent basis;

(e) Encourage intraregional co-operation to establish training institutions as joint ventures by interested countries in the training of professional and subprofessional personnel, *inter alia*, by the provision of teaching staff from water-development organizations within the region;

(f) Make provision for scholarships of long duration for graduate courses in subjects pertaining to water resources development as distinct from short-term fellowships included in specific projects;

(g) Make an inventory of regional institutions concerned with sanitary engineering and strengthen them by providing adequate personnel, funds and equipment;

(h) Consider the establishment of water resources development training centres on a subregional or regional basis to train specialists in various aspects of technology in the development of water resources at the post-graduate level for the benefit of graduates in engineering from existing universities or polytechnics, with provision for on-site training and refresher courses for engineers, including special courses in water resources management. In cases where these centres already exist they should be strengthened and no new ones should be established;

(i) Accord to scientists and engineers working in water resources development a status similar to professionals in other sectors of the national economies in order to ensure their retention;

(j) Establish, in co-operation with regional and international organizations, personnel exchange programmes to provide for experts and technicians from developing countries to serve in other countries which suffer from personnel shortages and to provide work experience for persons engaged in the operation of water management schemes at existing successive schemes in other countries, and to further encourage students engaged in graduate research to conduct their investigations in their own countries on topics appropriate to their countries' needs;

(k) Publish technical manuals and other guidance material in water-project design and construction, with particular relevance to local conditions;

(l) Ensure that university teachers and technical education institutions have enough practical experience and multidisciplinary training to improve their teaching and research;

(m) Take steps to encourage operational managers and supervisors to play their part, both individually and collectively, as non-professional and part-time trainers and instructors of their own subordinate staff.

International organizations and other supporting bodies should, as appropriate, and on request, take the following action:

(i) Conduct surveys on available manpower and needs in the field of water resource management and utilization;

(ii) Strengthen and expand the existing educational and training institutions at all levels including vocational training and improve the course content in subjects pertaining to the development of water resources;

(iii) Establish new training centres, as and when requested by countries;

(iv) Provide scholarships for undergraduate and graduate courses;

(v) Establish water resources development training centres in Africa for postgraduate specialization with special courses in the management of water resources and sanitary engineering;

(vi) Undertake regional studies in consultation with the countries concerned to identify the incidence of problems relating to the education and retention of staff. Thereafter, as appropriate, steps should be taken to formulate proposals to countries and to international agencies to meet identified needs. Countries are meanwhile urged to share their expertise and to offer appropriate training programmes as part of their own aid programmes.

Research needs

Properly planned research and its appropriate application play an important role in the resolution of water problems, and while the diversity of circumstances within the regions calls for specific programmes in most countries, there is also scope for the co-ordination of efforts. Considerable research is being carried out in research institutes, governmental and intergovernmental organizations and universities on problems related to the development of water resources. There is a need to review and evaluate the work carried out so far and to outline areas in which further research should be undertaken.

It is recommended that countries evolve, within the framework of national science policies, a particular policy for research work in the development, management and conservation of water resources. High priority should be accorded to research programmes that provide the knowledge necessary for the sound management of water resources. Suitable institutional forms should be developed to promote co-operation between water research and administration and to ensure that research endeavours respond first to priority problems as designated in national plans for the development of water resources. Research endeavours should first respond to important problems, by ensuring that duplication and overlapping are minimized and that results are disseminated in forms that can be readily interpreted and applied by other countries. Encouragement should be given to regional co-operation in hydrometeorological research and monitoring and to research promoting greater efficiency in water use, particularly in agriculture and industry. The results of long- and short-term basic and applied research should be adopted and utilized in order to solve specific problems and thus forge a closer relationship between research and development.

To this end it is recommended that countries should:

(a) Set up national steering committees comprising all relevant interested parties to make an inventory of problems in water resources development on which research has been, or is now being carried out, including research of subregional and regional organizations dealing with problems pertaining to water development;

(b) Co-ordinate research programmes at the national level by means of a systematic and scientific evaluation of the work carried out on those problems with a view to locating gaps in knowledge, avoiding overlap of research efforts and identifying areas in which further research is needed to advance the future development of water resources;

(c) Strengthen existing institutions, where gaps exist, and establish new ones, wherever necessary, for the specific purpose of conducting water resources research on problems closely related to developmental needs;

(d) Adopt and utilize the results of research to solve specific problems and thus forge a closer relationship between research and development;

(e) Make more use of existing institutional mechanisms and promote additional ones, where necessary, for continuous consultation and co-ordination among research workers in the field so that solutions will emerge to suit the water problems of the countries in particular regions;

(f) Promote research into problems of methodologies for the assessment of supplies of surface and ground-water resources, and for their use, development and management. Research organizations should use their resources first for applied research and application of research results already available to solve some of the most urgent national problems. As scientific personnel and equipment become available, more basic research may be undertaken and also research into high-technology fields;

(g) Promote research in areas related to their respective needs including where relevant:

Weather modification (should not be contrary to General Assembly resolutions 3475 (XXX) and 31/72)

Climatology and agroclimatology

Weather forecasting

Remote sensing

Possible effects of climatic change on water availability

Artificial recharge of aquifers

Soil-erosion and sediment control

Methods of increasing efficiency of water use in irrigation and rain-fed agriculture

Conservation of water in reservoirs and methods of operation of multi-purpose reservoirs

Physical modelling

Application of systems analysis techniques for water resources, planning and management

Desalination, with particular reference to the treatment of brackish water

Recycling of water

Water and waste treatment

Water pollution and water quality modelling

Water-associated diseases and health effects of water schemes

Use of brackish water in agriculture

Contamination of ground waters

Crop water requirements

Salt-tolerant crops

Aquaculture

Methods of increasing efficiency of flood control and drought mitigation

Prevention and mitigation of the effects of natural hazards like earthquakes, hurricanes, volcanic eruptions on water resources

Use and control of water in humid areas, or areas of large amounts of rainfall;

(h) Encourage multidisciplinary research in co-ordination with training programmes within the fields of water assessment, utilization, protection, conservation and management;

(i) Encourage the participation of national research institutes and the scientific community in international programmes and institutions, and the exchange of relevant information with other countries.

International organizations and other supporting bodies should, as appropriate, and on request, take the following action:

(i) Conduct a review and evaluation of the research work done so far with a view to outlining the directions of future research work needed;

(ii) Strengthen the existing research institutions and set up new ones, wherever needed, by offering technical assistance, funds, equipment and expertise;

(iii) Exchange information and experience and disseminate research results;

(iv) Prepare research projects, including global studies of environmental trends;

(v) Standardize methods of processing relevant data;

(vi) Investigate the possibilities of new technologies such as weather modification (in accordance with General Assembly resolutions 3475 (XXX) and 31/72), long-term weather forecasting, desalination and remote sensing to augment water availability.

G. *Regional Co-operation*

*Development of shared water resources**

In the case of shared water resources, co-operative action should be taken to generate appropriate data on which future management can be based and to devise appropriate institutions and understandings for co-ordinated development.

> **Countries sharing water resources, with appropriate assistance from international agencies and other supporting bodies, on the request of the countries concerned, should review existing and available techniques for managing shared water resources and co-operate in the establishment of programmes, machinery and institutions necessary for the co-ordinated development of such resources. Areas of co-operation may with agreement of the parties concerned include planning, development, regulation, management, environmental protection,**

---

*This term has been used only for the uniformity of the text and its use does not prejudice the position of the countries supporting the terms "transboundary waters" or "international waters" in any of the problems involved.

use and conservation, forecasting, etc. Such co-operation should be a basic element in an effort to overcome major constraints such as the lack of capital and trained manpower as well as the exigencies of natural resources development.

To this end it is recommended that countries sharing a water resource should:

(a) Sponsor studies, if necessary with the help of international agencies and other bodies as appropriate, to compare and analyse existing institutions for managing shared water resources and to report on their results;

(b) Establish joint committees, as appropriate with agreement of the parties concerned, so as to provide for co-operation in areas such as the collection, standardization and exchange of data, the management of shared water resources, the prevention and control of water pollution, the prevention of water-associated diseases, mitigation of drought, flood control, river improvement activities and flood warning systems;

(c) Encourage joint education and training schemes that provide economies of scale in the training of professional and subprofessional officers to be employed in the basin;

(d) Encourage exchanges between interested countries and meetings between representatives of existing international or interstate river commissions to share experiences. Representatives from countries which share resources but yet have no developed institutions to manage them could be included in such meetings;

(e) Strengthen if necessary existing governmental and intergovernmental institutions, in consultation with interested Governments, through the provision of equipment, funds and personnel;

(f) Institute action for undertaking surveys of shared water resources and monitoring their quality;

(g) In the absence of an agreement on the manner in which shared water resources should be utilized, countries which share these resources should exchange relevant information on which their future management can be based in order to avoid foreseeable damages;

(h) Assist in the active co-operation of interested countries in controlling water pollution in shared water resources. This co-operation could be established through bilateral, subregional or regional conventions or by other means agreed upon by the interested countries sharing the resources.

The regional water organizations, taking into account existing and proposed studies as well as the hydrological, political, economic and geographical distinctiveness of shared water resources of various drainage basins, should seek ways of increasing their capabilities of promoting co-operation in the field of shared water resources and, for this purpose, draw upon the experience of other regional water organizations.

Recommendations for particular regions

The Conference took note of all the specific regional recommendations emanating from the regional commissions in Africa, Asia and the Pacific, Europe, Latin America and Western Asia and referred them to the regional commissions concerned for appropriate action in the light of the other relevant recommendations approved by the Conference. These recommendations are reproduced in the annex to this section of the present chapter.

H. International Co-operation

Development of shared water resources

It is necessary for States to co-operate in the case of shared water resources in recognition of the growing economic, environmental and physical interdependencies across international frontiers. Such co-operation, in accordance with the Charter of the United Nations and principles of international law, must be exercised on the basis of the equality, sovereignty and territorial integrity of all States, and taking due account of the principle expressed, *inter alia*, in principle 21 of the Declaration of the United Nations Conference on the Human Environment.*

> **In relation to the use, management and development of shared water resources, national policies should take into consideration the right of each state sharing the resources to equitably utilize such resources as the means to promote bonds of solidarity and co-operation.**
>
> **A concerted and sustained effort is required to strengthen international water law as a means of placing co-operation among states on a firmer basis. The need for progressive development and codification of the rules of international law regulating the development and use of shared water resources has been the growing concern of many governments.**

To this end it is recommended that:

(a) The work of the International Law Commission in its contribution to the progressive development of international law and its codification in respect of the law of the non-navigational uses of international watercourses should be given a higher priority in the working programme of the Commission and be co-ordinated with activities of other international bodies dealing with the development of international law of waters with a view to the early conclusion of an international convention;

(b) In the absence of bilateral or multilateral agreements, Member States continue to apply generally accepted principles of international law in the use, development and management of shared water resources;

(c) The Intergovernmental Working Group of Experts on Natural Resources Shared by Two or More States of the United Nations Environment Programme be urged to expedite its work on draft principles of conduct in the field of the environment for the guidance of States in the conservation and harmonious exploitation of natural resources shared by two or more States;

(d) Member States take note of the recommendations of the Panel of Experts on Legal and Institutional Aspects of International Water Resources Development set up under Economic and Social Council resolution 1033 (XXXVII) of 14 August 1964 as well as the recommendations of the United Nations Interregional Seminar on River Basin and Inter-basin Development (Budapest, 1975).

---

*Report of the United Nations Conference on the Human Environment (United Nations publication, Sales No.: E.73.II.A.14), chap. I, sect. II.

(e) Member States also take note of the useful work of non-governmental and other expert bodies on international water law;

(f) Representatives of existing international commissions on shared water resources be urged to meet as soon as possible with a view to sharing and disseminating the results of their experience and to encourage institutional and legal approaches to this question;

(g) The United Nations system should be fully utilized in reviewing, collecting, disseminating and facilitating exchange of information and experiences on this question. The system should accordingly be organized to provide concerted and meaningful assistance to States and basin commissions requesting such assistance.

Financing arrangements for water development

A persistent and recurring problem in many countries is the mobilization and the obtaining of adequate financial resources to implement necessary improvements in the numerous aspects of water resources planning, development and management.

> **A better and increased flow of funds on the best possible terms can assist in achieving the goals associated with water resources planning, development and management. Arrangements should be made to provide adequate and timely financing for project planning, formulation and implementation on a sustained and long-term basis on easy and liberal terms.**
>
> **States which command surplus financial resources may establish joint or intergovernmental ventures as their constitutional regimes permit in the field of water management and development with developing countries. This may be done voluntarily on a country-by-country basis but should preferably be handled on a combined regional basis.**

To this end, it is recommended that countries should:

(a) Examine the various possibilities of mobilizing internal resources;

(b) Develop by 1980 an inventory of investment needs in the field of water resources and determine the relative priorities of these needs;

(c) Investigate the possibilities of making water projects, as far as possible, self-sustaining;

(d) Attempt to reduce project costs by greater involvement of the people, more extensive use of local labour, material and technology, more economic designs and the preparation and adoption of standard designs for structures, establishment of joint ventures for manufacturing pumps, gates, pipes, valves, etc., and formation of national consultancy firms, etc.;

(e) Improve the economic viability and the social effectiveness of projects by making them more efficient;

(f) Support where appropriate the work of non-governmental organizations engaged in the promotion of water management projects, particularly those which are low-cost and self-help based.

International agencies and other supporting bodies, particularly international financing agencies such as the World Bank, regional and subregional development banks, national development banks and other bilateral and multilateral agencies for development financing, should, where appropriate and within their respective areas of responsibility:

  (i) Co-ordinate their policies and activities in the matter of financing projects and plans for water resources development;

 (ii) Review their financing criteria and give sufficient weight to the socio-economic effects of the projects, including direct, indirect and social benefits;

(iii) Adopt flexible methods of project execution in order to encourage effective participation of national capacities and to promote regional co-operation;

 (iv) Enunciate well-thought-out, comprehensive and realistic policies for financial assistance, which will pave the way for the formulation of long-term programmes for the implementation of water projects;

  (v) Strengthen existing institutional arrangements at the subregional and regional levels through the provision of equipment, personnel and funds;

 (vi) Undertake such co-operative studies or joint action for the development of international river and lake basins as may be requested by basin countries;

(vii) To the extent possible, provide appropriate opportunities for tenders to be offered on an international basis for goods and services, entrusting the recipient countries with the responsibility of executing projects financed by these agencies provided cost-effectiveness is achieved;

(viii) To the extent possible, agree to the retention of local consulting firms capable of undertaking entire projects or project elements, channel foreign expertise into such firms while advising on specific aspects of the project at the request of the Governments concerned.

Technical co-operation among developing countries

The promotion of technical co-operation among developing countries will supplement, upgrade and give a new dimension to the traditional forms of bilateral and multilateral development co-operation to help the developing countries achieve greater intrinsic self-reliance. The development of water resources in developing countries provides a promising area where technical co-operation among developing countries can be achieved. Many developing countries have expertise and capacity which they can share with other developing countries. Alternate appropriate technologies have been developed and many developing countries have reached the stage of self-reliance in water-resource development to enable them to apply the more appropriate techniques using the latest know-how and promote better understanding among the countries concerned. This can be adapted to the needs of other developing countries by means of technical co-operation among developing countries.

> **Governments of developing countries should pursue, explore and build mechanisms in order to promote to the fullest extent, technical co-operation among themselves with a view to achieving collective self-reliance in the development of their water resources.**

> **Technical co-operation among developing countries will also facilitate the selection of appropriate technologies for each country and region according to local socio-economic and physical conditions.**

In the light of these considerations it is recommended that where appropriate countries should at the national, regional and subregional level:

(a) Develop an adequate information base so that the capabilities and requirements for technical co-operation in water resources development are known, and put to good use on a continuing basis;

(b) Co-operate in the preparation and upgrading of a register of experts and consultant services on a subregional/regional basis having particular knowledge of the problems confronting the development of water resources for that subregion/region, and who can be called upon as and where required by member Governments;

(c) Determine priority areas in water resources development, and identify institutes having facilities, capabilities and expertise in these areas to develop technologies appropriate for developing countries;

(d) Develop pilot projects for the region/subregion by mutual agreement among the countries concerned to comprise a group of engineers and experts in the field of water resources from the region/subregion who would travel from country to country to collect detailed information on the available resources and the need for mutual exchange of technical resources in the region to promote technical co-operation among developing countries in the water sector;

(e) Identify programmes for water resources development that can be achieved through technical co-operation among developing countries in specific sectors such as community water supply, irrigation, drainage, hydroelectric generation, the development and management of transboundary water resources, ground-water development, and means for the prevention and reduction of losses due to floods and droughts and pollution control, water legislation and training, transfer of technology suited to the requirements of the developing countries and the general development of such technology;

(f) The countries of the regions of Africa, Asia and Latin America are especially urged to study the possibility of research development and production of low-cost equipment and technology so as to achieve the objectives of a better and more comprehensive assessment of their water resources within the shortest possible time and at the least cost and to promote the exchange of information at the regional level.

International organizations and other supporting bodies should, as appropriate, and on request, take the following action:

(i) The Administrator of the United Nations Development Programme (UNDP) in close consultation with the whole United Nations system, should make a study on the feasibility of establishing an information referral system on the capacities available in the developing countries for technical co-operation with each other by means of the utilization of key water resources institutions in the developing countries. This system should form an integral part of the UNDP information referral system. It should be based on information supplied by Governments and by the United Nations system from institutions within each sector and should be managed by UNDP on behalf of the United Nations system as a whole;

(ii) Assistance should be given in the initiation and implementation of joint programmes and institutions for research and training in water-related activities on a regional or subregional basis, as well as for financing of pilot projects and field studies as and where appropriate;

(iii) Consideration should be given in the preparatory process for the United Nations Conference on Technical Co-operation among Developing Countries to the provision of assistance, as necessary, to appropriate institutions concerned with water management to allow them to attend the Conference.

Annex

SPECIFIC REGIONAL RECOMMENDATIONS

Africa: Institutional Problems

Institutional inadequacy has been one of the major constraints on the effective development of water resources in the past: increasing attention has been paid to this problem during the last decade and a number of measures have been taken to strengthen existing institutions, to create new ones where needed and to provide for co-ordination; however, much remains to be done by way of streamlining the organizations and providing effective mechanisms for implementation and co-ordination at the national, subregional and regional levels.

The problem of creating an adequate institutional infrastructure should be kept constantly under review at the national, subregional and regional levels, in order to streamline the existing organizations and create new ones, where necessary, in order to deal effectively with the problems of water development as they emerge from time to time.

To this end it is recommended that countries should:

(a) Consider strengthening existing subregional organizations according to their individual needs, in consultation with the organizations concerned;

(b) Consider the creation of regional teams of experts/consultants under either the Economic Commission for Africa or any other suitable African development agency; such teams should carry out similar tasks in adjacent African countries for ground-water assessment, studies on water demand, reconnaissance of dam sites, etc., so as to enable the countries to work together over an extended period of time under similar technical conditions;

(c) Encourage the formation of technical associations open to all who possess the necessary professional credentials to be organized regionally with annual all-African conferences focusing on specific problem areas and solutions;

(d) Consider the establishment of scientific institutes within the common river basins to promote scientific studies, to formulate basin-wide plans for integrated basin development and to promote manpower training and an institutional framework within the basin States so as to reduce progressively the dependence on foreign consultancy enterprises;

(e) Consider expanding the scope of various specifically African agencies, such as the Organization of African Unity or the Economic Commission for Africa, so as to encourage participation in water resources development programmes to a much greater extent than hitherto; such regional organizations are potentially the most effective for co-ordination at the regional level, and for the evaluation of the progress of projects and their implementation at specified intervals of time — such as every three to five years;

(f) Strengthen the secretariat of the Economic Commission for Africa in its water resources activities so as to assist in co-ordinating the activities of the United Nations bodies at the regional level and to follow up the recommendations for Africa in the field of water resources.

In connexion with the establishment of institutions to deal with drought management, the Economic Commission for Africa has recommended further that drought-affected or drought-prone countries should draw up programmes similar to those of the Permanent Inter-State Committee on Drought Control in the Sahel, and implement them as early as possible so as to mitigate human suffering and free African agriculture from its present almost total subjection to the vagaries of rain.

Europe

In the case of transboundary river basins, and other shared waters, the active co-operation of riparian countries should be promoted, in particular in water pollution control.* This international co-operation could usefully be established, *inter alia*, through regional conventions and the harmonization of different long-term national plans of riparian countries, and at a second stage, if necessary, take steps to develop a joint plan for the entire basin.

Co-operation at the regional and international levels should be developed along the following guidelines:

(i) Exchange of scientific and technical information and documentation;

(ii) Review and analysis of the existing situation and prospects concerning the use of water resources, including:

Improving forecasting methods of hydrological régimes and exchanging forecasts on a regional scale.

Research into water resources in transboundary river and sea basins to estimate the effects of human activity factors on water régimes and quality.

Intensification of research and development applied to water management, including the design and demonstration of new systems and instruments for measuring and monitoring water quality and quantity (remote sensing) as well as low cost, easily maintained and reliable technologies for use by all nations, and research on emerging technologies for non-conventional sources.

Intensification of national and international efforts designed to maximize the economic and social efficiency of all water inputs, including measures to heighten awareness, change attitudes and provide the technological means and incentives to conserve and protect available water.

---

*In the ECE region this co-operation is carried out in the spirit of the Final Act of the Conference on Security and Co-operation in Europe. See also, *Water Development and Management*, edited by Asit K. Biswas, Pergamon Press, Oxford, 1978.

Latin America

The work that the United Nations, its specialized agencies and other international bodies operating in the region have carried out or are carrying out has effectively contributed to the exploitation of water resources.

It is desirable that the work of the United Nations in the region should be continued, strengthened, co-ordinated with and complemented by the activities of other international bodies.

In particular it is recommended that:

(a) Co-ordination at the regional level among the bodies of the United Nations system, and co-ordination between them and the other international organizations operating in Latin America and the Caribbean should be strengthened;

(b) The Economic Commission for Latin America should continue its work on studies of the optimum and integrated use of water with appropriate and timely participation by professionals and technical experts from the countries involved; it should include in its programme projects dealing with the interaction between water and the other environmental components; and it should co-operate with national and international bodies in the training of human resources;

(c) The studies on water in relation to the environment begun by the United Nations Environment Programme, the Economic Commission for Latin America, and the United Nations Educational, Scientific and Cultural Organization should be continued and enlarged, and further topics of interest should be included among those specifically studied;

(d) The work carried out on similar subjects by the International Law Commission should also be continued and expanded;

(e) The Pan-American Sanitary Bureau and the World Health Organization should continue and strengthen their technical co-operation activities in the field of the supply of drinking water, waste-water disposal, and water quality generally;

(f) The Joint Inter-American Development Bank/Pan-American Sanitary Bureau project for the supply of water to small communities should be continued and strengthened;

(g) The Food and Agriculture Organization of the United Nations should attach special importance to the execution of drainage works in agricultural land;

(h) The Centre for Natural Resources, Energy and Transport, in collaboration with the Economic Commission for Latin America, should carry out a study of river transport systems, taking into account the interests of the countries which share navigable international waters;

(i) International agencies such as the Inter-American Development Bank and the World Bank should increase financing both for basic studies and for plans, feasibility studies, projects and the construction of necessary works for the exploitation of water resources, in view of the social benefits involved in such activities;

(j) Support should be given to the work of the Comité Regional de Recursos Hidráulicos del Istmo Centroamericano so that it can continue its activities on a permanent basis with an executive secretariat, and the United Nations bodies, especially the World Meteorological Organization and the Economic Commission for Latin America, can collaborate with the projects which that Committee may establish;

(k) Regional central American programmes for sanitary engineering and hydraulic resources in the Regional School for Sanitary Engineering in Guatemala City and the Chair of meteorology in Costa Rica should be strengthened and organizations of the United Nations should collaborate in their task through programmes of technical assistance, exchange with other similar regional centres and the granting of fellowships;

(1) An inventory should be made of the human resources in the countries of the region, while training in research and the development of water resources and exchange of personnel should be promoted in order to allow first-hand exposure to differing technologies and procedures;

(m) The Organization of American States should continue its technological efforts to help with the implementation of projects for the exploitation of water resources, in respect of which it provides regional technical co-operation, when so requested by the countries concerned;

(n) The Latin American Economic System (SELA) should be urged to give priority to its co-operation programmes for regional and subregional projects for the exploitation of water resources;

(o) The United Nations, availing itself of the experience of the Centro Interamericano de Desarrollo Integral de Agua y Tierra (CIDIAT), the Instituto Nacional de Ciencia y Técnica Hídricas (INCYTH) and other existing bodies specializing in the subject, to carry out research and the training of professional, subprofessional, technical and management staff in the various aspects of science and technology related to the development of water resources;

(p) Support should be given to the work being conducted by the institutional system of the River Plate Basin so that its activities may be continued and intensified with a view to attaining the objectives embodied in the River Plate Basin Treaty;

(q) The facilities of the programmes of the World Meteorological Organization, particularly the World Weather Watch, should be utilized with the view to supporting a better understanding of hydrometeorological phenomena in the region;

(r) Through appropriate action by the World Health Organization, the positive experience gained by the Centro Panamericano de Ingeniería Sanitaria y Ciencias del Ambiente (CEPIS) should be strengthened, increased and extended so that, through the establishment of similar centres, the developing countries of other geographical regions may enjoy similar benefits.

Western Asia

Because of the extreme importance of water resources for the future of the region it is imperative that measures be taken now to conserve and develop this vital resource in the most efficient and economic manner for the highest and best use of all nations.

> **It is recommended that there be formed a water resources council for Western Asia (hereinafter referred to as the council), composed of one representative from each of the following twelve states: Bahrain, Democratic Yemen, Iraq, Jordan, Kuwait, Lebanon, Oman, Qatar, Saudi Arabia, Syrian Arab Republic, United Arab Emirates and Yemen; that each representative on the council be qualified to speak for his country on water-related matters; that such representatives be named as soon as possible in order that an initial meeting be held**

soon thereafter; that in order to implement the programme of the council certain committees, task forces and boards, as noted below, for example, may need to be established on a permanent or temporary basis; that such committees, task forces and boards maintain full co-ordination with United Nations agencies and governmental and private agencies now working in water programmes; that task forces be phased out after completion of their mission; that task forces, boards and committees be established initially for the following areas, with others to be formed as needed:

Board for a water resources fund

This Board would be set up for the purpose of establishing a new fund or establishing access to existing funds to be used in the form of loans or grants to the States members of the Economic Commission for Western Asia, at the national, subregional and regional levels in water-related programmes. The Board could establish an appropriate organizational structure to handle such funds. It could also be the responsibility of the Board, with the approval of the Council, to disburse aid or to assist countries in securing funds for use in efficient and worth-while water-related programmes. Such programmes could include, but need not be limited to, the broad categories of education, manpower training, research, consultant services, implementation of data-collection systems, development and management of water resources and economic analyses of water priorities. Specialists may be employed to determine eligibilities of need for assistance from the fund. Upon acceptance of this concept and formation of the Board detailed procedures would be developed.

Task force for the establishment of the water resources technical training centre

This task force could establish as soon as possible a training centre (with location to be determined by the task force and approved by the Council) for the training of technical personnel urgently needed in the field of water resources. The initial size of the training centre could allow for a minimum of 10-15 representatives from each country, the length of the training period to be determined after detailed analysis. Training at the subprofessional and technical levels could be given in many areas related to water resources, including but not limited to the following:

(a) Training in proper techniques for installing data networks and the evaluation and assessment of such data; the networks would include climatological stations, stream-gauging stations, ground-water observations, etc.;

(b) Fundamentals and principles of hydrology and hydrogeology at the subprofessional level;

(c) The operation and maintenance of water systems, including desalination plants, municipal and rural drinking-water systems, and water-treatment plants; training in laboratory analysis and testing for chemical and biological materials would also be included;

(d) The training of well-drilling crews in proper techniques for the drilling and development of well production, which would include electric logging and material analysis and the proper selection of pumps, well screens and other pertinent items.

Task force on data collection networks

This task force could be responsible for determining the components of and for implementing an adequate data-collection network for each country desiring assistance. Specialists trained in this field could be sent to any country desiring assistance to analyse and assess the situation, recommend components for the system and recommend necessary action to see that the programme is carried out.

Committee for professional assistance

This committee could see that teams of consultants or specialists of professional stature are made available to any nation requesting assistance in water-related matters. Such matters could include, but need not be limited to, assistance in developing national water policy, long-range planning, water legislation, rules and regulations for water use, studies and recommendations on governmental infrastructure related to water resources, economic evaluation of priority of water use, assistance in assessing the magnitude and quality of surface-water and ground-water resources, water management techniques and other areas as deemed appropriate. Such teams would be paid for by the country requesting assistance or by the Fund, as considered appropriate.

Committee for applied research

This committee could examine research facilities at present available for water-related matters and could recommend the establishment of any other facilities deemed necessary to cover fully the needs of all 12 nations on the Council. The committee could also establish a centre for compiling and disseminating research findings, both regional and international, to each of the 12 countries comprising the Council. Research findings and scientific articles could be published in technical periodicals and professional journals to give prestige to the research programmes of the area. The committee could also establish and maintain a reference library for use by the States members of the Council and could establish and operate a data bank, including data on water resources data for the members of the Council. The committee could investigate the need for a data bank on trained manpower.

Committee on subregional streams and underground aquifers

This committee could assist in initiating studies related to streams, wadis or underground aquifers common to two or more States members of the Council. This committee would co-operate with existing committees and groups in the gathering and analysis of basic data and the development of guidelines and compacts governing the use of such resources.

Committee for environmental and health aspects of water resource development

The committee is not intended to duplicate existing programmes in health-related fields but would ensure that water-resource development is in harmony with environmental and health factors. Close co-operation could be maintained with health organizations. Consultants or specialists could be employed as required to examine projects proposed for implementation in order to assess and evaluate the effects, both beneficial and adverse, of such proposed programmes on the environment and health of the country concerned. Special attention could be given to the effects upon coastal and marine water from upstream development. This committee should investigate the desirability of requiring environmental impact studies for all water-resource projects.

Committee on higher education at the professional level in water-related fields

This committee would examine the facilities and curricula of existing higher educational institutions in Western Asia with a view to determining the adequacy of present quality and the coverage of courses relating to water resources and environmental fields at professional levels. Where deficiencies are noted, action could be taken to bring such schooling up to adequate and acceptable levels. It would not be expected that each country would provide such training, but somewhere in the region there should be sufficient institutional facilities to fill the needs of the region. This programme could be co-ordinated with existing educational and scholarship programmes within the region.

RESOLUTIONS

I. Assessment of Water Resources

The United Nations Water Conference,

Recognizing that for the plans of action adopted by the Conference for the intensification and improvement of water use and development in agriculture and for providing safe drinking water and sanitation for all human settlements by 1990, a proper assessment is necessary of water resources in all countries of the world, and in particular in developing countries,

Considering that this assessment can be achieved only if all countries strengthen and co-ordinate arrangements for the collection of data in accordance with the recommendations of the Conference,

Resolves that:

(a) All efforts should be undertaken at the national level to increase substantially financial resources for activities related to water-resources assessment and to strengthen related institutions and operational services as necessary and appropriate at the national and regional levels;

(b) Training programmes and facilities for meteorologists, hydrologists and hydrogeologists should be established or strengthened;

(c) National scientific infrastructure for water-assessment activities be strengthened or established, particularly in developing countries;

(d) International co-operation aimed at the strengthening of water-resources assessment, particularly within the International Hydrological Programme and Operational Hydrological Programme be keyed to the targets set by the United Nations Water Conference and appropriately supported by national and international governmental and non-governmental institutions.

II. Community Water Supply

The United Nations Water Conference,

In view of the course taken by the discussions and the aspirations of the countries represented at the United Nations Water Conference and in view also of what was proposed at Habitat: United Nations Conference on Human Settlements, and

Considering that:

(a) All peoples, whatever their stage of development and their social and economic conditions, have the right to have access to drinking water in quantities and of a quality equal to their basic needs;

(b) It is universally recognized that the availability to man of that resource is essential both for life and his full development, both as an individual and as an integral part of society;

(c) To a significant extent similar considerations apply to all that concerns the disposal of waste water, including sewage, industrial and agricultural wastes and other harmful sources, which are the main task of the public sanitation systems of each country;

(d) The fundamental challenge facing all mankind can be met only with full international co-operation in all its aspects, entailing the mobilization of physical, economic and human resources;

(e) It is imperative to facilitate ways of achieving this essential co-operation, so that water is attainable and is justly and equitably distributed among the people within the respective countries;

(f) Those countries which are in a position to provide assistance, as well as international or regional organizations, should undertake to do so until the objective is attained, seeking to simplify regulations and administrative arrangements;

(g) Organizations of the United Nations system and other international organizations are making progress towards possible establishment of a consultative group mechanism on community water programmes.

Recommends:

(a) That where human needs have not yet been satisfied, national development policies and plans should give priority to the supplying of drinking water for the entire population and to the final disposal of waste water; and should also actively involve, encourage and support efforts being undertaken by local voluntary organizations;

(b) That Governments reaffirm their commitment made at Habitat to "adopt programmes with realistic standards for quality and quantity to provide water for urban and rural areas by 1990, if possible";

(c) That with a view to achieving these ends, the nations which need to develop their systems for providing drinking water and sanitation should prepare for 1980 programmes and plans to provide coverage for populations and to expand and maintain existing systems; institutional development and human resources utilization; and identification of the resources which are found to be necessary;

(d) That the United Nations agencies should co-ordinate their work efforts to help Member States, when they so request, in the work of preparation referred to in subparagraph (c) above;

(e) That in 1980 the national programmes which have been implemented for that purpose, and the extent to which the countries concerned have succeeded in mobilizing local and national support should be reviewed by an appropriate mechanism to be determined by the Economic and Social Council and based on the use of existing machinery, with a view to attaining co-ordinated action toward agreed targets;

(f) That in accordance with the decisions of the existing structures of the Economic and Social Council, appropriate external assistance should be available in order to assist in building, operating and maintaining these systems;

(g) That the Plan of Action formulated below should be implemented in a co-ordinated manner at the national and international levels.

PLAN OF ACTION

In order to be able to reach the targets of Habitat recommendation C.12, drastic measures have to be taken. This will need firm commitment on the part of countries and the international community.

A. *Priority areas for action*

1. Action must focus on promoting (a) increased awareness of the problem; (b) commitment of national Governments to provide all people with water of safe quality and adequate quantity and basic sanitary facilities by 1990, according priority to the poor and less privileged and to water scarce areas; and (c) larger allocation to this sector from the total resources available for general economic and social development.

2. Action must be taken to remedy constraints of manpower shortage (especially at the intermediate and lower levels), inadequacies in institutions and organization, and lack of appropriate and cost-effective technology.

3. New approaches should be developed which will result in larger flows of national, international and bilateral funds on more favourable and flexible conditions, so as to enable countries to increase the speed of implementation and, more important, enable the more effective use of the additional resources.

4. Communities must be provided with effective education on domestic hygiene and must be motivated and involved as appropriate at every level of the programme, including the planning, construction, operation, maintenance and financing of services, and the monitoring and safeguarding of the quality of the water supplied.

B. *Recommendations for action at national level*

5. Each country should establish goals for 1990 which match as far as possible the global targets adopted. In order to attain these goals, each country should:

(a) Develop national plans and programmes for community water supply and sanitation, and identify intermediate milestones within the context of the socio-economic development plan periods and objectives, giving priority attention to the segments of the population in greatest need;

(b) Immediately initiate engineering and feasibility studies on projects that are considered to be of the highest priority, and are based on a cost-effective technology appropriate to local conditions, with community participation, good management, and provision for operation and maintenance;

(c) Assess the manpower situation and, on the basis of this assessment, establish training programmes at the national level, to meet the immediate and future needs for additional professional staff, intermediate level technicians and, most important, village technicians;

(d) Promote massive national campaigns to mobilize public opinion regarding the provision of basic sanitary services, and develop appropriate procedures to ensure the active participation of communities in the programme;

(e) Establish appropriate institutions, if these do not exist, and assign to them specific responsibilities for the planning, implementation and monitoring of progress of the programme;

(f) Co-ordinate the efforts of all sectors active in rural areas, utilizing the manpower and other resources available, to ensure the provision of technically and socially acceptable sanitary facilities in rural areas;

(g) Develop a national revolving fund, in the first instance financed from substantially increased loans and grants from national and foreign sources, for water supply and sanitation which will encourage both the mobilization of resources for this sector and the equitable participation of beneficiaries; discourage wasteful consumption; and include a flexible combination of rates and, where necessary, explicit subsidies or other measures designed to achieve the economic and social objectives of the programme.

C. Recommendations for action through international co-operation

6. To achieve the Habitat targets, the international community must adopt new approaches to support increased national commitments with particular reference to the least developed and most seriously affected countries. It is, therefore, recommended that:

(a) Financial contributions be increased to strengthen the capabilities of international and bilateral agencies co-operating with Governments in the extension of community water supply and sanitation;

(b) At the request of national Governments, co-operation be extended to the formulation and implementation of high priority projects and programmes for community water supply and sanitation, with analysis of goals, methods and resources;

(c) Collaboration with the ongoing activity of the World Health Organization for monitoring and reporting on the status and progress of community water supply and sanitation be intensified.

7. The international community should give high priority to collaborating with Governments with regard to manpower surveys, the establishment of national training programmes (to meet immediate and future needs for professional staff, intermediate level technicians, and village technicians), research, and the promotion of community participation.

8. There should be even greater emphasis on social benefits. Multilateral and bilateral financing institutions should recognize the need for a higher level of grants and low interest-bearing loans to community water supply and sanitation programmes and, where this practice is already accepted, increase the proportion of such loans. They should be prepared to shoulder a higher proportion of local costs when financing community water supply and sanitation, increase their total allocations especially to rural water supply and sanitation, and complement local efforts in the rehabilitation and maintenance of systems.

9. Developing countries should foster co-operation among themselves, *inter alia*, in the establishment of intercountry training facilities; the development of appropriate technologies and of methodologies for training and management, and the exchange of experts and information, so that experience available elsewhere can be adapted to local conditions.

10. An effective clearing-house mechanism should be developed through international co-operation, by strengthening existing mechanisms if available, at the national, regional and international levels, to provide for the communication of selected information concerning all elements of community water supply and sanitation. An interrelated communication function should be included at every stage in all community water supply and sanitation projects.

11. Regular consultations should be held among Governments, international organizations, the international scientific community and relevant non-governmental organizations to ensure co-ordinated and accelerated action in the area of rural water supply and sanitation.

12. Co-ordination within the United Nations system should be improved at country level in order to ensure (a) a multidisciplinary approach in the development of community water supply and sanitation services; and (b) that rural water supplies and sanitation form part of integrated rural development projects.

III. *Agricultural Water Use*

The United Nations Water Conference,

Recognizing that the enormous deficit of food and agricultural production identified by the World Food Conference of 1974 calls for solutions of similar magnitude,

Accepting the vital role of water in expanding and intensifying agricultural production and in providing improved livelihood for the populations of developing countries,

Realizing that the scale of action required is immense in terms of investments and manpower for land areas to be developed and improved,

Considering that considerable national and international resources have to be allocated for the development of institutional services and human skills to provide the technical, managerial, administrative and farming expertise to meet the future demands of agriculture,

Recommends that the Action Programme on Water for Agriculture formulated below should be implemented with high priority in a co-ordinated manner at the national and international levels.

ACTION PROGRAMME ON WATER FOR AGRICULTURE

1. Faced with the enormous and continuing deficit in the production of food and of agricultural products revealed at the World Food Conference in 1974, and in recognition of the potential role of water development in correcting this deficit through activities proposed in the resolutions of that Conference, attention is drawn to the now urgent need for action to initiate a world-wide programme for the intensification and improvement of water development in agriculture.

2. Such a programme should in particular, though not exclusively, be directed at:

   (a) The improvement of existing irrigation with the objectives of raising productivity with minimum cost and delay, improving the efficiency of water use and preventing waste and degradation of water resources;

   (b) Developing efficient new irrigation for the further expansion of production;

   (c) Improving and extending rain-fed agriculture and livestock production, through both better soil moisture management and the opening up of new land through the provision of water supplies to human settlements and livestock;

   (d) The protection of agricultural land against the harmful effects of flooding and waterlogging and, where necessary, its reclamation;

   (e) The introduction or expansion of fish rearing in conjunction with over-all rural development activities.

3. As an indication of a major programme component, that of irrigation and drainage development, the magnitude of a 15-year global programme is estimated at some 45 million hectares of improved and 22 million hectares of new irrigation development.

A. *Recommendation on phased action programmes*

4. It is recommended that national action, where appropriate with supporting assistance from the international community, be directed at formulating phased programmes for action in the development and use of water for agriculture, showing the activities required, the estimated costs and the timing, and that reports on progress made in this area should be regularly reviewed by the appropriate intergovernmental bodies.

5. It is therefore proposed that national programmes be prepared containing the essential elements for:

   (a) Analysis and assessment of the problem, its magnitude and potential for development;

   (b) Planning for agricultural water development within a co-ordinated framework for national development, agricultural and over-all water planning;

   (c) Financing, with indications of the role of national finance and needs for external aid;

   (d) Building-up of national advisory services in government and private sectors for project planning, design, construction, operation and maintenance within the framework of the programmes envisaged;

(e) Training, extension, research and strengthening of formal education to support the heavier technical demands;

(f) Establishing and improving institutions for management, administration and legislative support.

B. *Recommendations on financing*

6. It is recommended that national efforts be concentrated on the sound formulation and planning of attractive programmes for water use and development for agriculture, and that the mobilization of local sources of finance be encouraged. It is further recommended that, within two years of the United Nations Water Conference, phased programmes of financial requirements be available for presentation to the appropriate intergovernmental bodies.

7. It is recommended that the attention of international financing agencies be drawn to the need to adapt to the intensified programme, in recognition in particular of the severe constraints imposed by current methods of project financing for the development of water in agriculture. This calls for a shift in the apportionment of funds giving higher priority to water for agriculture. It also requires more flexibility in local currency financing and in introducing integrated programme financing in addition to traditional project financing, together with the development of new evaluation criteria and methodologies. Finally this requires greater use of national and regional financing facilities and of local human and material resources.

C. *Recommendations on training, extension and research*

8. It is recommended that, in conjunction with the formulation of agricultural water development programmes, and immediately following the United Nations Water Conference, the present and future needs for trained manpower should be assessed. These requirements should not be limited only to directly water-related activities, but should include supporting disciplines in agriculture and associated subjects and the development of necessary interdisciplinary skills. The manpower needs for the three distinct components of technical training, extension services and research must be evaluated at the national level. Additionally, where necessary, attention must be given to the improvement of basic levels of formal education to facilitate subsequent training.

9. Co-ordinated research programmes should be undertaken to meet selected complex research requirements of the global water-development programme. A report should be prepared for presentation to the appropriate intergovernmental bodies on world training and research facilities and activities. This report should be available within two years of the United Nations Water Conference, and should include proposals for mobilizing and expanding such resources, and for the establishment of new facilities and programmes as and where appropriate. The report should also include the continual review of progress of all training and research programmes in the field of water resources to ensure their adequacy and appropriateness in support of development. The potential role of the United Nations University should also be considered.

D. *Recommendations for the promotion of national advisory services*

10. With the objective of building up technical and administrative capabilities to cope with the large-scale programmes envisaged, the full use of national manpower potential and material resources should be encouraged in the planning,

design, construction, operation and maintenance of water-development programmes. It is further recommended that immediate action be taken to develop the appropriate services, utilizing the skills and resources available in both public and private sectors. This would include consulting and supply services as well as development of local industries geared to the agricultural sector.

11. International aid for professional and technical training should give highest priority to the acquisition of skills in support of this specific objective, and organizations providing financial or material resources should clearly indicate their preference for the employment of local goods and services, as appropriate. The national advisory services should give particular attention to, and should be supported in the development of, technologies and the adaptation of methods and material most appropriate to local needs in the over-all aim of deriving optimal benefits from available investment, expertise and manpower.

E. *Recommendations on international programme support*

12. Recognizing the importance of international co-operation and support for implementing the proposed actions at the national level, it is recommended to co-ordinate international support programmes for the mobilization, planning, co-ordination and monitoring of international financial and technical assistance in the field of water development and use for agriculture. For this, it is proposed that support be given to:

(a) The co-ordination of international financial assistance to the activities of the programme;

(b) The co-ordination of technical assistance and backstopping of the programme, including analysis and assessment of the problem, planning for agricultural water development and establishing and improving institutions;

(c) Reporting to the appropriate intergovernmental bodies on progress made on the implementation of the programme on water for agriculture.

IV. *Research and Development of Industrial Technologies*

The United Nations Water Conference,

Bearing in mind the need to adopt rational water management methods,

Considering that rational water management entails not only using it economically and in the manner best calculated to prevent wastage and squandering but also using it properly so as to avoid in so far as possible the deterioration of the resource, to facilitate recycling and to maintain its potential usability for all the purposes for which it is intended,

Noting that industrial water use is one of the factors which are most intensively conducive to the qualitative degradation of water and its quantitative reduction in terms of its over-all use, contributing not only to the deterioration of the resource considered specifically and in relation to its various uses but also to the general pollution of the environment,

Recognizing that technology can contribute decisively to minimizing these negative effects of industrial water use,

Recommends that both Governments and international bodies, to the extent their competence, include in their economic, environmental and technological policies measures to facilitate, promote and stimulate research and development of industrial technologies requiring the least possible use of water and to facilitate recycling and even the replacement of methods entailing the use of water or other liquids by the use of other non-polluting liquids or by dry methods, so as to eliminate environmental contamination in so far as possible.

V. *Role of Water in Combating Desertification*

The United Nations Water Conference,

Bearing in mind the recommendations of the United Nations Conference on the Environment held in Stockholm in June 1972,

Taking into account the urgent need for concerted action to combat desertification and the forthcoming United Nations Conference on Desertification,

1. *Urges* all Governments to support and participate fully in the United Nations Conference on Desertification and in its preparatory meetings, including the regional meetings, in order to ensure the achievement of the objectives of the Conference;

2. *Considers* that water is one of the main factors limiting production and settlement in dry lands; and that lack of water, lack of the development of, or wasteful uses of, this resource are fundamental causes of many problems of desertification and environmental degradation;

3. *Considers* that proper planning, adequate development and wise management of water resources should receive priority in the efforts to combat desertification, to prevent environmental deterioration and to promote economic and social development in arid and semi-arid regions;

4. *Recommends* that nations should formulate specific action programmes to be considered by the forthcoming United Nations Conference on Desertification;

5. *Recommends further* that in most countries facing problems of desertification, urgent action is necessary to:

(a) Clearly define water policy in the current efforts to combat desertification and to formulate a comprehensive programme for the development and management of water resources, outlining both short-term and long-term specific objectives and targets for the future;

(b) Intensify and improve the arrangements existing for the assessment of water resources — surface as well as ground water;

(c) Consider, on the basis of prior environmental and health impact studies, a programme of surface and ground-water use and conservation with intensive mobilization of public participation on the basis of self-help. Such a programme should provide for the construction and maintenance of existing small dams or wells, with appropriate national and international assistance;

(d) Prepare feasibility studies for specific water projects expeditiously within the framework of over-all policies and programmes to combat desertification;

(e) Set up appropriate institutional arrangements at the national and regional levels in order that adequate attention be given to the problems of management and development of surface and ground-water resources in arid and semi-arid regions, including collation of related policies, promotion of efficient use of water by developing appropriate technologies, including the application of water-saving technologies;

(f) Promote research into all aspects of water-resources technology, with special reference to the problems and needs of arid and semi-arid areas;

6. *Urges* that international assistance be given to assist member Governments in the formulation of specific plans and projects for the development and management of water resources to combat desertification, the location of sources of financing for the implementation of projects for use in combating desertification, and the preparation and execution of training programmes at all levels.

VI. Technical Co-operation among Developing Countries in the Water Sector

The United Nations Water Conference,

Recalling General Assembly resolutions 3201 (S-VI) and 3202 (S-VI) of 1 May 1974, containing the Declaration and the Programme of Action on the Establishment of a New International Economic Order, 3281 (XXIX) of 12 December 1974, containing the Charter of Economic Rights and Duties of States, and 3362 (S-VII) of 16 September 1975 on development and international economic co-operation,

Noting the recommendations contained in the report of the *Ad Hoc* Group of Experts on Technical Co-operation among Developing Countries in Water Resources Development,*

Convinced that the management and development of water resources provides a promising area where technical co-operation among developing countries can be achieved,

Aware that alternate appropriate technologies in the field of the water sector have been developed by some developing countries and may be usefully applied by other developing countries,

1. *Welcomes* the convening of the United Nations Conference on Technical Co-operation among Developing Countries in Argentina in 1978;

2. *Urges* that all Governments support and participate fully in the United Nations Conference on Technical Co-operation among Developing Countries, as well as in the preparatory process for this Conference;

3. *Invites* the Administrator of the United Nations Development Programme to formulate immediately, and in consultation with the Governments concerned, a pilot project in water-resource management** and submit his proposal to the Governing Council of the United Nations Development Programme at its twenty-fourth session, if possible;

---

*E/CONF.70/12, see *Water Development and Management*, edited by Asit K. Biswas, Pergamon Press, Oxford, 1978.
**Defined in document E/CONF.70/12, para. 54.

4. *Further recommends* that, at the request of the Governments concerned, the regional commissions put forward proposals for the strengthening or, where appropriate, the establishment of regional institutes for training and research in the water sector;

5. *Recommends further* that the United Nations Development Programme in co-operation with the regional commissions and the United Nations system assist in promoting programmes of technical co-operation among developing countries in the field of water-resources development, which may include such areas as surface and ground-water development, drainage and reclamation, hydropower development and inland navigation;

6. *Recommends further* that all Governments, particularly those of developing countries, and the relevant United Nations agencies submit information to the United Nations Conference on Technical Co-operation among Developing Countries indicating the progress made in implementing recommendations for technical co-operation among developing countries in the water resource sector as delineated at the United Nations Water Conference with a view to defining future action and specific objectives in this area.

VII. River Commissions

The United Nations Water Conference,

Bearing in mind the relevant recommendations of the United Nations,

Recommends to the Secretary-General to explore the possibility of organizing meetings between representatives of existing international river commissions involved that have competence in the management and development of international waters, with a view to developing a dialogue between the different river-basin organizations on potential ways of promoting the exchange of their experiences. Representatives from individual countries which share water resources but yet have no established basin-wide institutional framework should be invited to participate in the meetings. The regional commissions should be called upon to facilitate this task at the regional level.

VIII. Institutional Arrangements for International Co-operation in the Water Sector

The United Nations Water Conference,

Recognizing the imperative need for accelerated progress in the investigation and development of water resources, and its integrated management for efficient use,

Aware of the efforts being undertaken by the United Nations system at various levels to assist the countries in their endeavours to achieve these objectives,

Recognizing the difficulties in the area of co-ordination which affect the United Nations bodies in execution of their tasks,

Further recognizing the complementary roles of global and regional bodies in the United Nations system, and the role of the regional commissions as outlined in Economic and Social Council resolution 2043 (LXI) of 5 August 1976,

Deeply conscious of the fundamental importance of water for economic and social development,

Requests the Economic and Social Council, in particular in its consideration of the restructuring of the economic and social sectors of the United Nations system, to give priority consideration to the following recommendations:

(a) That at the intergovernmental level the Economic and Social Council, the Committee on Natural Resources and the regional commissions within their respective regions, should play a central role in the promotion of intergovernmental co-operation as a follow-up to the Plan of Action on integrated water resources development and management recommended by this Conference;

(b) That for this purpose, among other measures, steps be taken to intensify the work in the water sector of the Economic and Social Council and the Committee on Natural Resources through, *inter alia*, strengthening the secretariat support services to these organs by all United Nations organizations and bodies involved in the water resources sector and, if required, through the convening of special or subject-oriented sessions;

(c) That the proposals for interagency co-ordination presented to the Conference in the report of the Administrative Committee on Co-ordination and the Environment Co-ordination Board* be examined by the Committee on Natural Resources at its fifth session with a view to submitting its recommendations to the Economic and Social Council at its sixty-third session for consideration and implementation;

(d) That the regional commissions should, taking into account the central role of the Economic and Social Council and the Committee on Natural Resources at the global level, and the special needs and conditions of the respective regions:

(i) Assist the United Nations Development Programme and the United Nations specialized agencies and organizations, at the request of the Governments of developing countries concerned, in identifying intersectoral subregional, regional and interregional projects and preparing programmes;

(ii) Intensify their efforts in the water sector, and, with the assistance of the competent organizations of the United Nations system and at the request of the Governments concerned, enlarge co-operation among the countries in the water field at the subregional, regional and interregional levels;

(iii) Assign specific responsibility on water to an existing intergovernmental committee within the regional commissions, or if necessary, create a new one, and establish or strengthen, as appropriate, the secretariat units of the commissions dealing with water, which would serve as the secretariat of the intergovernmental committee referred to in this subparagraph;

(iv) Establish *ad hoc* groups of experts, as and when necessary, who should preferably be drawn from the countries of the region concerned;

(e) That, for the purposes outlined in the preceding paragraphs, the General Assembly should consider providing, as necessary, additional resources to the regional commissions and other relevant sectors of the United Nations within the budget of the United Nations;

---

*Present and future activities of the United Nations system in water resources development (E/CONF.70/CBP/4), see *Water Development and Management*, edited by Asit K. Biswas, Pergamon Press, Oxford, 1978.

(f) That at the country level, under the leadership of the United Nations Development Programme resident representatives, the United Nations system should intensify the co-ordination of projects and programmes undertaken at the request of the Governments of developing countries.

IX. Financing Arrangements for International Co-operation in the Water Sector

The United Nations Water Conference,

Realizing the gravity of the problem of water resources and the crisis that mankind may have to face unless timely action is taken to avert it,

Recognizing that the Action Plan recommended by the Conference is designed to promote activities at the national, regional and interregional levels to avert such a crisis,

Further recognizing that the implementation of the Plan will require, *inter alia*, mobilization of increased financial resources,

Taking note of the suggestion for the establishment of a voluntary fund for the development and management of water resources,

Aware of the need for additional resources required for the implementation of the Action Plan,

1. *Requests* the Secretary-General to prepare, on the basis of consultations with Governments and competent organizations within the United Nations system, a study of the most effective and flexible mechanisms to increase the flow of financial resources specifically for water development and management through existing organizations and proposed mechanisms and to present the study to the General Assembly at its thirty-second session, through the Economic and Social Council at its sixty-third session;

2. *Recommends* that additional financial allocations be made to existing:

(a) Organizations within the United Nations system, particularly the United Nations Development Programme, in order to increase the funds available to all developing and in particular the least developed countries to meet their needs in technical assistance and programmes related to water resources development;

(b) Bilateral, subregional, regional and international organizations and programmes, including the International Bank for Reconstruction and Development and the regional development banks, within their respective areas of responsibilities, and recommends that they review their terms and conditions in view of the economic and social implications of water development projects with the objective of providing the best possible terms, taking into account the results of the United Nations Water Conference;

3. *Recommends further* that priority be given to projects for the development and management of water resources based on co-operation among developing countries.

X. Water Policies in the Occupied Territories

The United Nations Water Conference,

Recalling General Assembly resolution 3171 (XXVIII) of 17 December 1973, entitled "Permanent sovereignty over natural resources", and taking into consideration the statements made by the representatives of the United Nations Council for Namibia and the Palestine Liberation Organization,

Further recalling General Assembly resolution 31/186 of 21 December 1976, entitled "Permanent sovereignty over national resources in the occupied Arab territories",

Noting with great concern the illegitimate exploitation of the water resources of the countries and peoples subject to colonialism, alien domination, racial discrimination and *apartheid*, to the detriment of the indigenous peoples,

1. *Affirms* the inalienable right of the people of the countries under colonial and alien domination in their struggle to regain effective control over their natural resources, including water resources;

2. *Recognizes* that the development of water resources in territories subjected to colonialism, alien domination, racial discrimination and *apartheid* should be directed for the beneficial use of the indigenous peoples who are the legitimate beneficiaries of their natural resources, including their water resources;

3. *Denounces* any policies or actions by the colonizing and/or dominating Powers contrary to the provision of paragraph 2 of the present resolution, and particularly in Palestine, Zimbabwe, Namibia and Azania.

OTHER RESOLUTIONS

XI. Question of the Panama Canal Zone

The United Nations Water Conference,

Considering that:

(a) The sovereign use of natural resources, as a fundamental element of the economic, social and political development of peoples, is a principle recognized by the United Nations,

(b) Both the system of ownership of water and jurisdiction over that resource are of special significance for the purposes of planning and development of water resources,

(c) Those principles are closely linked to the objectives of the United Nations Water Conference,

(d) The problem of the so-called Canal Zone of Panama constitutes one of the principal impediments to the full development of water resources in the areas surrounding the cities of Panama and Colón,

Resolves to express its earnest wishes that the negotiations being conducted by the Republic of Panama and the United States of America will culminate at the earliest possible time in a just and equitable solution that will permit the Republic of Panama fully to exercise its sovereign rights in the part of its territory known as the Canal Zone and, consequently, to formulate a national policy for the full development of water resources.

14th plenary meeting
23 March 1977

XII. *Expression of Thanks to the Host Country*

The United Nations Water Conference,

Recognizing the importance of international co-operation aimed at improving the development of water resources for efficient use through an integrated approach,

Convinced that the United Nations Water Conference which took place at Mar del Plata from 14 to 25 March 1977 represents a significant contribution to the efforts of the international community to find appropriate means to improve the quality and supply of water for the use of mankind,

Expresses its profound appreciation to the Government and people of Argentina, of the province of Buenos Aires and, in particular, of the City of Mar del Plata, for making possible the holding of this Conference and for their generous hospitality and their great contribution to the successful outcome of its work.

16th plenary meeting
25 March 1977

Index

Action Plan 19, 147, 203, 204
Afghanistan 35
Africa 1, 4, 9, 13, 20, 21, 35, 37, 38, 39, 40, 42, 57, 60, 99, 101, 111, 117, 119, 120, 121, 122, 138, 178, 181, 185, 186, 187
  West xiii, 32
African Group 16
Agriculture xv, 5, 10, 11, 12, 13, 18, 45, 53, 55-59, 65, 66, 67, 69, 73, 79, 84, 85, 89, 99-101, 102, 104, 105, 107, 110, 112, 114, 128-130, 143, 149, 155, 160, 166, 179, 192
  Rain-fed 173, 179, 197
Agrigentum xi
Agroclimatology 179
Aid
  Bilateral 20, 175, 183, 196, 204
  Multilateral 175, 183, 196
Alien domination 205
Alkalinization xvi, 58, 100
America
  Central 35, 37, 100
  Latin 4, 9, 35, 38, 39, 42, 51, 57, 60, 100, 101, 111, 119, 121, 122, 138, 140, 181, 185
  North 1, 35, 37, 38, 39, 40, 42, 57, 59, 60, 61, 102, 104, 106, 119, 138
Antarctica xiii, 38, 119
Apartheid 205
Aquaculture 157, 180
Aquifer 33, 34, 36, 39, 43, 45, 47, 69, 101, 104, 110, 118, 121, 122, 137, 145, 148, 151, 173, 191
  Artesian 33
  Coastal 41
  Recharge 121, 122, 123, 137, 148, 179
Arabia 122
Arab World 22
Arctic 119
Argentina 7, 19, 116, 117, 120, 122, 124, 127, 130, 137, 138, 140, 141, 146, 201, 206

Arid Land xiv, 25, 34, 41, 55, 65, 99, 107, 115, 116, 118, 122, 123, 142, 200, 201
Aristotle xi
Arizona 124
Arsenic 48
Asia 1, 35, 37, 38, 39, 40, 41, 42, 57, 60, 100, 111, 119, 121, 138, 139, 181, 185
  South-East 98
  West 111, 181, 189, 192
Aswan 32, 121, 122, 135
Atlantic 146
Atmosphere xii, 8, 29, 75, 91, 119, 142, 148
Australia 38, 39, 42, 57, 115, 117, 118, 119, 122, 123, 125, 130, 134, 137, 139
  South 115, 139
Austria 117, 123, 125, 126, 132, 134, 136, 137
Avalanche 136, 137, 155
Azania 205

Baharin 189
Bali 73
Bangkok 126
Bangladesh 17, 97, 129, 139
Barrage 103
Basic Human Needs xiv, 12, 19, 21, 25, 39, 166, 193
Basin *see* Catchment
  Laguna de Bay 135
Baumgartner, A. 29, 37, 38
Bavaria 128
Benin 122
Benthic Organisms 34
Berkol, F. 14
Beyer, M. 12
Bicarbonate 41
Bioaccumulation 163
Biochemical Oxygen Demand xiii, 34, 41, 54
Biocides 163
Biodegradation 163
Bioprocessing 67
Biosphere xi

Index

Bisenzio 103
Biswas, Asit K. xi, 22, 23, 27, 69, 71, 91, 111, 113, 187, 201, 203
Biswas, Margaret R. 7, 23, 152
Bonem 54
Bore-hole 33, 118, 147, 173
Botswana 35, 118
Bower, B. 55
Brain Drain 176
Brazil 18, 59, 97, 122, 130
Budapest 182
Buenos Aires 15, 206
Bulgaria 53
Burundi 139
Byelorussian SSR 113, 115, 132, 135

Cadmium 136, 164
Calcium 41
California 124
Canada xii, xiii, 15, 21, 59, 111, 113, 114, 115, 116, 137, 138-139
Canal
  Jonglei 121, 129
  Lining 66
  Panama 19, 205-206
  Zone 205-206
Caracas 92
Carbon Absorption 143
Carcinogen 26, 48, 136
Caribbean 57, 188
Catchment 31, 60, 75, 83, 84, 85, 86, 93, 122, 130, 138, 139, 161, 165, 166, 172, 181, 184
Cement, Asbestos 170
Centre
  International Water Management Training and Research 140
  Water Research 140
Centro Interamericano de Desarrollo Integral de Agua y Tierra (CIDIAT) 189
Centro Panamericano de Ingenieria Sanitaria y Ciencias des Ambiente (CEPIS) 189
Chad 14
Charter of Economic Rights and Duties of States 201
Chemicals
  Man-made 34
  Toxic xiii, 26, 48, 63, 76, 104, 121, 135, 157, 163, 164
Chicago 127
China xi, 7, 15, 21, 35, 37, 43, 50, 57, 59, 102, 104
Chloride 41
  Polyvinyl 170

Chlorination 136, 144, 162
Cholera xiii, xv
Climatic Change 31, 32, 40, 41, 67, 75, 179
Climatology 179
Cloud-seeding see Weather Modification
Coastal Zone 43, 91, 116, 125, 142, 155, 162, 192
Code of Conduct 5
Coliform Organisms see Organisms, Coliform
Colon 205
Colonialism 205
Colonial Powers 14
Comité Regional de Recursos Hidráulicos del Istmo Centroamericano 188
Commoner B. 80
Community Participation see Public Participation
Computer 31, 140, 141, 142, 144, 145, 148, 149, 164, 176
Concrete, Prestressed 170
Congo 35
Conjunctive Use 142, 151
Conservation xiv, 9, 62, 81
Consumptive Use 39, 45, 53, 64, 114, 131, 159
Contamination, Bacteriological 34, 136
Costa Rica 189
Cost-Benefit Analysis 83, 89, 90, 124, 134, 137, 144, 157, 164, 165, 166, 171, 194, 195
Council for Mutual Economic Assistance (CMEA) 94
Countries, Landlocked 160
Cropping Intensity 64
Cuba 35
Cyclone 72, 74
Czechoslovakia 53

Data
  Banks 149
  Collection 78-79, 86, 119, 120, 123-124, 147, 148, 172, 190, 191
  Hydrological 28, 30, 31, 79, 120, 142, 147, 148, 160, 172
  Meteorological 31, 79, 147, 160, 172
  Network 30, 32, 68, 78, 190
  Processing 120, 141, 147, 148, 149
  Storage 120, 147
da Vinci, Leonardo 25
DDT xiii, 164
Decade
  International Drinking Water Supply and Sanitation 19, 21, 152

Index

International Hydrological 31, 37, 38, 119, 120
  Second Development 49, 50, 51, 52, 54
Delta, Burdekin 123
Denmark 113, 116, 125, 134
Desalination 8, 13, 30, 43, 66, 74, 124, 132, 140, 142, 175, 179, 180, 190
  Multistage Flash 124
  Reverse Osmosis 124
Desertification 65, 174, 200-201
Development 95
  Alternative Patterns 12, 65, 175
  Economic 1, 73, 74, 89, 95, 105, 106, 107, 115, 142, 153, 162, 165, 168, 200
  Environmental 165
  Industrial 104, 164
  Regional 83, 84, 85, 144, 162, 165
  Resource 173
  Rural 11, 21, 56
  Social 1, 73, 74, 89, 95, 105, 106, 107, 115, 142, 162, 165, 200
  Technological 106
Diarrhea xv
Dietrich, B. 15
Dinaric Karst Region 115, 131
Disaster Relief 98
Dissolved Oxygen see Oxygen, Dissolved
Drainage 10, 11, 21, 41, 43, 44, 45, 58, 59, 67, 77, 84, 99, 101, 108, 118, 129-130, 154-155, 157, 185, 191, 202
  Basin see Catchment
Draw-down 33
Dredging 103
Drought xi, xiv, 8, 14, 25, 31, 67, 72, 80, 83, 91, 97-99, 100, 101, 109, 112, 113, 120, 136-137, 145, 156, 173-174, 180, 181, 185, 187
Dry Farming 100, 101
Dysentery xv
  Bacillary xiii

Earthquakes 97, 113, 136, 138, 141, 145, 180
East
  Far 10, 57
  Near 57
Ecclesiastes xi
Education 112, 174-178

Efficiency of Water Use see Water Use, Efficiency
Effluent
  Charges 110, 163
  Control 67, 84, 109
  Disposal 110, 136, 162, 182
  Standards 67
Egypt xi, xvi, 13, 57, 121, 122, 129, 135, 139
Empedocles xi
Energy 8, 59-61, 67, 83, 84, 89, 95, 103, 104, 106, 112, 115, 116, 124, 131, 150, 159, 163
  Electrical 81
  Geothermal 67, 131
  Nuclear 61, 103, 106, 110, 131, 132, 134, 144, 162
  Solar 13, 67
  Thermal 77, 104, 114, 132, 134, 144, 162
  Wind 67, 103
England xiii, 103
Environment 2, 9, 10, 12, 14, 31, 34, 59, 63, 65, 67, 72, 75, 76, 80, 81, 86, 87, 88, 96, 105, 107, 110, 112, 116, 133-136, 141, 144, 151, 155, 158, 159, 160-164, 165, 170, 171, 180, 182, 188, 191, 192, 199, 200
Environmental Implications xvii, 18, 66-68, 83, 91, 108, 110, 136, 140, 180, 200
Epidemiology 162
Equity 90
Erosion xvi, 18, 26, 41, 42, 67, 72, 75, 76, 80, 83, 91, 130, 137, 156, 161, 172, 179
Estuary 162
  Tejo 135
Ethiopia 13, 136, 137, 139
Eurasia 100
Europe 1, 17, 35, 37, 39, 42, 57, 59, 60, 61, 100, 102, 104, 106, 111, 118, 119, 121, 138, 181, 187
  Eastern 57
  Western 57
European Economic Community 94
Eutrophication 134, 163
Evaporation 13, 28, 29, 31, 32, 35, 38, 39, 41, 43, 45, 61, 67, 74, 119, 129, 148, 174
  Reduction 66
Evapotranspiration 31, 32, 36, 39
Excreta Disposal xii, 49, 50, 51-52, 95, 102, 112, 162

Falkenmark, M. 146

Fano, E. 22
Fertilizers 22, 160, 163
Filariasis xiv
Finland 115, 121, 125, 126, 132, 134, 138
Fisheries 62, 63, 67, 161, 162, 197
Fleming, J. E. 146
Flood xi, xiv, 8, 10, 11, 14, 31, 44, 56, 60, 62, 65, 72, 73, 74, 75, 76, 77, 83, 84, 91, 97-99, 101, 112, 113, 120, 136-137, 138, 145-156, 157, 162, 172-173, 174, 180, 181, 197
  Evacuation 173
  Insurance 62, 137, 145, 173
  Proofing 98, 137, 145, 173, 174
  Risks 137, 145, 172, 173, 174
  Warning 62, 98, 108, 109, 173, 181
  Zoning 137, 145, 172-173, 174
Florence 103
Fluoride 41, 48
Fog Drip Augmentation 66
Food and Agricultural Organization (FAO) xv, 10, 22, 56, 57, 58, 188
Forecasting Methods see Methods, Forecasting
Forestation 63
Forests, Tropical 28
Fossil Fuels 40, 60, 61, 67, 103, 106, 131
France 11, 14, 18, 53, 113, 120, 122, 131, 134, 135, 140, 141
Fund
  Fertiliser 22
  for Water Development 16
Fungicides 63

Gambia 130
Gambian Sleeping Sickness xiii
Gash 122
Gastro-enteritis xiv, 12
Georgia 146
Germany
  Democratic Republic of 53, 121, 123
  Federal Republic of 16, 17, 53, 117, 122, 128, 129, 130, 136
Glaciers xii, 8, 29, 148
Great Britain see United Kingdom
Ground-water xii, xv, 8, 16, 25, 26, 28, 29, 30, 31, 32-33, 36, 37, 39, 40, 41, 52, 56, 65, 67, 68, 72, 75, 76, 79, 91, 96, 109, 110, 112, 116, 117, 118, 119, 121-123, 124, 126, 136, 137, 141, 142, 145, 147, 148, 149, 151, 154, 155, 163, 164, 173, 174, 179, 185, 186, 190, 191, 200, 201, 202
  Pollution 43
  Recharge 33, 43, 56, 69, 76, 78, 137, 142
Guatemala 189
Guinea Worm xiii
Guyana 127, 129

Habitat see United Nations Conference on Human Settlements
Habitat
  Aquatic 44, 59, 63, 104, 105, 157
  Wetland 44
  Wildlife 45, 67
Hail Suppression 75, 124
Haiti 35
Harambee 13
Harbours 103
Health
  Environmental 18, 26, 53, 72, 171
  Human xiii, 2, 18, 48, 52, 53, 63, 65, 67, 80, 84, 89, 90, 95, 96, 112, 133, 136, 144, 153, 154, 155, 157, 158, 159, 160-164, 165, 171, 172, 175, 195, 200
Helsinki 126
Hepatitis xiii
Herbicides 63, 129
Herodotus xi
Herring gulls xiii
Holy, M. 11, 58
Holy See 18, 113
Honduras 35
Horning, H. M. 10
Humidity 32, 36
Hungary 46, 53, 116, 123, 125, 134, 135, 137, 138
Hurricane 180
Hussain, M. I. 12
Hydrocarbons, Chlorinated xiii
Hydroelectric 2, 4, 7, 13, 15, 18, 44, 45, 59-61, 62, 63, 67, 77, 91, 103-105, 106, 113, 114, 119, 120, 131, 143, 150, 152, 159, 165, 166, 185, 202
Hydrologic
  Cycle 25, 29, 40, 43, 155
  Network 35
Hydrometeorology 37

Ice-age 32

Iceberg Transport 43, 66
Ice-cap 8, 29
Ice-career 41
Ice, Polar xii
Imagery
  Infra-red 141
  Multispectral 141
Income Redistribution 65, 81
India xi, xiii, 11, 14, 53, 59, 97, 122, 146
Indonesia 14, 18, 128
Industrial Revolution xii
Infiltration 76, 122, 123, 164
Inga 115
Institute for Water Economics, Legislation and Administration 140
Institutional Arrangements 16, 69, 84, 86, 94, 105, 107, 117, 128, 141, 167, 170, 174, 179, 180, 184, 185, 194, 202-204
Instituto Nacional de Ciencia y Técnica Hidricas (INCYTH) 189
Inter-American Development Bank 187
International Association for Water Law 92
International Bank for Reconstruction and Development see World Bank
International Commission on Irrigation and Drainage 11
International Development Association 16
International Development Research Centre 51
International Fertilizer Supply Scheme 22
International Fund for Agricultural Development (IFAD) 16, 22
International Joint Commission 139
International Labour Organization (ILO) 12
International Law Association 93, 94
International Law Commission 18, 182, 188
International Law Institute 93
International Reference Centre for Community Water Supply 128
Intestinal Worm Infections xv
Invertebrate xiii
Iran 17, 113, 114, 116, 117
Iraq 113, 114, 189
Iron 41, 125
Irrigated Area xv, 33, 55-59, 64, 100, 101, 152, 156, 197

Irrigation 7, 9, 10, 11, 13, 14, 15, 18, 20, 21, 22, 26, 41, 44, 45, 47, 55-59, 60, 61, 62, 66 69, 77, 82, 84, 85, 99, 100, 101, 103, 114, 118, 119, 120, 122, 128-130, 132, 143, 154, 155, 157, 185, 191
  Drip 10, 58
  Efficiency 58
  Gravity 10
  Sprinkler 10, 58
Isolines 31
Israel 10, 53, 116, 129, 132
Italy 103, 113, 115
Ivory Coast 35, 122

Japan xiii, 35, 53, 59, 113, 115, 118, 124, 126, 132, 136, 146
Jauregui, L. U. 7, 9
Jordan 189

Kelian Subak 73
Kenya 13, 120, 130, 139
Kuwait 35, 43, 124, 189

Lagoon 148
  Aerobic 128
  Anaerobic 128
Lake
  Chad 40
  Kyoga 139
  Michigan xiii
  Mobutu-Sese-Seko 139
  Nasser 32
  Victoria 139
  Volta 31
Lakes xii, 8, 29, 30, 39, 40, 63, 73, 76, 96, 105, 119, 125, 148, 162, 184
  Great 132
  Oligotropic 76
Land
  Classification 156
  Degradation 26, 58, 155, 161
  Reform 59
  Subsidence 118, 138
  Transport 44
  Use 44, 60, 62, 76, 86, 98, 108, 130, 137, 148, 155, 157, 158, 164, 173, 175, 176
Latin American Economic System 189
Law, International 26
Lebanon 189
Leningrad 38
Liberia 13, 139
Libya 14, 57
Lima Declaration 158

Livingstone, D. A. 41
Locks 61
Locusts 97
Lvovich 37, 38, 41, 42, 58

Machinery
  Economic 80
  Financial 80
  Institutional 80
  Legal 80
  Technical 80
Madrid 126
Mageed, Y. A. 1, 7, 8, 9, 19, 21, 22, 23
Magnesium 41
Malaria xiv, xv, 12
Malnutrition 81
Malthaus xvi
Manganese 125
Manpower 175, 176, 190, 194, 195
Mar del Plata 7, 23, 147, 206
Mauritania 14
Mendez-Arocha, J. L. 146
Mendoza 140
Mercury xiii, 136, 164
Mesopotamia xi, 102, 105
Metals, Heavy xiii, 34, 41, 134
Methods
  Forecasting 120, 140, 142, 148, 172, 173, 174, 181, 187
  Nuclear 148
Mexico 53, 113, 114, 124, 141
Middle Ages 102
Minimata Bay xiii
  Disease 136
Models
  Analogue 34, 148
  Analytical 46
  Hydrologic 174
  Mathematical 31-32, 34, 40, 117, 123, 130, 131, 134, 138, 140, 141, 142, 148, 149, 151, 165, 166, 176, 179
  Numerical 141
  Parametric 135, 144, 164
  Physical 34
  Simulation 40, 131, 134, 135, 144, 164
Mongolia 53
Montreal xii
Morocco 13, 59
Morse, B. 15
Moscow 38, 42
Mosquitoes 12
Munich 29, 38
Mutagenic 26, 48

Nairobi 3
Namibia 205
National Commission on Water Quality xiii
Navigation 2, 44, 45, 59, 61-62, 63, 74, 75, 77, 79, 101-103, 105, 106, 113, 133, 160, 182, 188, 202
Nepal 35
Network
  Communication 81
  Density 36, 37, 120, 147
New Delhi 146
New International Economic Order xvi, 3, 8, 201
New South Wales 115, 139
Newspapers 175
Niger 13
Nigeria 13
Nitrate 41, 48
Nitrogen 34
Non-point Sources 34, 62
Norway 17, 59, 125, 127, 135, 138
Nubariya xvi
Nutrients 34, 69
Nutrition 100, 156

Ocean xiii, 8, 28, 29, 30, 38, 39, 41, 43, 72, 76-77
  Arctic 41
  Pacific 119
Oceania 57, 60, 119
Oman 189
Onchocerciasis xiv
Optimization 117, 131, 134, 155, 159
Organic Materials 34, 136
Organic Synthetic Compounds xiii, 41, 48, 54, 72
Organisation of Economic Cooperation and Development 18, 94
Organisms
  Coliform xiii, 34, 41
  Pathogenic 43, 48
Organization of African Unity 186
Organization of American States 189
Organoleptic Substances 157
Osaka 118, 126, 136
Overgrazing 18, 65, 173
Oxfam 97
Oxygen, Dissolved 34
Ozonation 143
Ozone 40

Pacific 1, 100, 111, 181
  South-West 35, 37
Pakistan 14
Palestine 205

Liberation Organization 205
Pampas 141
Panama 35, 205-206
Pan-American Sanitary Bureau 188
Paris xii, 3
Penguins xiii
Pesticides xiii, 63, 160
Philippines 14, 135
Phosphorous 34
Phreatophyte 43, 66
Pindar xi
Plan of Action 17
Plato xi, 103
Point Sources xiii, 34, 62
Poland 53, 115, 117, 118
Polar Ice-Caps see Ice-Caps, Polar
Pollution xi, 2, 4, 8, 9, 10, 18,
  25, 63, 72, 74, 75, 76, 83, 84,
  87, 89, 91, 96, 105, 106, 109,
  114, 121, 125, 133, 135, 141,
  158, 160, 163, 168, 175, 176,
  179, 181, 190
 Air 61
 Control xiv, 47, 63, 68, 94, 110,
  114, 115, 116, 134, 138, 140,
  144, 159-160, 163-164, 185, 187,
 Microbiological 76
 Noise 61
 Transfrontier 17, 94
Polychlorinated Biphenyl 164
Portugal 135
Potassium 41
Precipitation xiii, 29, 30, 31, 32,
  36, 37, 38, 39, 41, 58, 63, 75,
  119, 122, 124, 148
 Acid 135, 144, 164
Primary Treatment see Treatment,
 Primary
Prince Edward Island 116
Programme
 International Hydrological 120,
  148, 192
 Operational Hydrology 148, 192
Programming, Nonlinear 131
Project
 Golodnaya 128
 Kakhovka 128
 Karshinskaya 128
 Kazyal-Orda 128
 Kuban 128
 Saratov 128
Public Participation 12, 18, 51, 80,
  87, 88, 106, 109, 117, 167, 169,
  170, 172, 183, 195, 200

Oatar 189

Racial Discrimination 205
Radiation 32, 36
Radio 175
Reclamation 10, 11, 26, 56, 128, 155,
  157, 197, 202
Recreation 44, 61, 62, 63, 67, 72,
  73, 75, 77, 91, 113, 122, 132,
  133, 134, 136, 144, 150, 159, 161,
  163
Recycling 10, 53, 54, 56, 66, 74,
  101, 104, 132, 143, 144, 150, 157,
  158, 166, 179, 199
Reforestation 155
Reichel, E. 29, 38
Remote Sensing 122, 123, 141, 142,
  145, 148, 149, 179, 180, 187
Reservoirs 39, 109, 116, 138, 141,
  161
 Operation 132, 143, 159, 172, 179
Resolutions 192-206
Rhizomata xi
Riparian
 Consumption 75
 States 17, 187
 Wells 33
Risks 76, 104, 143, 152, 165, 173,
  175
River
 Ara 115
 Brahmaputra 61, 139
 Chao Phraya 127
 Colorado 58, 124
 Columbia 94
 Congo 11
 Danube 61, 64, 102, 134, 135
 Darling 139
 Dez 49
 Dnieper 115
 Don 61
 Elbe 61, 102
 Euphrates xi, 99
 Gaja Creek 116
 Gambia 130
 Ganges 61, 139
 Huang-Ho xi
 Indus xi, 11, 94, 99
 La Plata 119
 Main 102
 Mano 139
 Mekong 99, 128
 Mississippi 61, 102, 105
 Moldau 134
 Murray 139

Nile xi, 11, 32, 61, 99, 121, 122, 139
Notec 117
Oder 102
Odra 115
Ohio 34
Paranaiba 130
Plate 11, 189
Rhine 36, 61, 102, 134
Salt 64
São Francisco 59
Seine xi, 61
Senegal 94
Siberian 116
Tigris xi, 99
Tisza 64
Tone 115, 126
Torina 138
Vistula 115
Volga 59, 61, 115
Yangtze 99
Yellow 99
Yodo 126
Zaire 115
River Commissions 18, 202
Romania 14, 113, 115, 117, 125, 134
Rome 3
Ruhr 117
Rural Development *see* Development, Rural
Russia *see* USSR
Rwanda 138

Sahara 33
Sahel 13, 14, 65, 98, 120, 122, 187
Saint-Marc, P. 80
St. Pierre and Miquelon 35
Saldanha, E. C. 146
Salinity 34, 40, 67, 113, 129-130, 137, 141, 143, 151, 155, 156
Salinization xvi, 12, 18, 26, 58, 76, 83, 100, 113, 130, 156
Salt
  Dissolved 41
  Suspended 41
Salt-water Intrusion 41, 43, 76, 130, 155, 157
Sanitation 19, 21, 84, 95, 96, 126, 127-128, 136, 144, 152, 153, 154, 168, 175, 177, 192, 193, 194, 195, 196
Santiago 51
Satellites 140-141
Saudi Arabia 15, 189
Schistosomiasis xiii, xiv, 12

Sea
  Black 102
  Caspian 39, 40
  Mediterranean 140
  North 102
Second World War 1, 14
Sediments xiii, 34, 35, 37, 41, 42, 44, 67, 130, 137, 161, 179
Seepage 60, 174
Self-purification 72
Self-reliance 170, 174, 183, 184, 200
Semi-arid Land 34, 40, 47, 65, 99, 107, 123, 200, 201
Sewage 177, 193
Sewell, W. R. D. 55
Shared Water Resources *see* Water Resources, Shared
Siberia 10
Sierra Leone 35
Silting 60
Singapore xv
Smirnov, B. S. 146
Snails 12
Snowfall 36, 149
Snowmelt 120
Social Implications xvii, 65, 106, 116, 144, 165, 184
Social Response 106
Sodium 41
Soil
  Conservation 59, 63, 130, 143, 155, 156, 157
  Fertility 106
  Loss 18, 69
  Moisture xii, 8, 11, 29, 36, 44
Solar Energy *see* Energy, Solar
Solids, Dissolved 34, 42
Somalia 35, 122
South America *see* America, Latin
Soviet Union *see* USSR
Spain 73, 116, 118, 119, 126, 140
Sri Lanka 18
Standardization 181
  Designs and Plans 171, 183
  Equipment 171
  Methods 180
  Specifications 171
Steel 170
Stockholm 3, 17, 200
Storage 31, 56, 60, 61, 100, 101, 114, 116, 128, 137, 145, 151, 159, 162
  Pumped 159
Strait, Bering 40
Stratosphere 40

Streams xii, 8, 63
Subsidies 80, 90, 150
Sudan 7, 13, 22, 39, 57, 97, 116,
    121, 122, 129, 139
Sudano-Sahelian Zone 32
Sudd 39, 121
Sulphate 41
Swamps xii, 8, 29, 77, 155, 157
Swan Coastal Plain 122
Swaziland 97
Sweden 14, 17, 18, 122, 123, 133,
    134, 135, 138, 140
Switzerland 11, 138
Syria 189
Systems Analysis *see* Models

Tanzania 13, 16, 21, 53, 113, 114,
    120, 127, 139
Technical Assistance 97, 149, 154,
    170, 174, 189, 199, 204
Technical Cooperation 14, 17, 141,
    171, 178, 181, 184-185, 201-202
Technology
  Appropriate 141, 145, 169-170,
    171, 184, 196, 201
  Capital-Intensive 170
  Change 66-67
  Choice 64, 104, 110
  High 179
  Imported 170
  Labour-Intensive 15, 20, 97, 170
  Traditional 170
  Transfer 15, 97, 105, 106, 113,
    128, 141, 145, 153, 170, 185
Television 175
Teratogenic 48
Territories
  British Caribbean 35
  Occupied 205
Texas 33
Thailand 118, 126, 127, 128, 131
Theamatic Papers 19, 113
Third World 13, 21
Thomas, F. 146
Tokyo 126
Tolba, M. K. 12, 17
Tourism 73, 102, 132, 133, 134,
    144, 159, 161
Toxic Chemicals *see* Chemicals, Toxic
Trace Metals 104
Training 112, 139-140, 145, 148,
    149, 154, 156, 166, 174-178,
    181, 185, 190, 192, 195, 198, 201
Transportation 29, 31, 45, 95, 103,
    133, 135, 144, 150, 160, 166,
    174, 188

Treatment, Primary xii
Treaty
  Boundary Water 94, 138-139
  Columbia 94
  Indus 94
  Plate 189
  Senegal 94
Trypanosomiasis xiii
Tsetse Flies xiii
Tsunamis 97
Tunnel, Päijänne 126
Turbidity 34, 63
Turbines 15, 103
Turkey 97
Typhoid xiii
Typhoons 97

Uganda 59, 139
Ukrainian USSR 14, 113, 114, 115,
    120, 123, 133
Underdevelopment 6
Underemployment 81, 170
Undernourishment
Unemployment 81, 170
USSR 10, 17, 35, 37, 38, 53, 57, 59,
    60, 111, 113, 115, 116, 117, 118,
    119, 120, 121, 123, 127, 128, 132,
    133, 134, 135, 138, 146
United Arab Emirates 189
United Kingdom 14, 36, 53, 117, 132,
    140
United Nations xvi, 1, 4, 6, 7, 8, 9,
    15, 16, 19, 20, 21, 22, 27, 51,
    53, 54, 56, 59, 94, 111, 139, 146,
    152, 161, 175, 182, 183, 185, 187,
    188, 189, 190, 193, 194, 196, 202,
    203, 204, 205
  Administrative Committee on
    Coordination 17, 203
  Bodies
    CNRET 188, 203
    UNDP 15, 17, 37, 51, 185, 201,
      202, 203, 204
    UNDRO 14
    UNEP 12, 17, 18, 182, 188
    UNESCO 31, 163, 188
    UNICEF 12, 51
    UNIDO 158
    UNU 198
    Regional Economic Commissions 17,
      18, 111, 181, 202, 203
    ECA 186, 187
    ECE 187
    ECLA 188
    ECWA 189, 190

Centre on International Rivers 17
Committee on Natural Resources 3, 7, 16, 17, 22
Conference on
    Desertification 12, 19, 201-202
    Food 7, 10, 22, 23, 57, 196, 197
    Human Environment 7, 161, 163, 182, 200
    Human Settlements 7, 19, 20, 21, 23, 127, 143, 152, 154, 193, 194, 195
    Population 7, 22, 23
    Science and Technology for Development 171
    Technical Cooperation Among Developing Countries 15, 19, 185, 201, 202
    Water 1, 5, 7, 8, 9, 12, 19, 20, 22, 23, 71, 92, 94, 111, 146, 171, 181, 192, 193, 196, 198, 199, 200, 201, 202, 204, 205, 206
Economic and Social Council 7, 9, 16, 17, 22, 71, 171, 182, 194, 202, 203, 204
Environment Coordination Board 203
General Assembly 7, 16, 179, 180, 201, 203, 204, 205
Water Resources Board 17
United States xiii, xv, 9, 10, 14, 18, 36, 41, 51, 53, 54, 59, 60, 64, 111, 113, 114, 115, 116, 120, 124, 125, 127, 128, 130, 131, 132, 133, 135, 137, 138-139, 140, 146, 206
  Commission on Water Quality 41
Upper Silesia 117
Urbanization 11, 58, 62, 67, 72, 81, 126

Valencia 73
Valley, Alpine 136
Value, Social 81
Vancouver 3, 5
Van Laethem, G. 9
Venezuela 146
Victoria 130, 139
Vienna 102
Vietnam 14
Volcanic Eruptions 97, 180

Waldheim, K. 8

Ward, B. 20
Waste
    Agricultural 193
    Discharge 34, 53, 54, 63, 67, 73, 74, 76, 135, 138, 163
    Disposal xv, 44, 54, 61, 72, 73, 101, 103, 104, 128, 150, 152-154, 165, 188, 193
    Industrial 63, 67, 103, 105, 193
    Municipal 63
    Organic xiii, 41, 163
    Radioactive 18, 160
    Treatment 18, 63, 66, 67, 150, 153, 154, 158, 170, 175, 179
Water
    Balance 29, 31, 32, 33, 36, 38, 43, 68, 148
    Brackish 13, 43, 66, 124, 142, 179
    Collection Journey xiii, xiv
    Conflicts 72-73
    Conservation xvi, 8, 46, 55, 66, 80, 83, 91, 96, 104, 105, 106, 107, 108, 109, 112, 114, 130, 132-133, 143, 144, 151, 152, 155, 156, 157, 165, 166, 168, 174, 175, 176, 178, 181, 187, 200
    Crisis 7, 8
    Demand xiii, xvii, 7, 10, 11, 28, 30, 31, 39, 41, 43, 46-50, 52, 56, 57, 58, 61, 64-68, 71, 74, 77, 89, 96, 97, 106, 108, 109, 112, 114, 116, 121, 122, 123, 125, 131, 132, 143, 151-152, 165, 166, 186
    Geothermal 43, 124, 140
    Global Stock 25
    Ground see Ground-water
    Infrastructure 13
    Law 87, 91-92, 94, 108, 110, 118, 140, 142, 150, 168-169, 183, 185
    Potable xii, xiv, 11, 63
    Pricing 66, 80, 89, 90, 91, 96, 108, 109, 113, 126, 143, 150, 153, 154, 155, 158, 166
    Quality 34, 36, 37, 41-43, 45, 54, 56, 60, 62, 63, 64, 66, 67, 72, 75-76, 80, 83, 94, 96, 101, 104, 105, 106, 109, 112, 116, 119, 124-125, 133, 134, 135, 136, 147, 148, 158, 163-164, 168, 181, 187, 188, 194, 199
        Bacteriological 28, 62, 163
        Biological 34, 104, 136, 163
        Chemical 28, 34, 62, 104, 163
        Mineral 28, 123, 142, 148
        Monitors 36, 147, 164, 175

Radiological 104
Standards 17, 29, 48, 76, 108, 110, 143, 150, 164
Stations 35
Rights 26, 58, 80, 93, 108, 109, 118, 155, 168
Resources, Shared xi, 2, 5, 9, 17, 18, 22, 68, 93, 94, 112, 124, 138-139, 148, 180-183, 184, 187, 188, 191, 202
Reuse 30, 43, 52, 56
Saline 34, 52
Shortages 71, 107, 165, 170, 171, 173, 175, 194
Supply xvii, 54, 55, 63, 64-68, 71, 72, 77, 89, 95-97, 99, 106, 110, 115, 119, 150
  Community 2, 5, 8, 18, 20, 21, 49, 50, 84, 96, 99, 106, 112, 113, 124, 126-127, 128, 141, 143, 152-154, 162, 170, 185, 193-194, 196
  Village 12, 21, 110, 113, 127, 143, 167, 196
Table 41
Transfer, Interregional 72, 74, 83-84, 87, 116, 166, 173
Transport 61-62, 132-133
Treatment 34, 67, 81, 143, 150
Use xv, 7, 11, 14, 28, 30, 41, 43-45, 46, 47, 52, 55, 56, 65, 66, 69, 72, 73, 77, 83, 90, 91, 93, 96, 101, 108, 109, 113, 116, 119, 121, 128, 138, 142, 149-151, 155, 158, 160, 165, 167, 173, 176, 179, 180, 187, 188, 191, 192, 198
  Agriculture xv, xvi, 8, 19, 20, 21, 55-59, 62, 64, 66, 80, 83, 91, 100, 106, 113, 115, 122, 128, 141, 143, 152, 154-157, 165, 177, 178, 196-199
  Domestic 8, 61, 62, 65, 80, 89, 90, 95-97, 101, 110, 115, 150, 161, 165, 192, 193, 196
  Efficiency xii, xvi, 10, 12, 18, 26, 47, 58, 64, 90, 96, 99, 100, 104, 107, 109, 114, 129, 143, 149-151, 153, 155, 156, 158, 174, 178, 179, 191, 201, 202
  Fisheries 58, 91, 99, 115, 150, 157
  Industrial xv, xvi, 8, 14, 52-55, 62, 63, 83, 94, 104, 113, 122, 123, 124, 126, 131-132, 141, 152, 157-158, 165, 177, 178, 179, 199
  Irrational xvi, 90, 100, 106, 155, 175, 199, 200
Water-borne Diseases xiii, xv, 12, 20, 48, 83, 95, 175, 176
Waterlogging xvi, 11, 12, 26, 58, 100, 129, 130, 143, 156, 197
Water-mills 103
Water-related Diseases xiv, 18, 67, 95, 100, 106, 113, 148, 156, 161, 162, 176, 179, 181
Waterschappen 117
Watershed Management 30, 98, 110, 155
Water-wheels 103
Weather
  Forecasting 174, 179, 180
  Modification 30, 43, 66, 74, 75, 98, 124, 140, 141, 142, 179, 180
Weeds 129, 134, 161
Western Nations 20
White, A. U. 48
White, G. F. 25, 44
Wind 32, 36
Wollman, N. 54
Women, Role of xiii, xiv, 170
World Bank 15, 19, 51, 183, 188, 204
World Energy Conference 60
World Health Organization xiv, 15, 19, 21, 22, 48, 49, 50, 51, 188, 189, 195
World Meteorological Organization 16, 31, 35, 37, 41, 77, 188, 189
World Weather Watch 189

Yemen 35, 189
  Democratic Republic of 14, 35, 189
Yield 33, 123
Yugoslavia 113, 114, 115, 116, 117, 131

Zaire 115, 134
Zambia 13
Zimbabwee 205